THEN & NOW®

SWAMPSCOTT

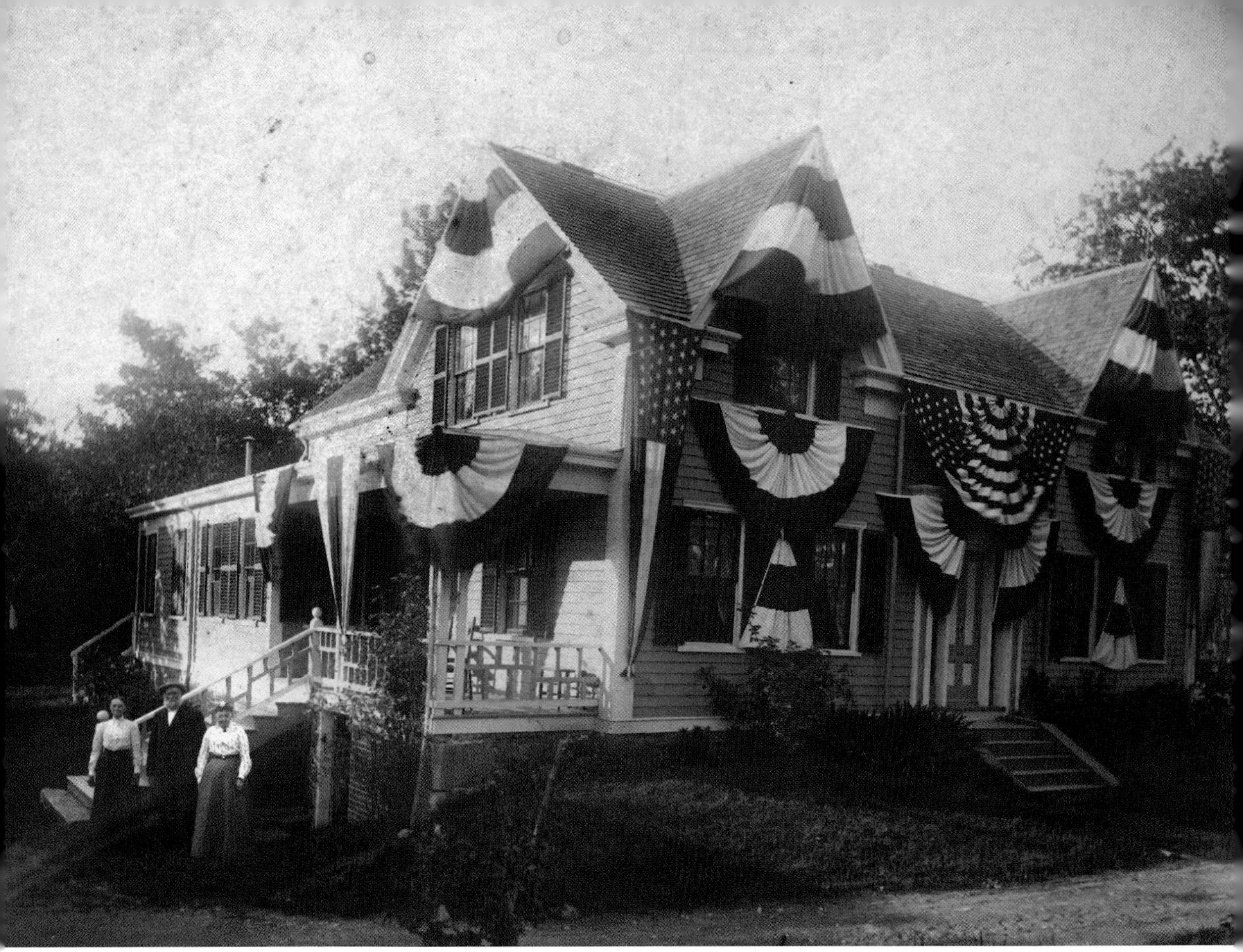

Swampscott likes to hold grand celebrations, especially when it comes to marking the birthday of the town, May 21, 1852. Back in 1902, when the town celebrated 50 years, private homes and businesses went all out, just as the Harris family did at their Humphrey Street home. (Courtesy Swampscott Historical Commission.)

Then & Now®

Swampscott

Sue Ellen Woodcock

Arcadia Publishing

ISBN 978-0-7385-1056-9

Published by Arcadia Publishing
Charleston, South Carolina

Printed in the United States of America

Then and Now is a registered trademark and is used under license from Salamander Books Limited

Library of Congress Catalog Card Number: Applied for.

For all general information contact Arcadia Publishing at:
Telephone 843-853-2070
Fax 843-853-0044
E-mail sales@arcadiapublishing.com
For customer service and orders:
Toll-Free 1-888-313-2665

Visit us on the Internet at www.arcadiapublishing.com

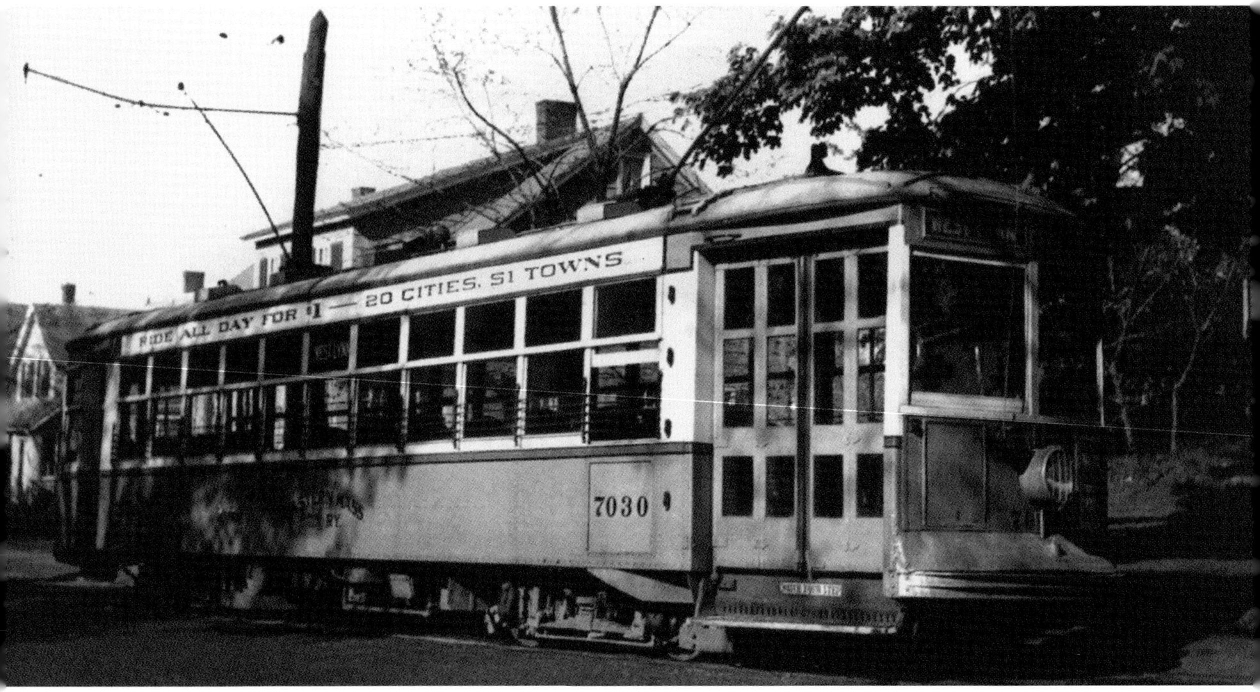

Imagine riding the trolley all day for just a dollar. You could do that in Swampscott and the North Shore in 1937. This trolley traveled from West Lynn to the Beach Bluff section of town and surely brought many visitors to Swampscott's pristine beaches and grand hotels. (Courtesy Swampscott Historical Society.)

Contents

Acknowledgments

Years ago, when I met Louis A. Gallo through my work at the Swampscott Reporter, it was evident that in addition to his artistic talents he was also a walking reference book on Swampscott. We started a column in the *Swampscott Reporter* called "Then & Now," and it was hugely popular. Gallo would drop off some old photographs, and we would drive around town looking for the "now" picture. I would like to thank him once again for helping with this *Then & Now* project.

I would also like to thank the Swampscott Historical Commission and the Swampscott Historical Society for providing inspiration and photographs included in this book. The Swampscott Public Library was also helpful in lending some of the images used, as was Police Chief Ron Madigan.

It should also be noted that numerous volunteers and history buffs keep local history alive through Internet Web sites, presentations, continued research, writing, and preservation of historic sites in town. Swampscott's history runs deep and is by no means boring. The more people get turned on to local history, the longer it will be kept alive.

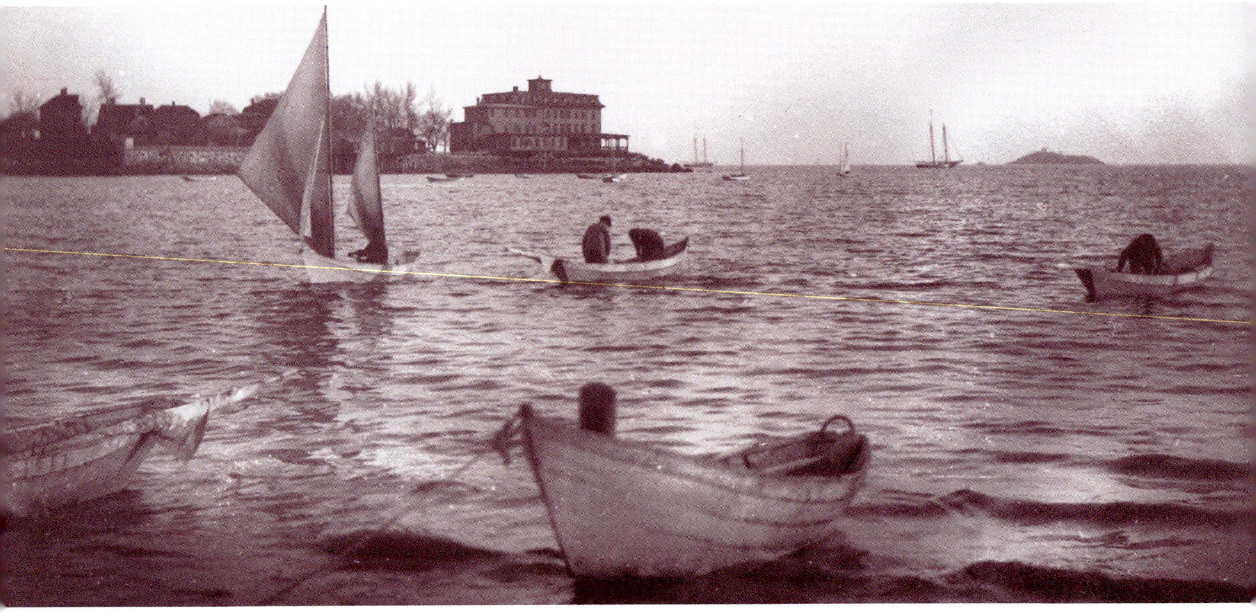

Swampscott photographer Stuart P. Ellis captured this image of fishermen working off Fisherman's Beach in sail-powered dories in 1895. In the distance is the Lincoln House Hotel. (Courtesy Swampscott Public Library.)

Introduction

When a few Swampscott visionaries led the charge in breaking away from the city of Lynn, who would have thought that 150 years later, landmarks, buildings, coastlines, and streets would be recognizable today?

Sometimes, when driving down Humphrey Street, it is hard to imagine that it was once a thoroughfare teeming with horses and carriages. With the invention of the automobile and the reliability of the train and trolley system, summer visitors flocked to the town known as the gateway to the Gold Coast. During the summer destination peak, Swampscott boasted more than six major hotels, including the world-famous, 582-room New Ocean House and several other small establishments. Imagine what it must have been like to move your entire family to spend the summer at one of Swampscott's many estates or to spend a week at the New Ocean House, where the hotel staff made sure all needs were met.

While the Swampscott of today is known more as a bedroom community than as a tourist destination, it still holds all the attractive features vacationers look for: the ocean, the beaches, the fine restaurants, a topnotch golf course (yes, even though the clubhouse is in Marblehead), public tennis courts, parks, and plenty of places to take a leisurely stroll or bicycle ride.

In today's fast-paced world, it is easy not to notice the changes happening in a community. It is easier to be consumed by the present than to look back, and without looking back it is hard to see how we got to where we are today. As the town celebrates its 150th anniversary (1852–2002), *Then & Now: Swampscott* is intended to provoke a second look at Swampscott. Raised here or not, almost anyone who has spent time in this seaside town will be able to recognize areas that have undergone change. Some changes have been good; some have been not so good. Imagine the town today if the grand hotels had survived. Think about Elihu Thomson's cofounding of General Electric and the hundreds of Swampscott residents who were employed by this world-renowned company. At one time, just about every other person in town worked at or had a connection to General Electric in Lynn; today, due to company cutbacks, they are retired or at other jobs.

As you thumb through the pages of this book, you will see that some things have changed very little—some images will be recognizable. You will also see images of some things that are long gone and live only in memories.

Author Willa Cather once wrote, "There are all those early memories, one cannot get another set." It is hoped that this book will rekindle early memories of Swampscott, for it is important that those memories be passed on to family and friends.

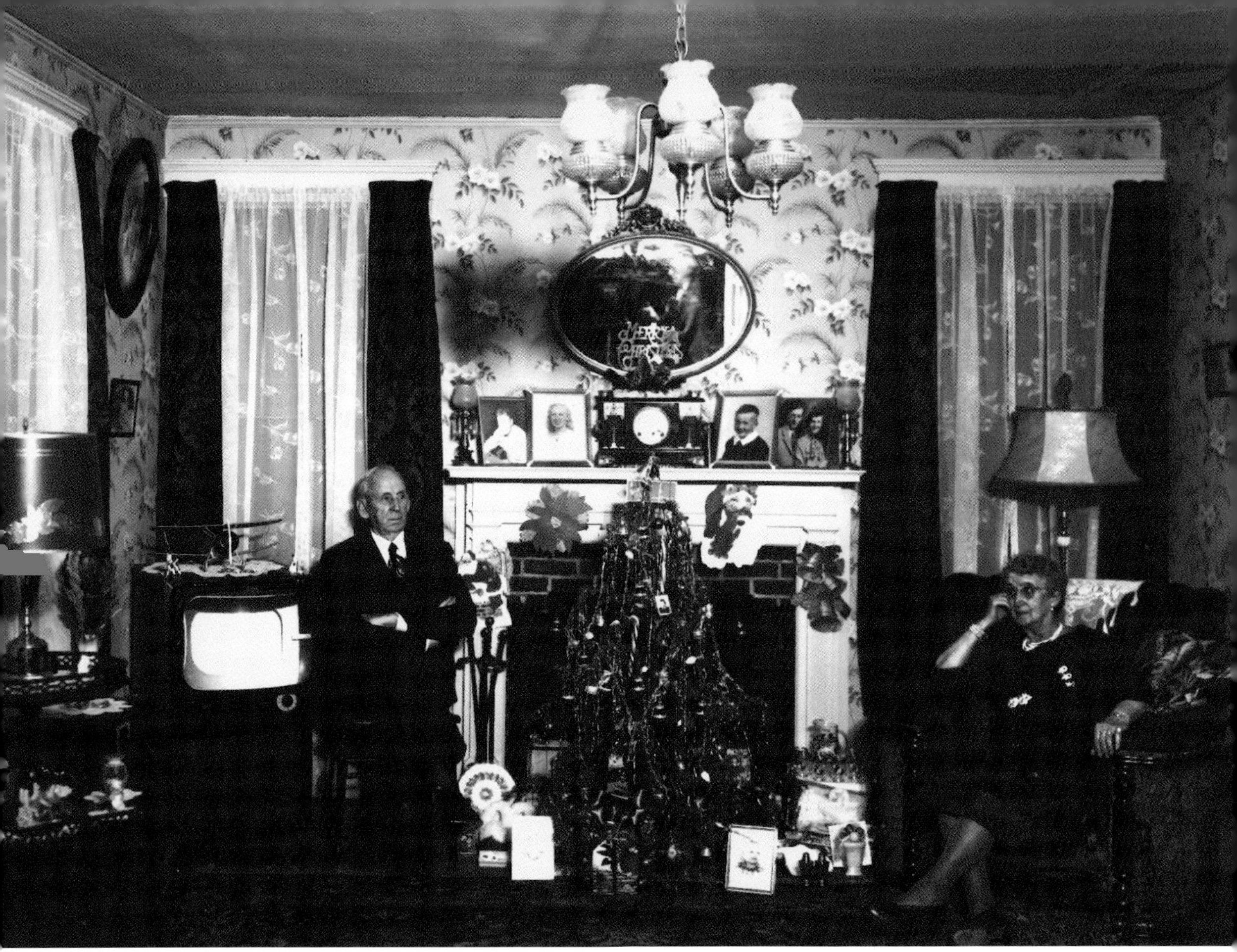

During simpler times, before Christmas succumbed to the commercialism of today, the holiday would have been depicted as in this image of Christmas at the home of Swampscott residents Mr. and Mrs. Fred Sullivan in 1951. (Courtesy Swampscott Historical Society.)

The home of shoe manufacturer and banker Herbert E. Gale, also known as Graystone Hall, was built in 1915–1916 and was demolished in 1944–1945. Located at 391 Puritan Road, the estate covered 17 acres and included a seven-car garage, a cow barn, a poultry house, a sports pavilion, gardens, and orchards. It is pictured in 1928. (Courtesy Swampscott Public Library.)

Chapter 1

A Different Place and Time

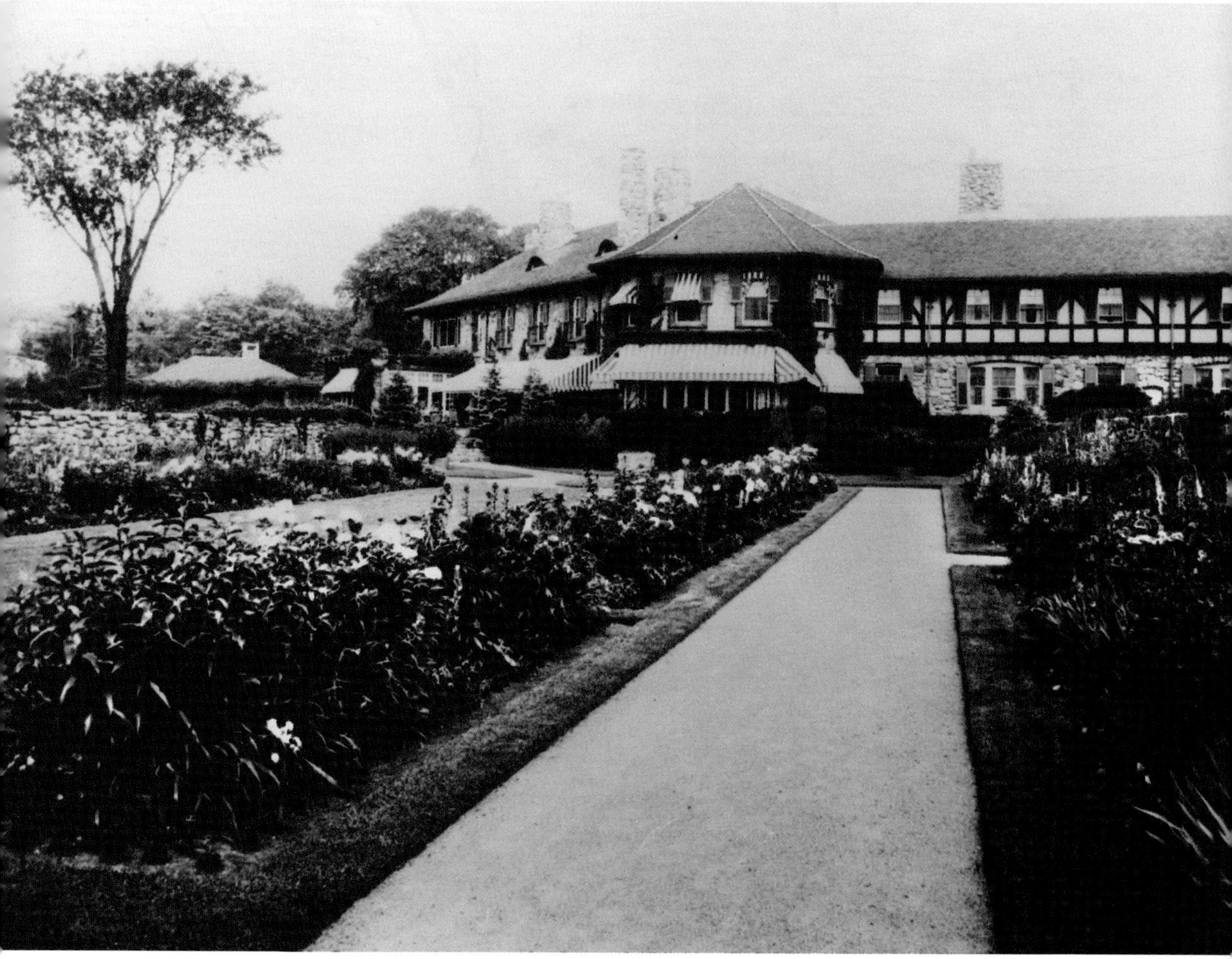

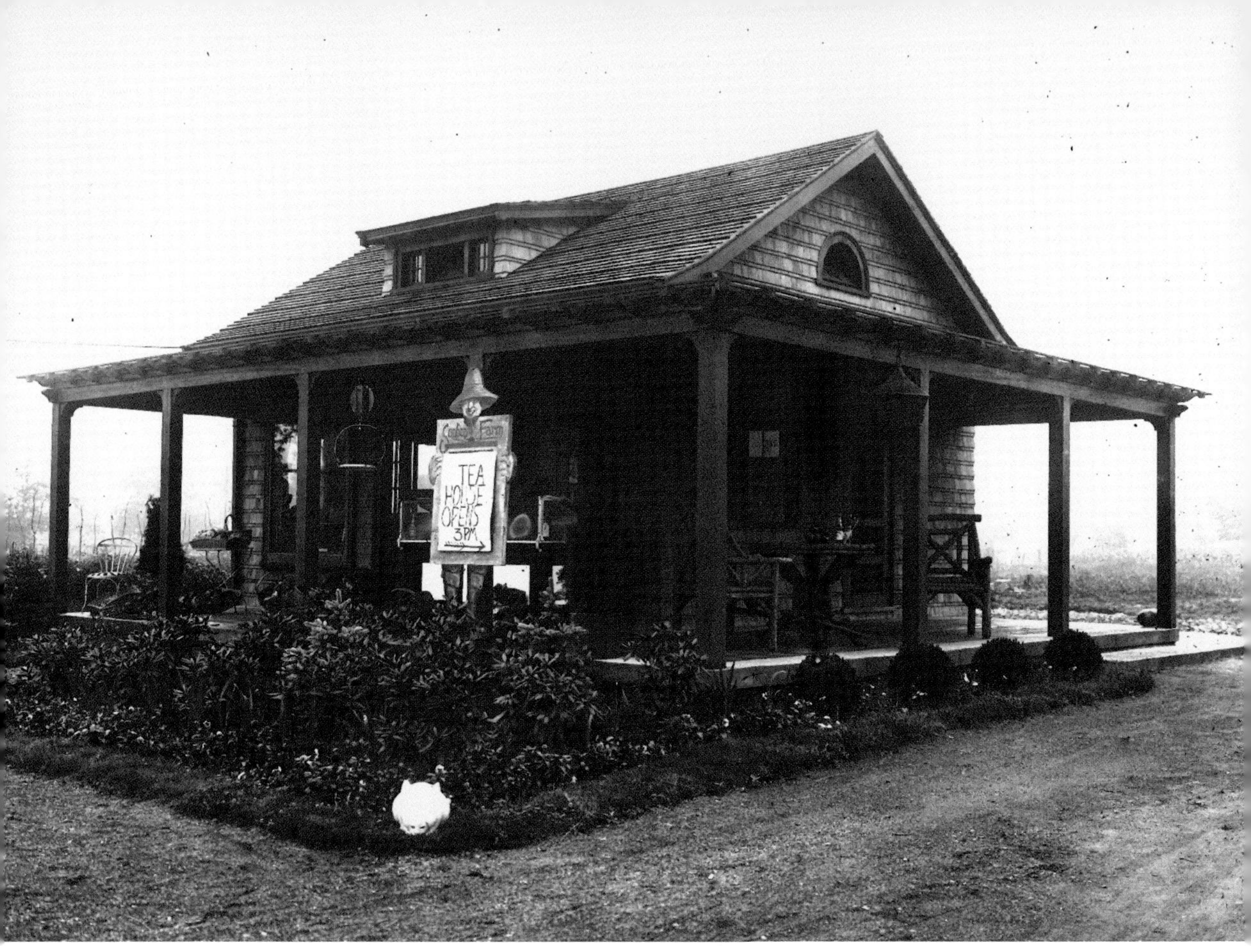

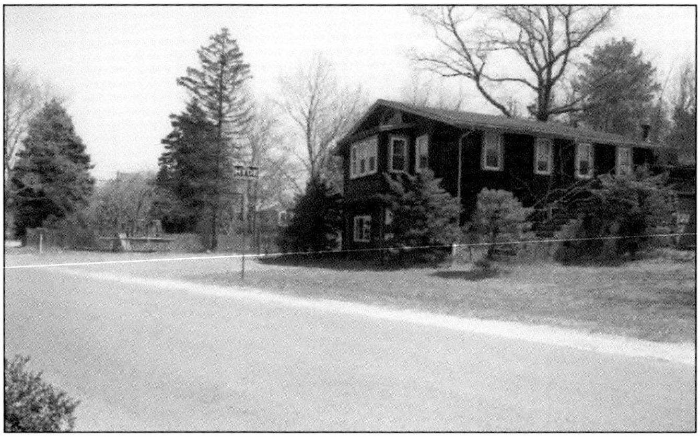

The Sunbeam Inn was more than a stop along the State Road (Paradise Road); it also included a teahouse and a vegetable store (above). Built on the General Glover farm property, now known as Vinnin Square, the inn existed from the 1920s to 1955. Today, the only glimpse of the historic site is a house on Sunbeam Lane, which locals know as the back entrance to the Marshall's side of Vinnin Square. (Courtesy Swampscott Public Library.)

Lillian A. Little can be credited with restoring General Glover's one-time home on the Swampscott-Salem-Marblehead line into a popular teahouse (below), visible behind two unidentified women. In 1957, the establishment became the General Glover Restaurant, owned by Anthony Athanas. The restaurant closed in the late 1990s and remains vacant today. (Courtesy Swampscott Public Library.)

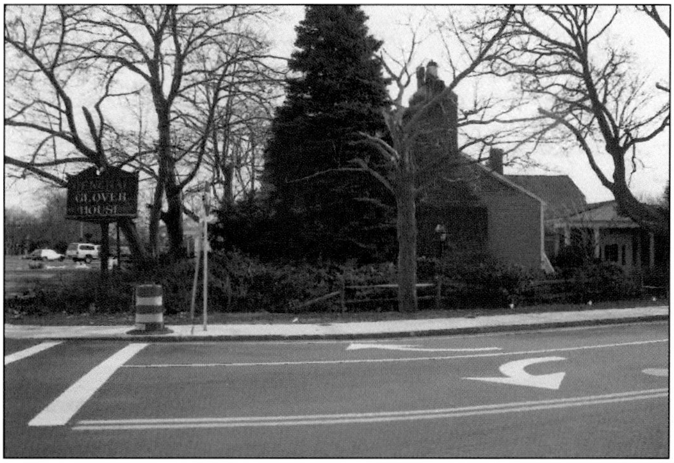

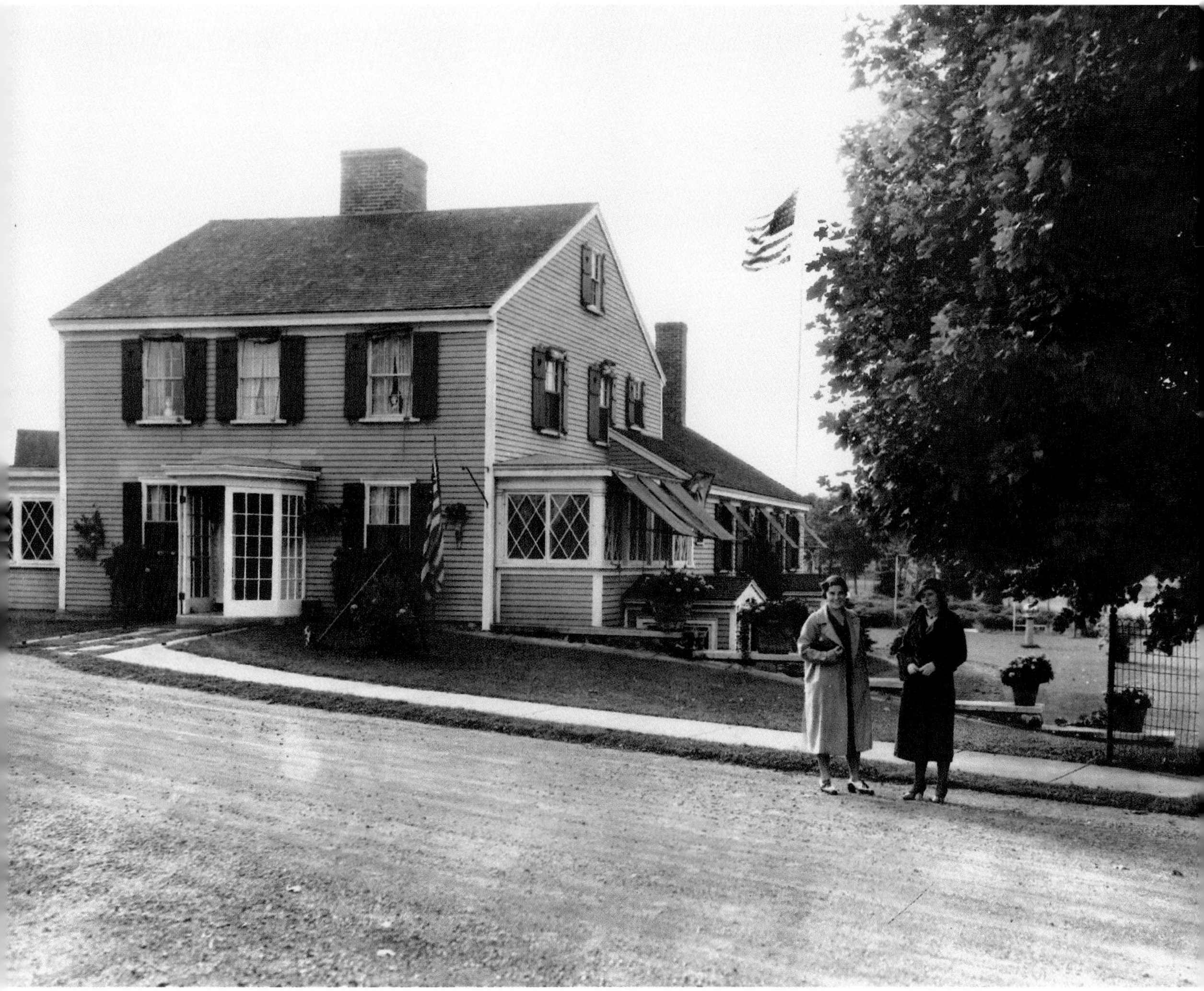

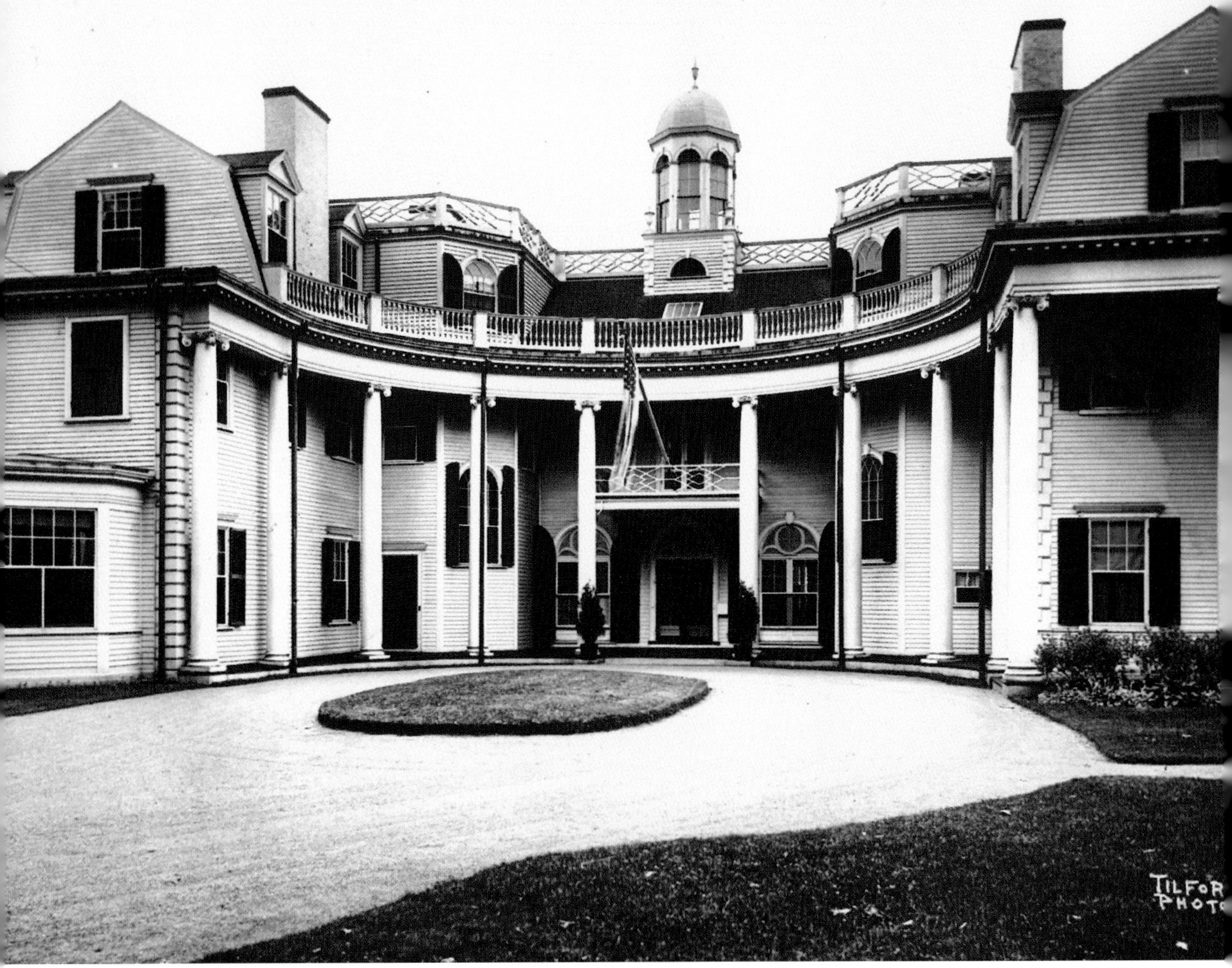

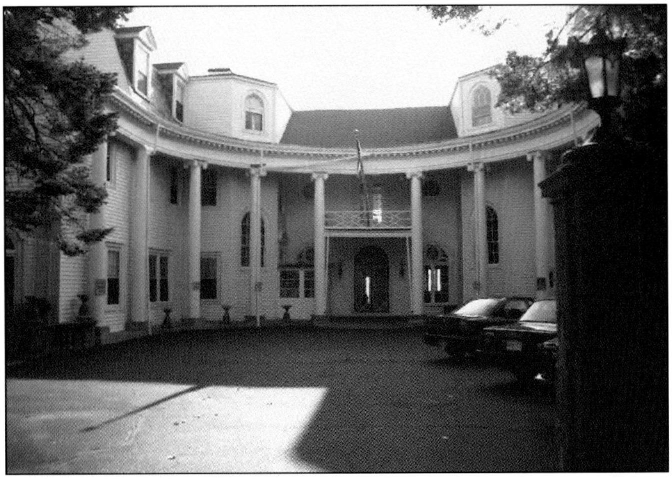

Pres. Calvin Coolidge and first lady Grace Coolidge called White Court on Little's Point their summer White House in 1925. Built in 1895 for an Ohio businessman, the house is known today as Marian Court College and retains much of its ocean-side charm. (Courtesy Swampscott Historical Commission.)

The ocean side of White Court shows verandas and patios for relaxation in the sun. In addition to being a college, the building has also been home to a small group of nuns. Summers in Swampscott for the Coolidges (below) were more than lazy days by the ocean. A couple of Little's Point neighbors join the president and his wife for a walk through the gardens that once grew in abundance around the property. (Courtesy Swampscott Historical Commission.)

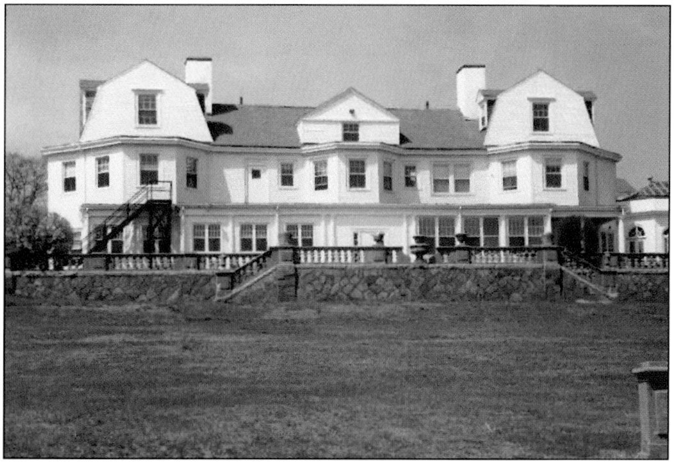

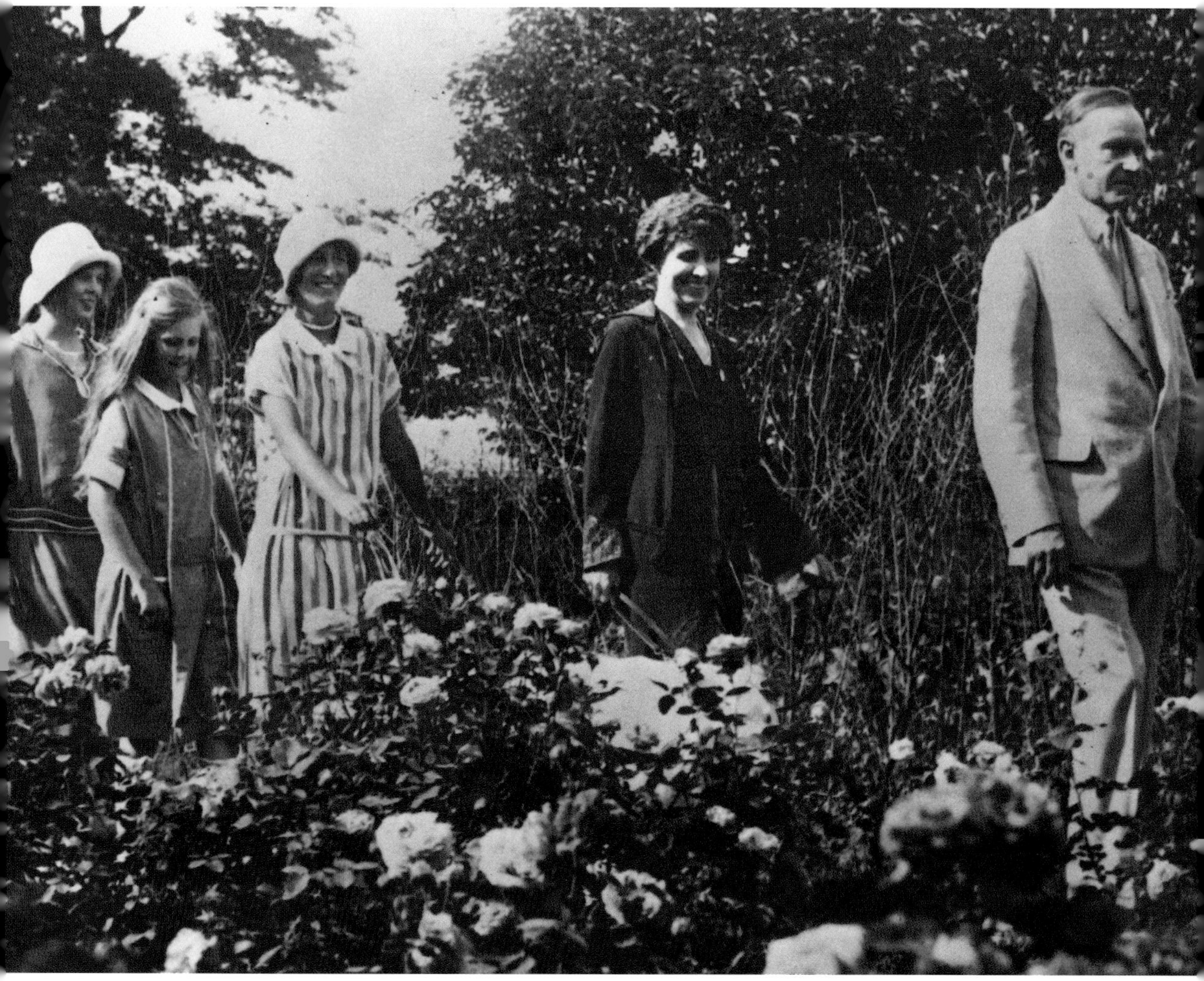

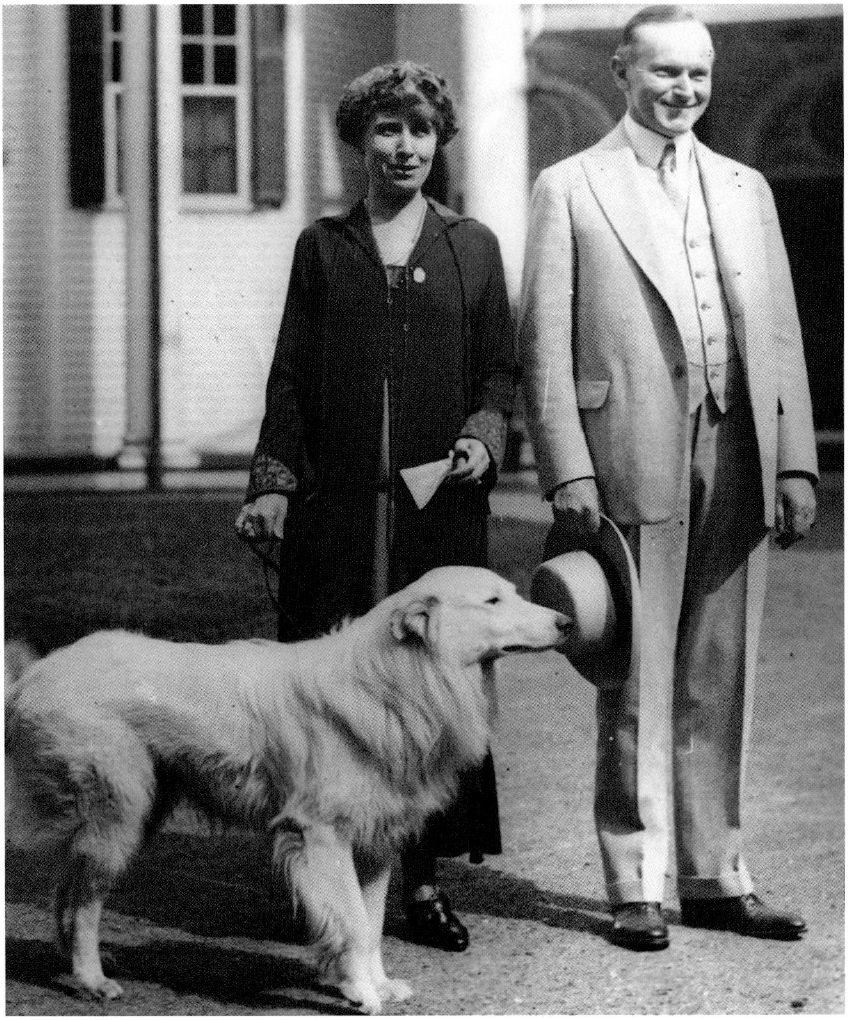

President and Mrs. Calvin Coolidge and their dog Rob Roy pose outside White Court in 1925. It was not uncommon for the Coolidges to take a daily walk past the New Ocean House Hotel on Puritan Road. Grace Coolidge stops for a photograph near the hotel entrance where the Washington press corps used to stay. (Courtesy Swampscott Historical Commission.)

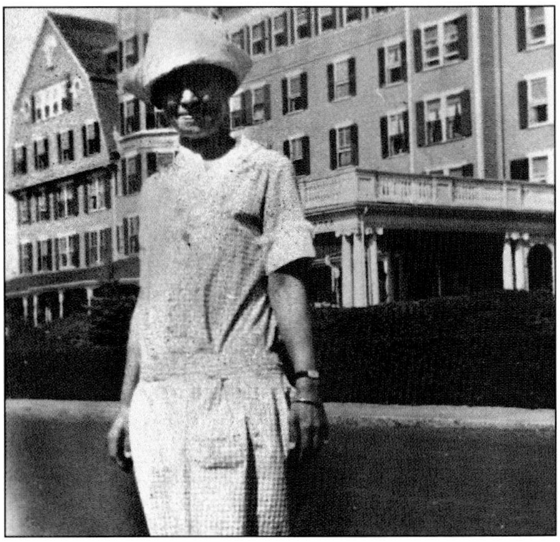

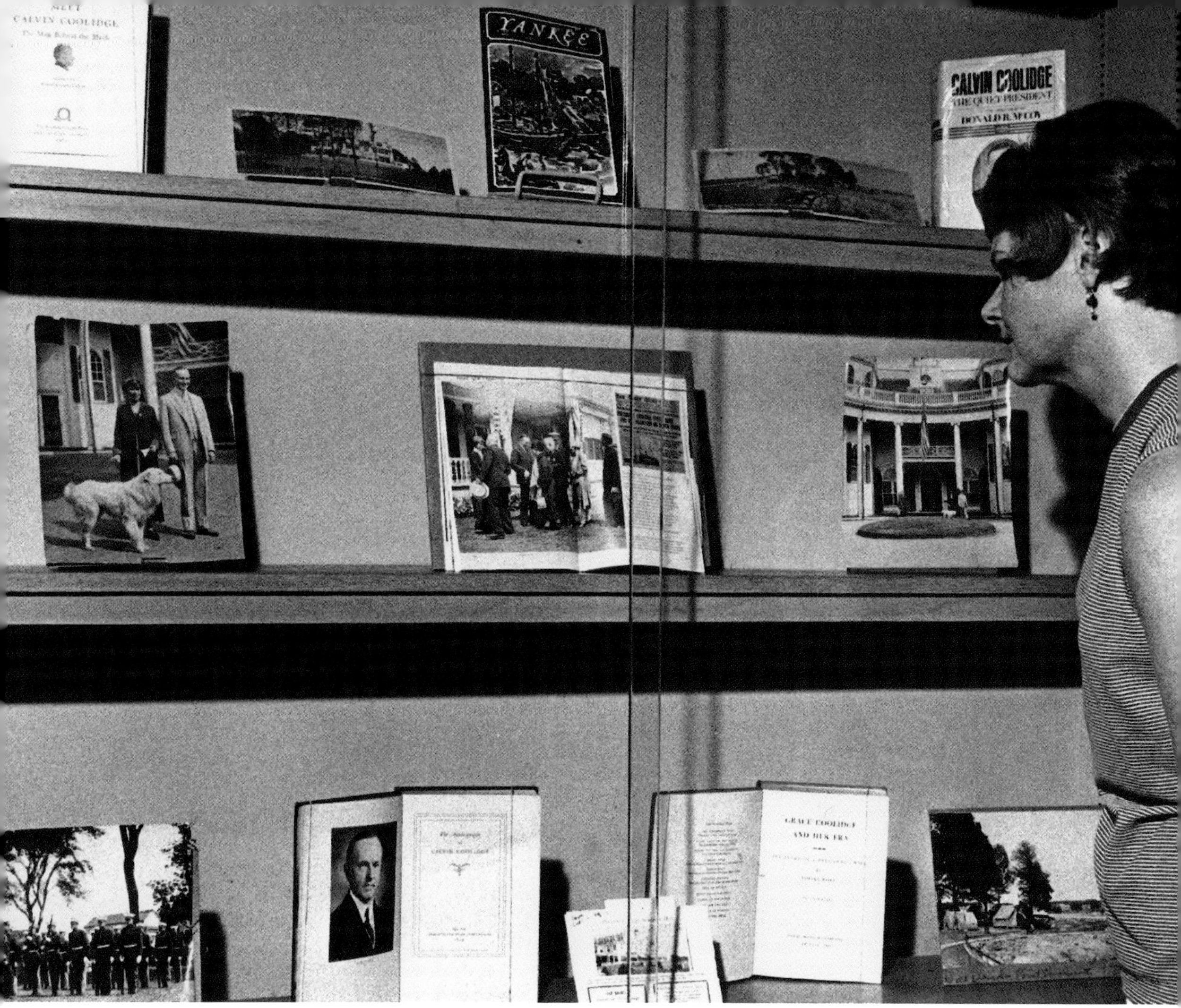

During the president's stay in Swampscott, the Swampscott Public Library made sure to offer a special display of information on the Coolidges, including *Yankee Magazine* and several books. (Courtesy Swampscott Public Library.)

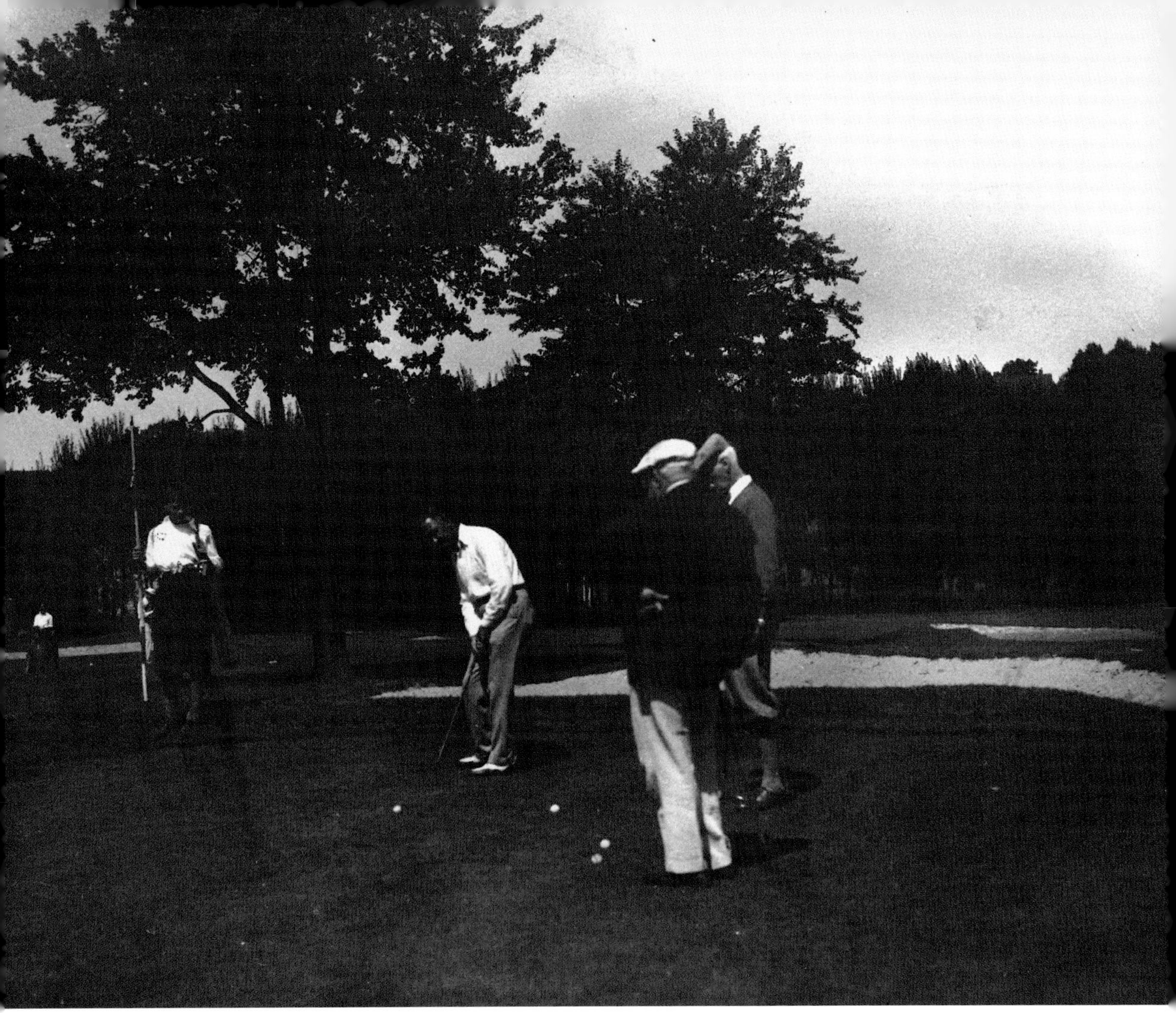

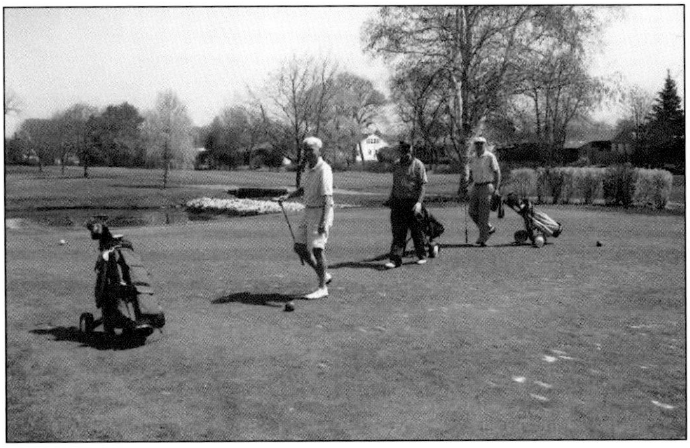

The New Ocean House Hotel, on Puritan Road, included a nine-hole golf course behind the hotel (above). Today, the only place in town to play 18 holes of golf is at the Tedesco Country Club. Although the clubhouse is in Marblehead, the golf course spreads across Salem Street into Swampscott. (Courtesy Louis A. Gallo.)

While golf may have attracted some guests, it was the New Ocean House Hotel itself that held an allure for many. The 582-room hotel was originally built in 1835 and was known as the Ocean House. Two fires followed and, in 1902, new owners and renovations turned it into the New Ocean House. After the hotel burned in 1969, developers built condominiums on a portion of the property. The only glimpse of the old hotel property is the cement exedra seat on the Puritan Road side where the swimming pool used to be. (Courtesy Swampscott Public Library.)

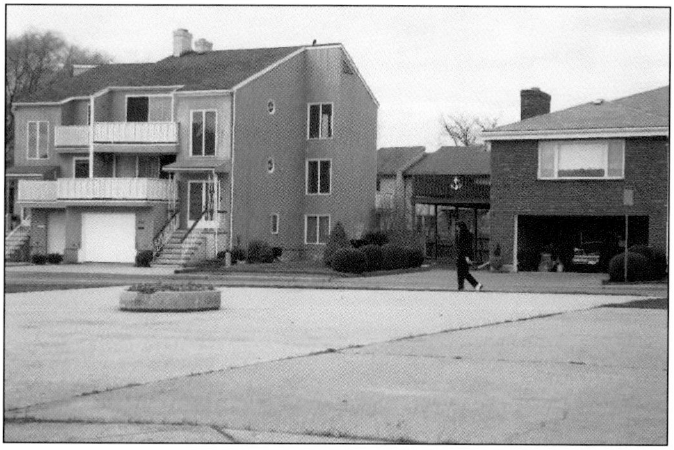

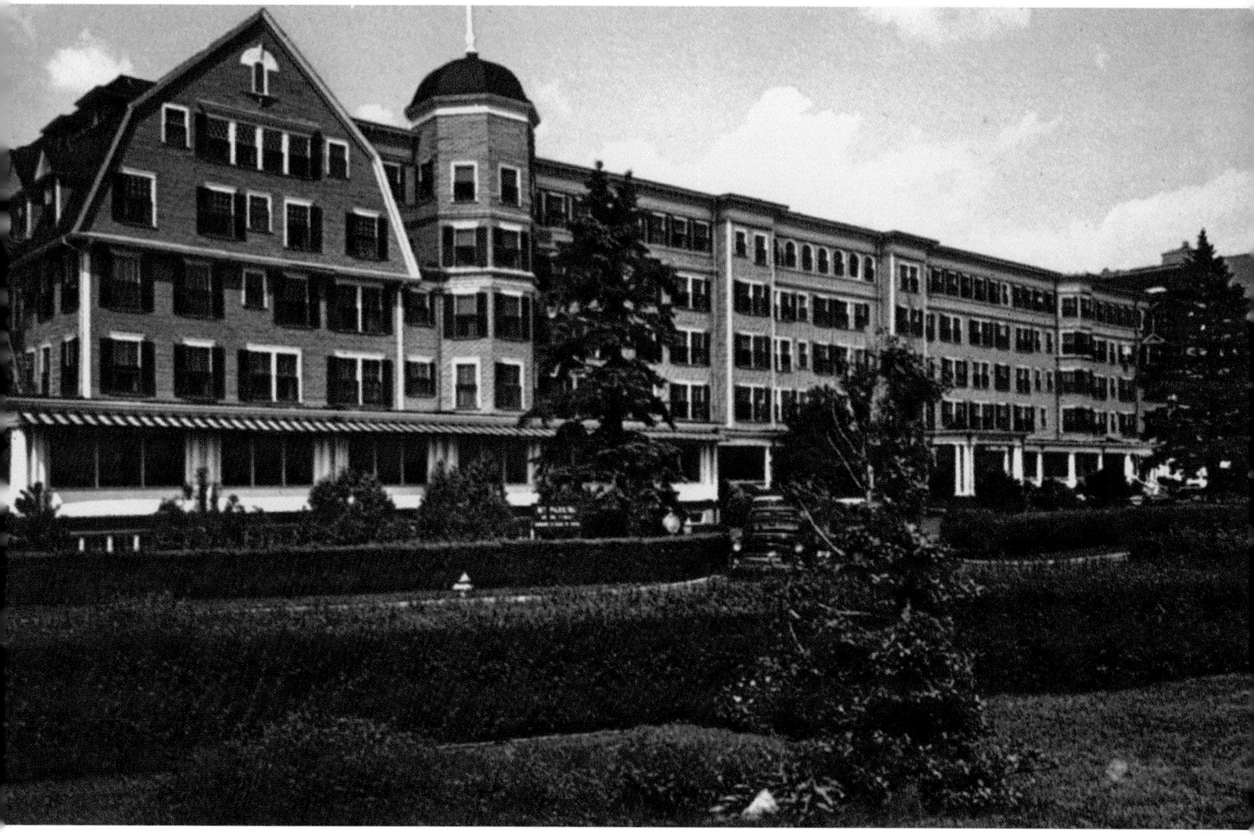

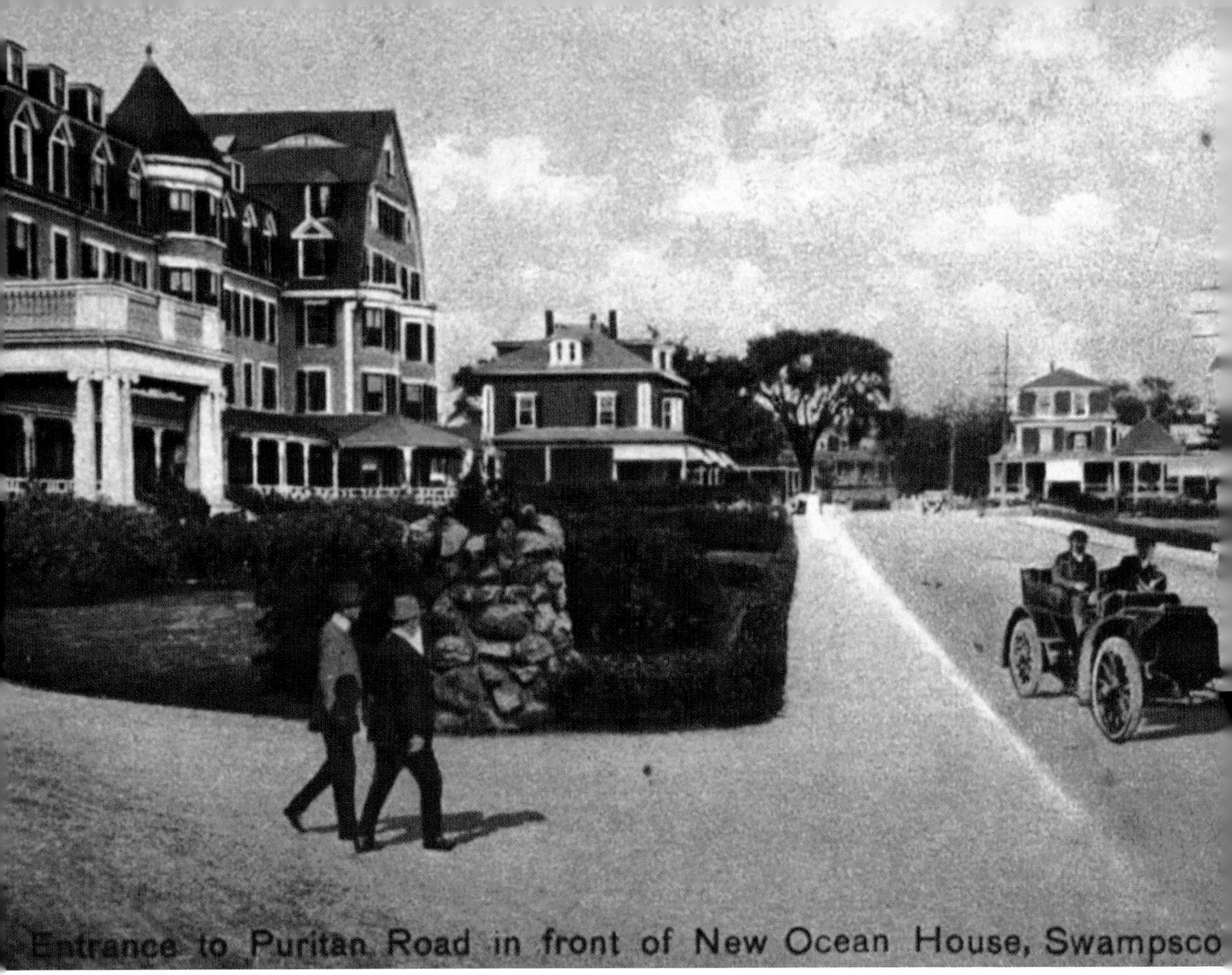

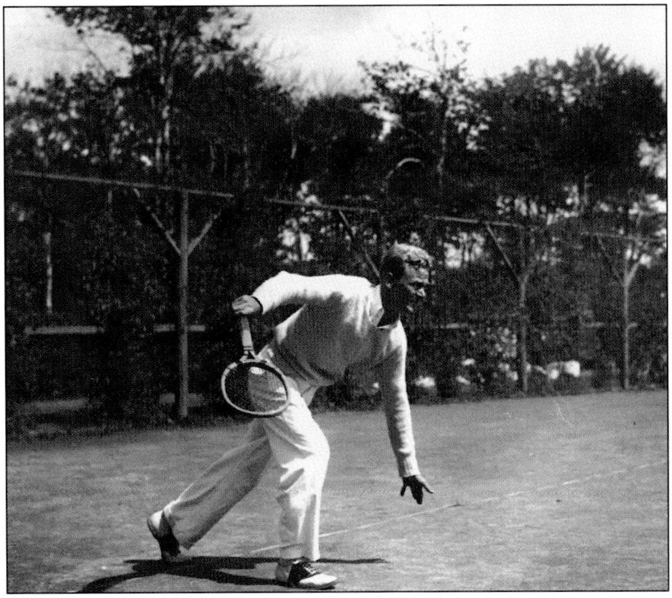

The early-1900s postcard (above) shows the Puritan Road entrance to the New Ocean House Hotel. The grassy area on the right side remains today as an entrance to Whales Beach. In addition to golf, the hotel retained tennis pro Sydney Dufton. (Courtesy Louis A. Gallo.)

Hotel guests approach the back of the New Ocean House after visiting the Exhibition Center, located closer to Humphrey Street. Today, the 22 acres of land have been used by the town for recreation and by a private developer for an assisted living facility. (Courtesy Louis A. Gallo.)

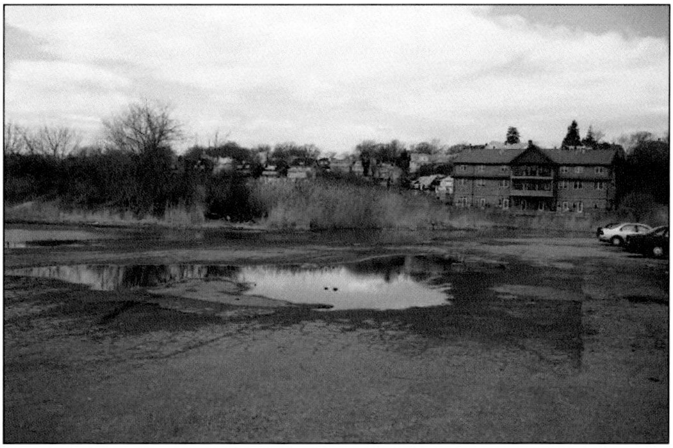

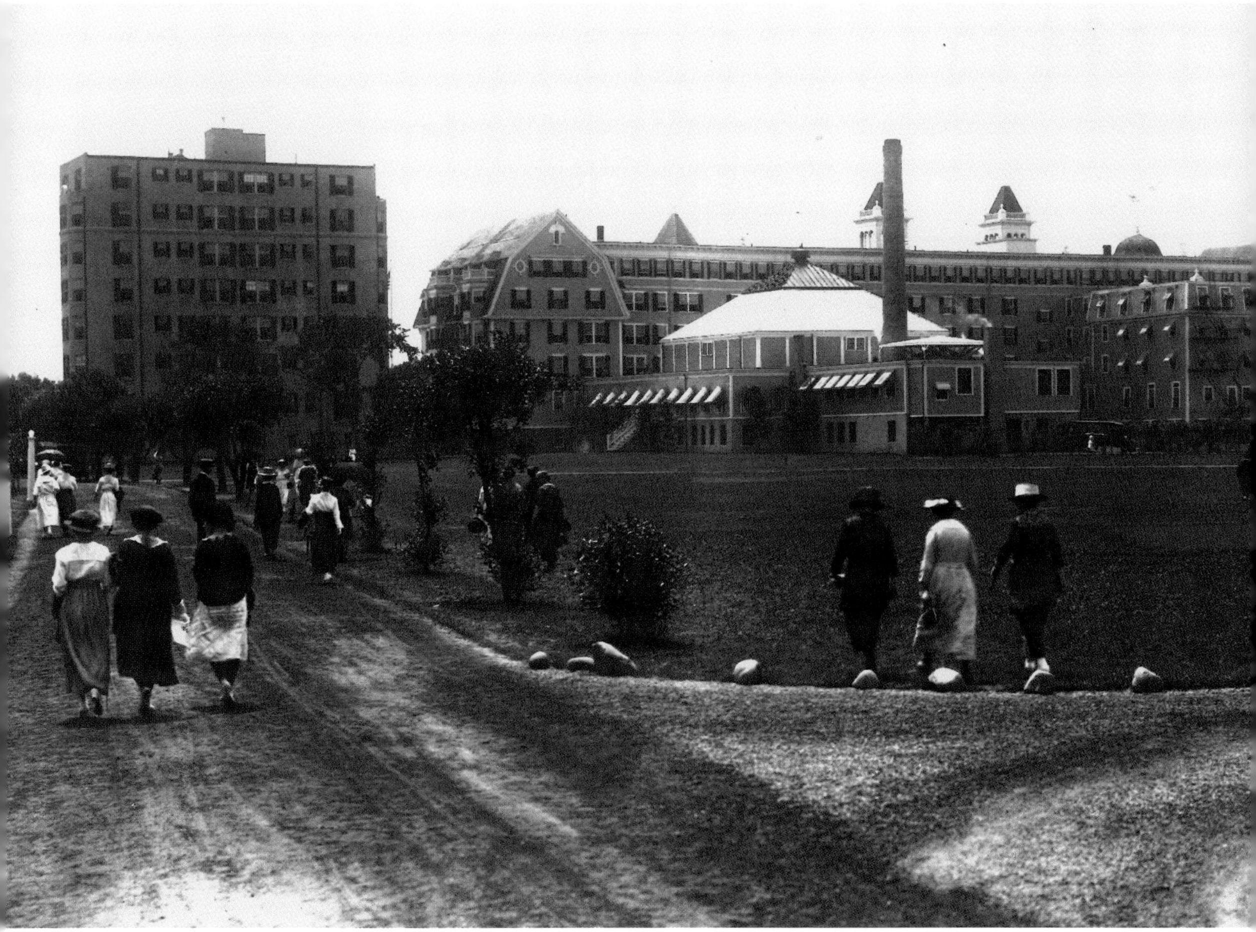

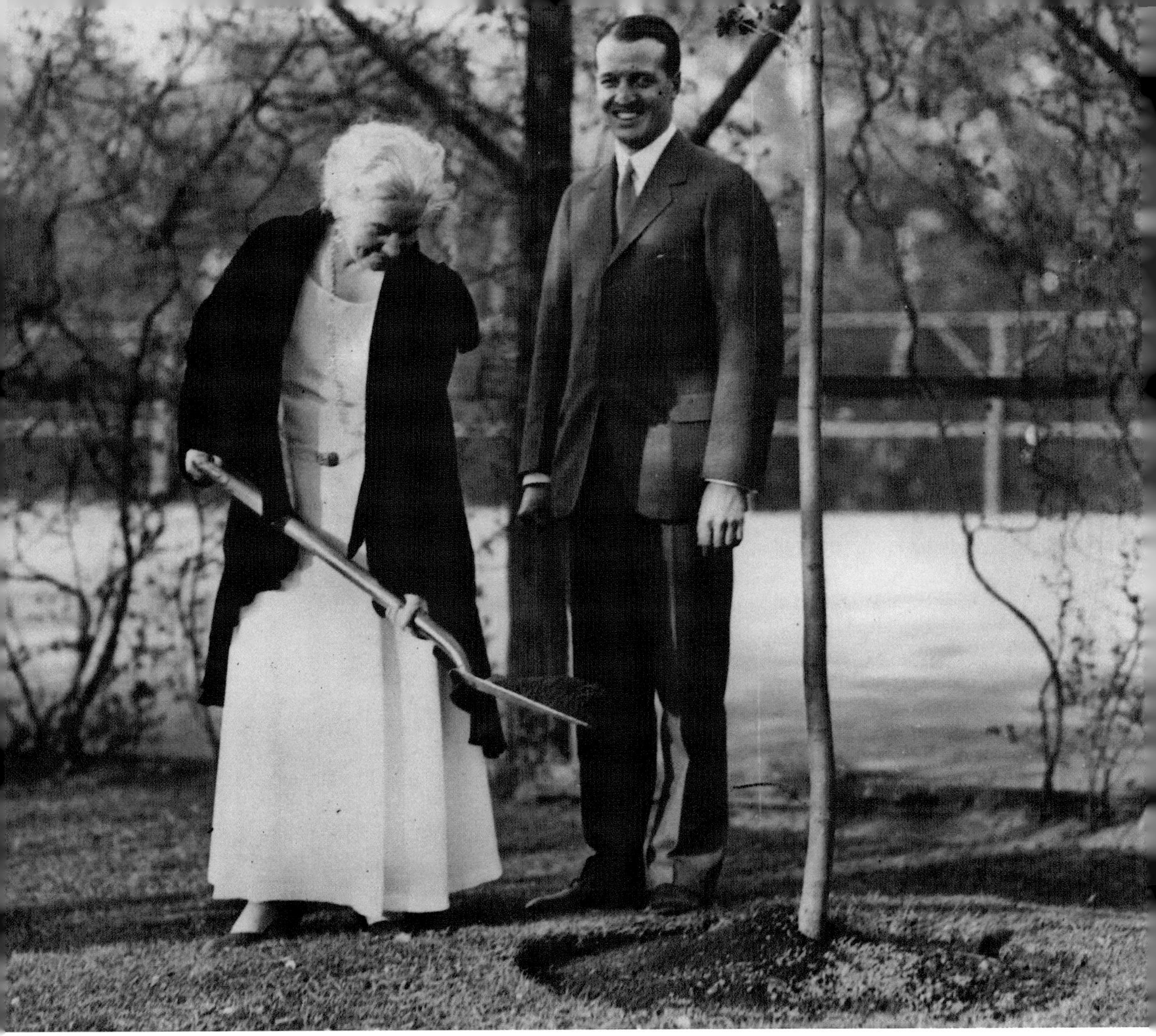

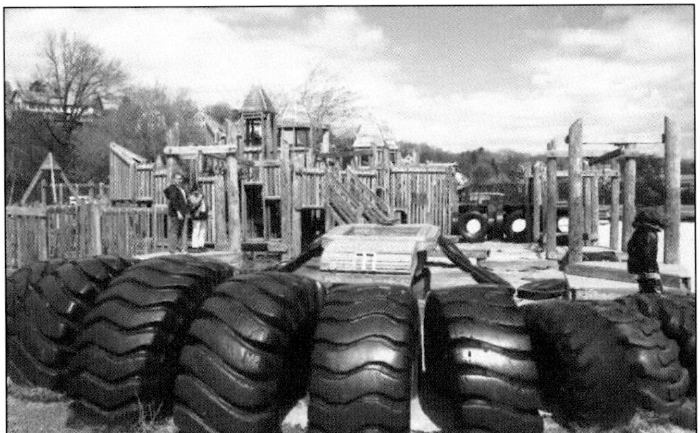

An unidentified woman helps hotel owner Clement Kennedy plant a tree near the hotel tennis courts in the mid-20th century. Trees from numerous famous spots around the United States were planted on the grounds. This particular tree was from Mount Vernon, the Virginia home of George Washington. Today, the playground known as Kids' Cove makes its home on the old hotel property. (Courtesy Louis A. Gallo.)

Children who were guests at the hotel had plenty of activities, including grand costume parties. These privileged children pose on Puritan Road, facing Whales Beach. (Courtesy Louis A. Gallo.)

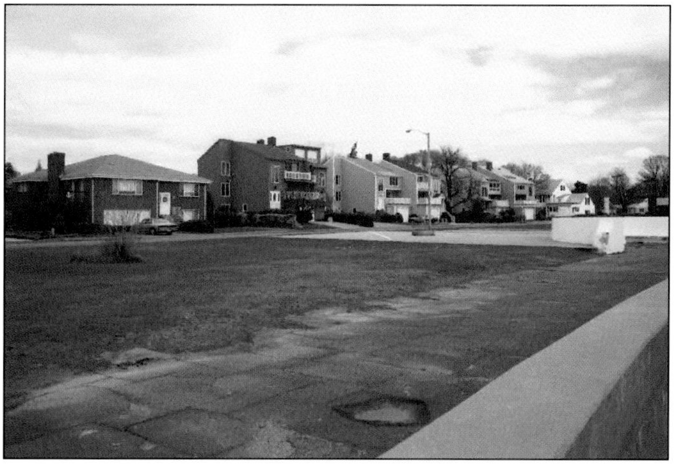

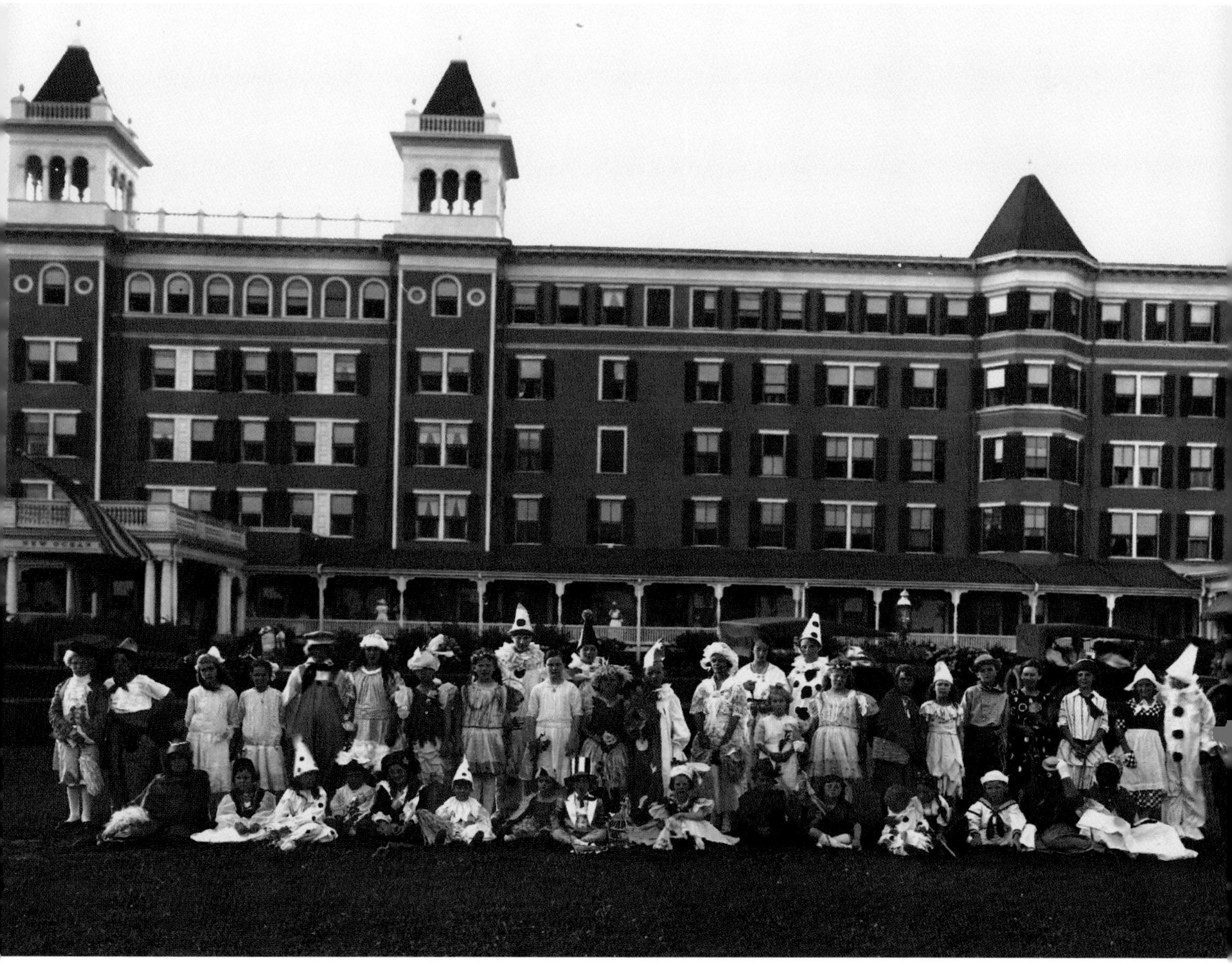

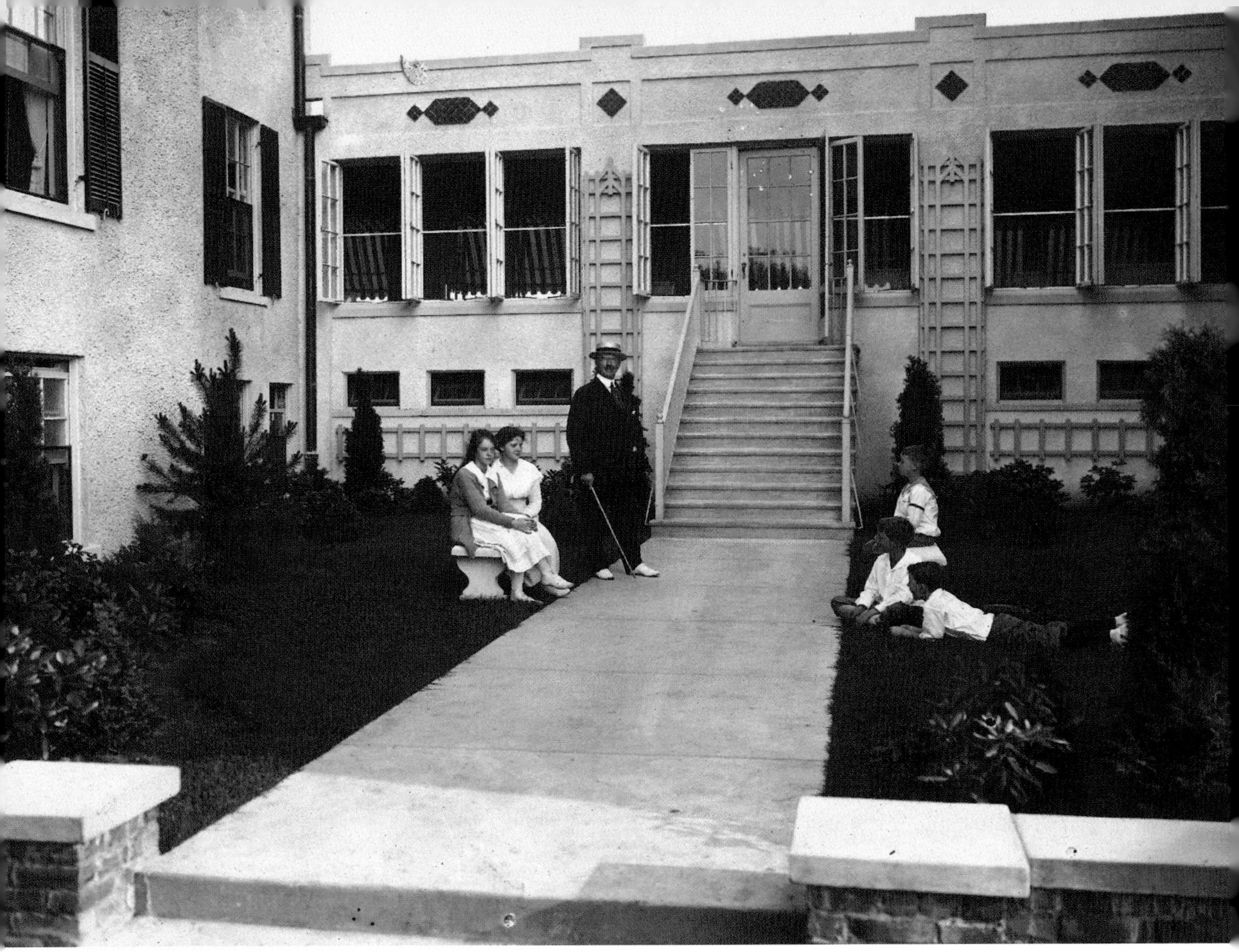

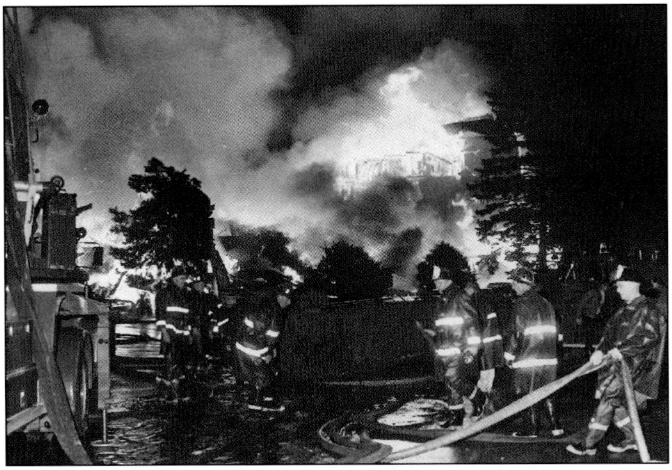

In the mid-1900s, a visiting family gathers behind the connecting hall of the New Ocean House Hotel and Puritan Hall, which was added in 1917. The father dons a straw hat and fashionable white summer shoes, and one of the boys wears a sailor suit. Years later, on May 8, 1969, the hotel went up in flames. (Courtesy Louis A. Gallo.)

The morning after the fire, Swampscott firefighters keep the embers wet. Even the hotel's pool was used as a source of water to put out the mass of flames. Firefighters from all over the North Shore worked together to fight the fire. (Courtesy Swampscott Historical Society.)

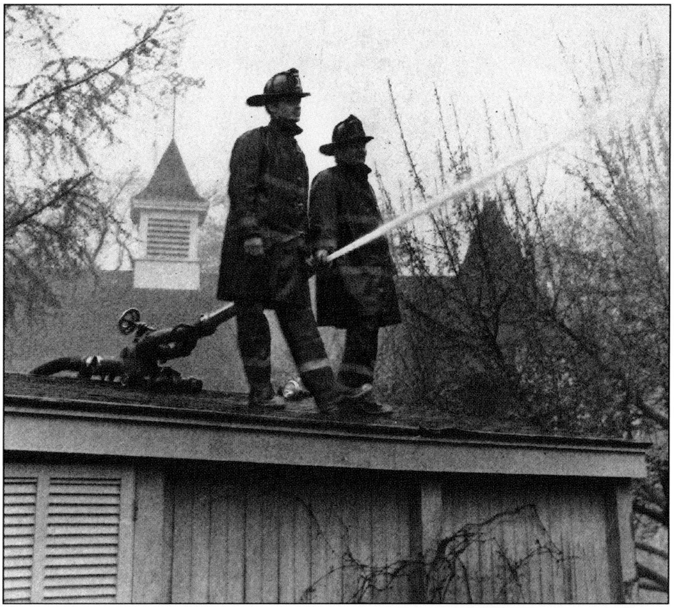

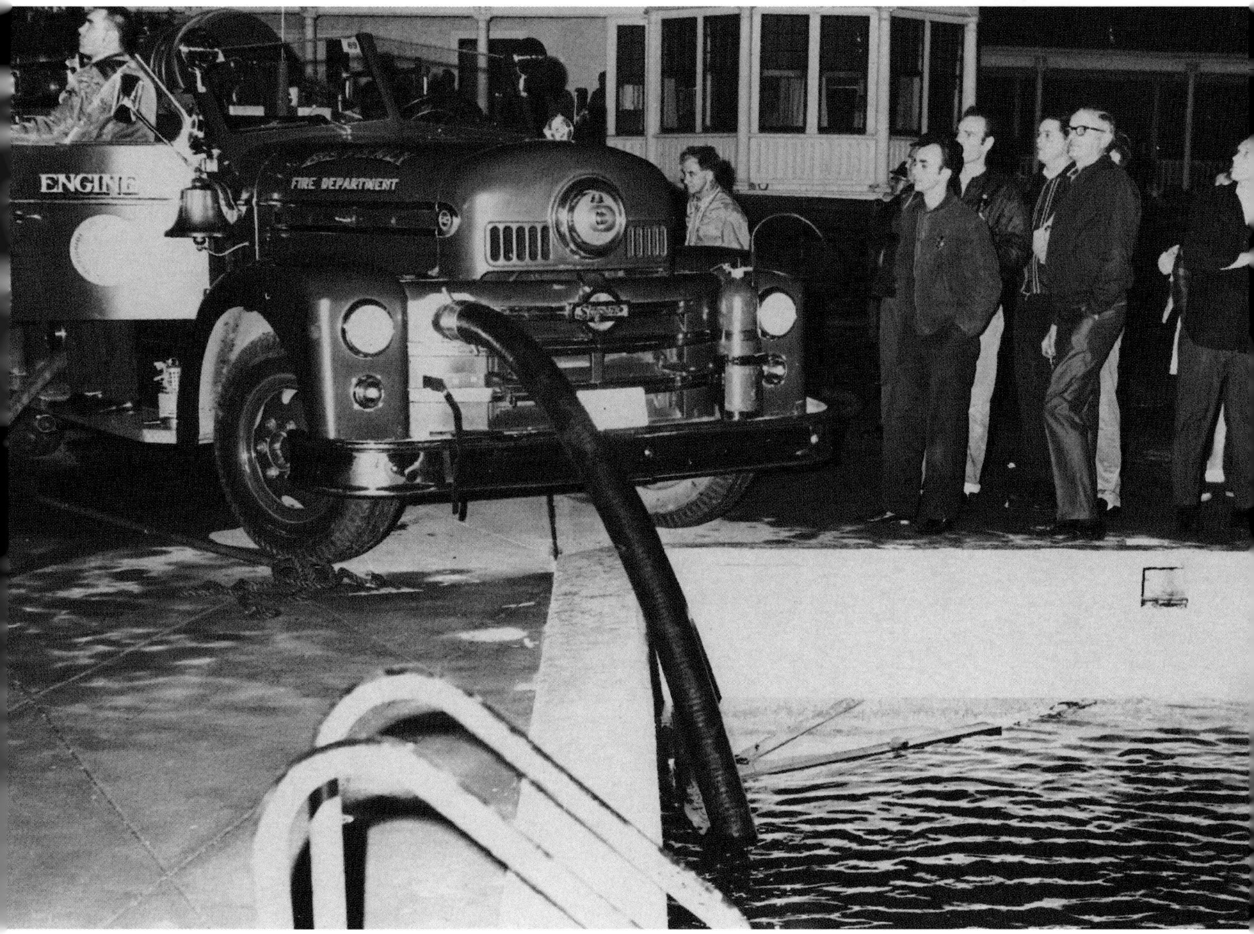

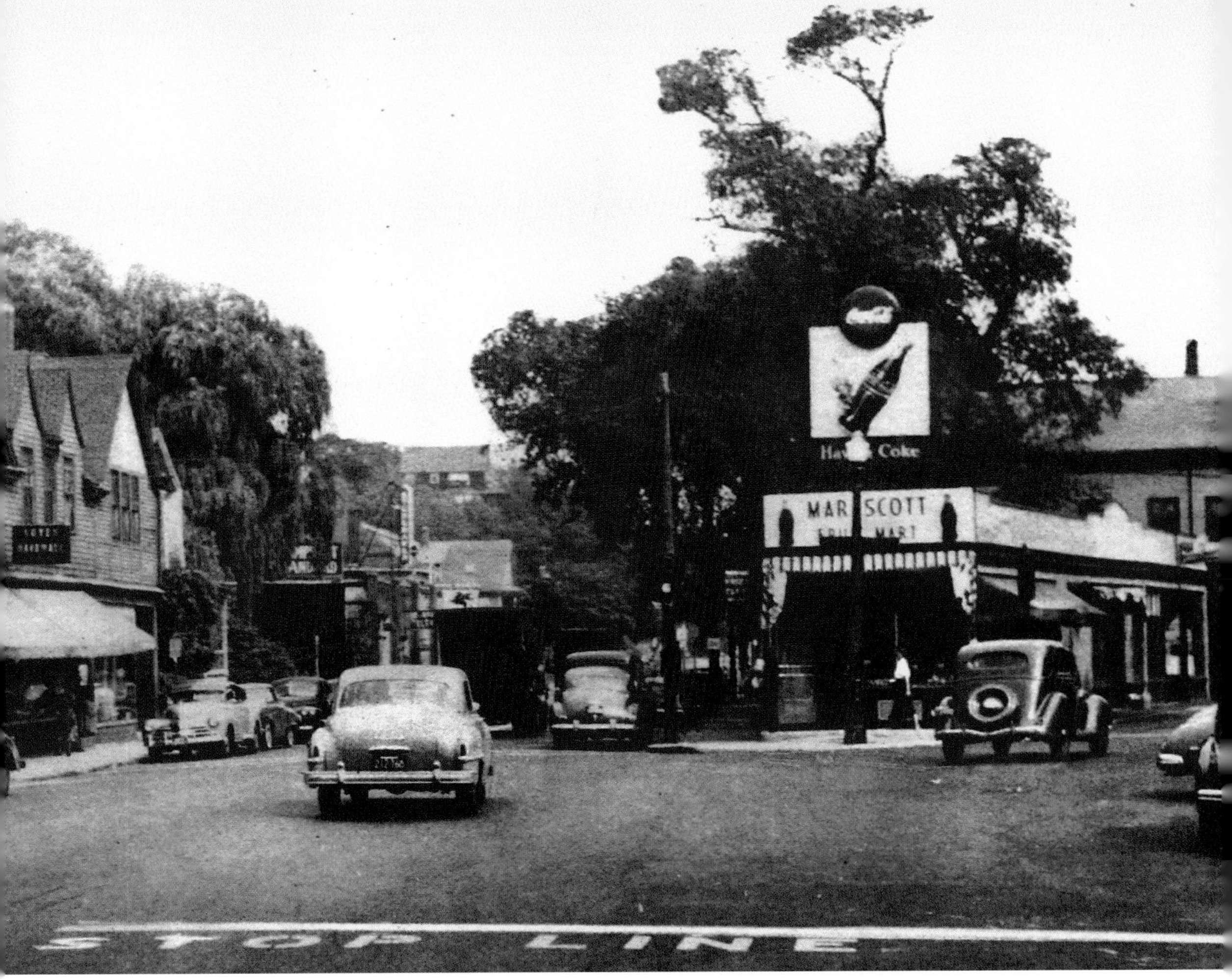

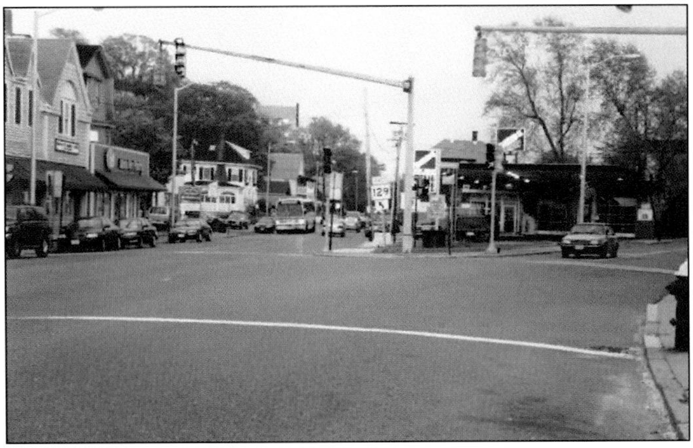

The intersection of Humphrey Street and Puritan Road, also known as Hayscales Corner, is still familiar today. In the mid-1900s, the Mar-Scott Fruit Market, owned by Eva Peretsman and her brother, stood where the Gibbs gas station is located today. Eva Peretsman became a familiar face at town meeting, known for attending in a Santa Claus suit to get a point across. (Courtesy Louis A. Gallo.)

The Swampscott Mall has taken on new life in the past decade, with its strong anchor stores and front entrances. Built in 1955 and later torn down and rebuilt, the mall at one time was enclosed, as shown in the 1977 view (below). (Courtesy Swampscott Historical Commission.)

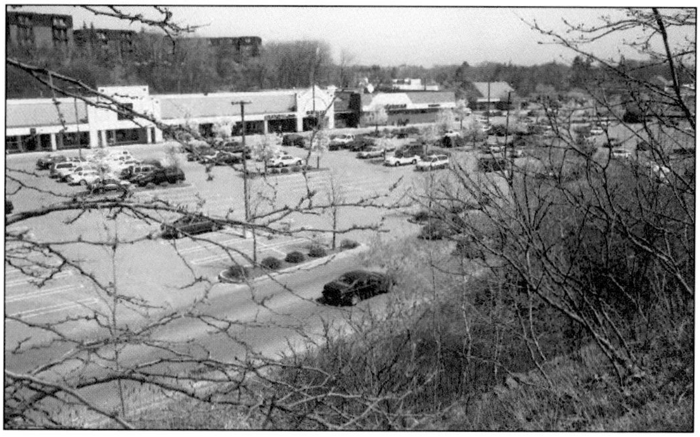

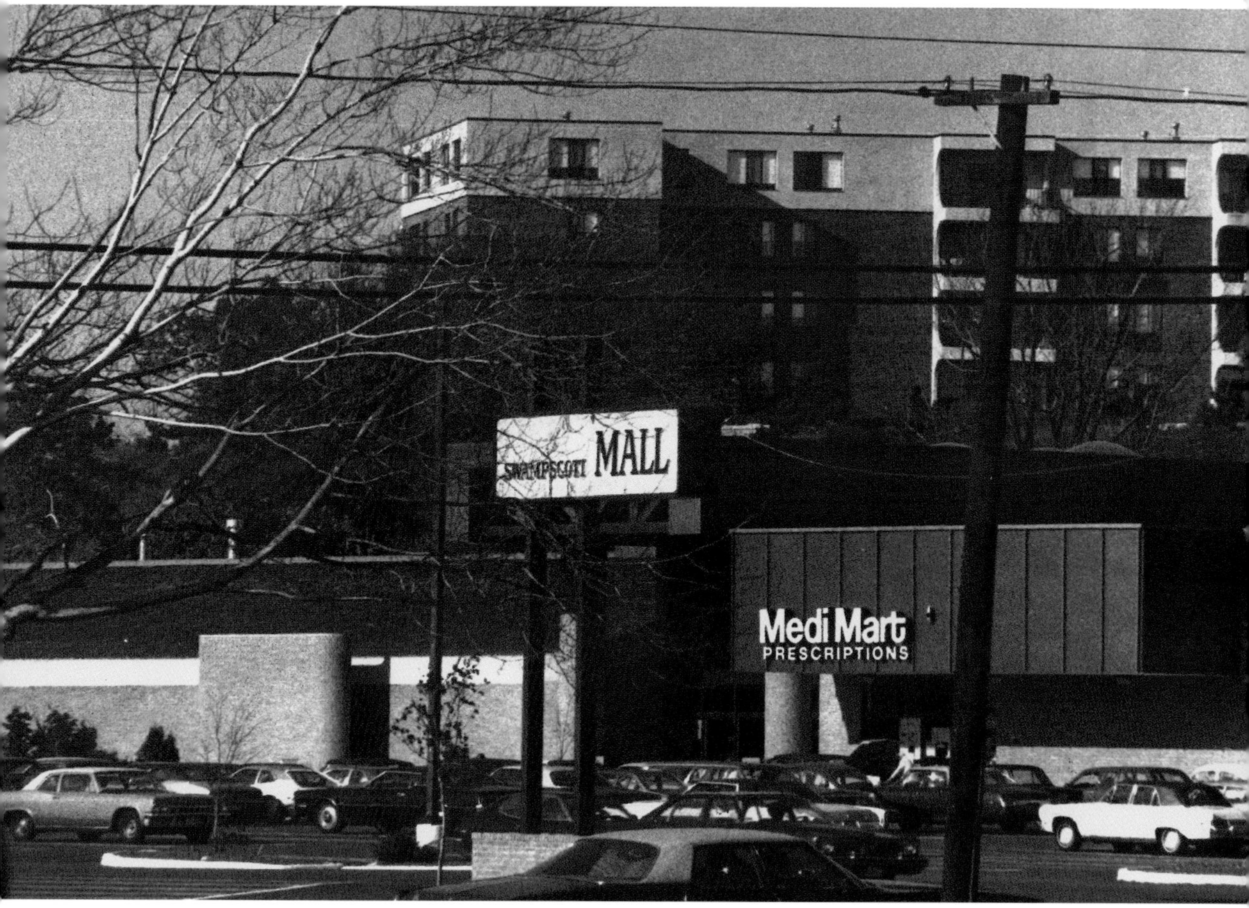

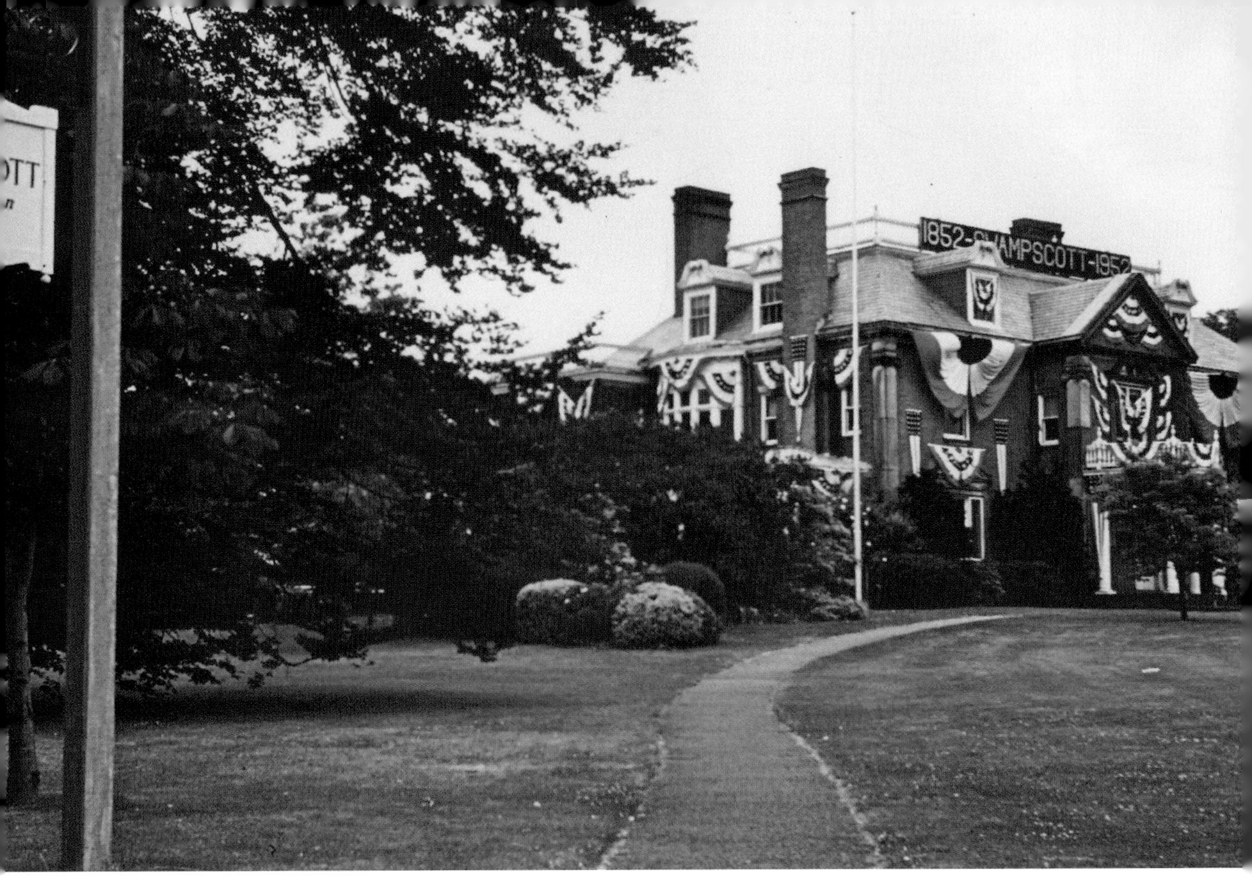

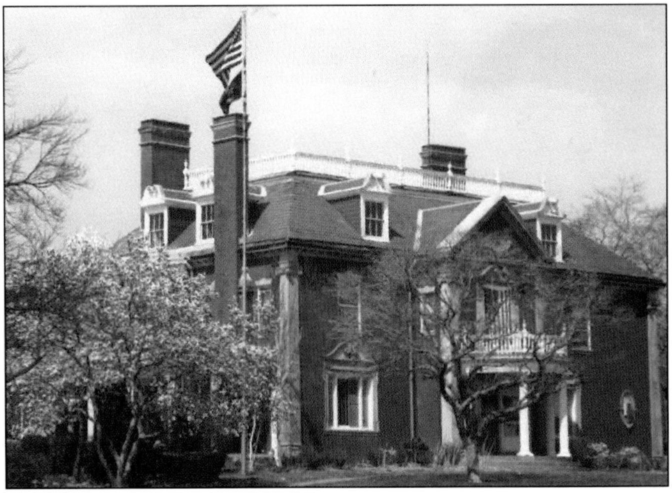

In honor of the town's 100th birthday in 1952, the town hall—once the home of General Electric cofounder Elihu Thomson—is decked out in red-white-and-blue bunting (above). Although some of the landscaping has changed over the years, the patriotism has not. The flag hanging in the middle of the building was added after September 11, 2001. (Courtesy Swampscott Historical Commission.)

The 50th anniversary of Swampscott prompted many residents in town to decorate their homes with American flags and red-white-and-blue bunting. Even Edmund Russell, owner of 189 Burrill Street, went all out in 1902. (Courtesy Swampscott Historical Commission.)

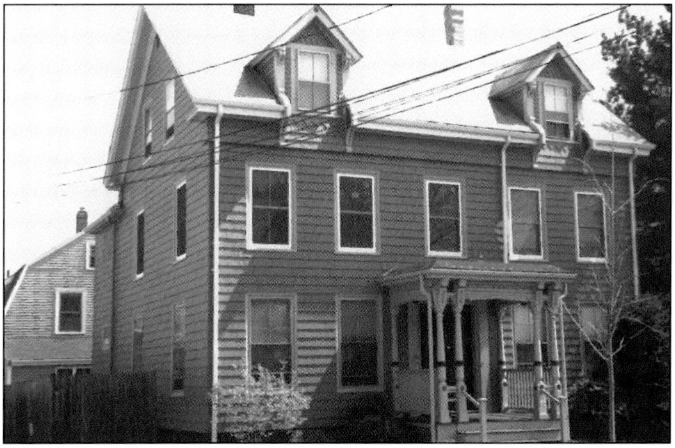

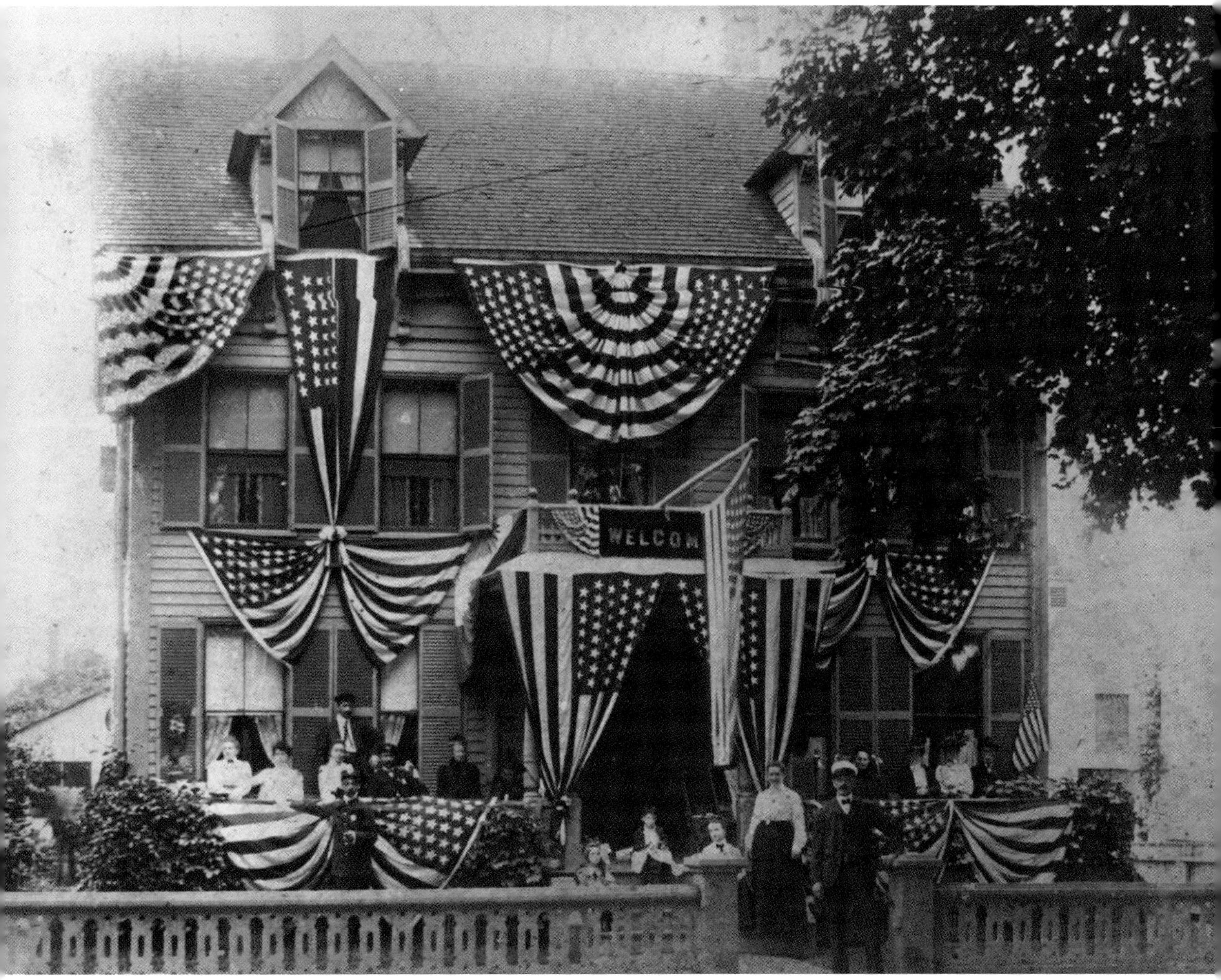

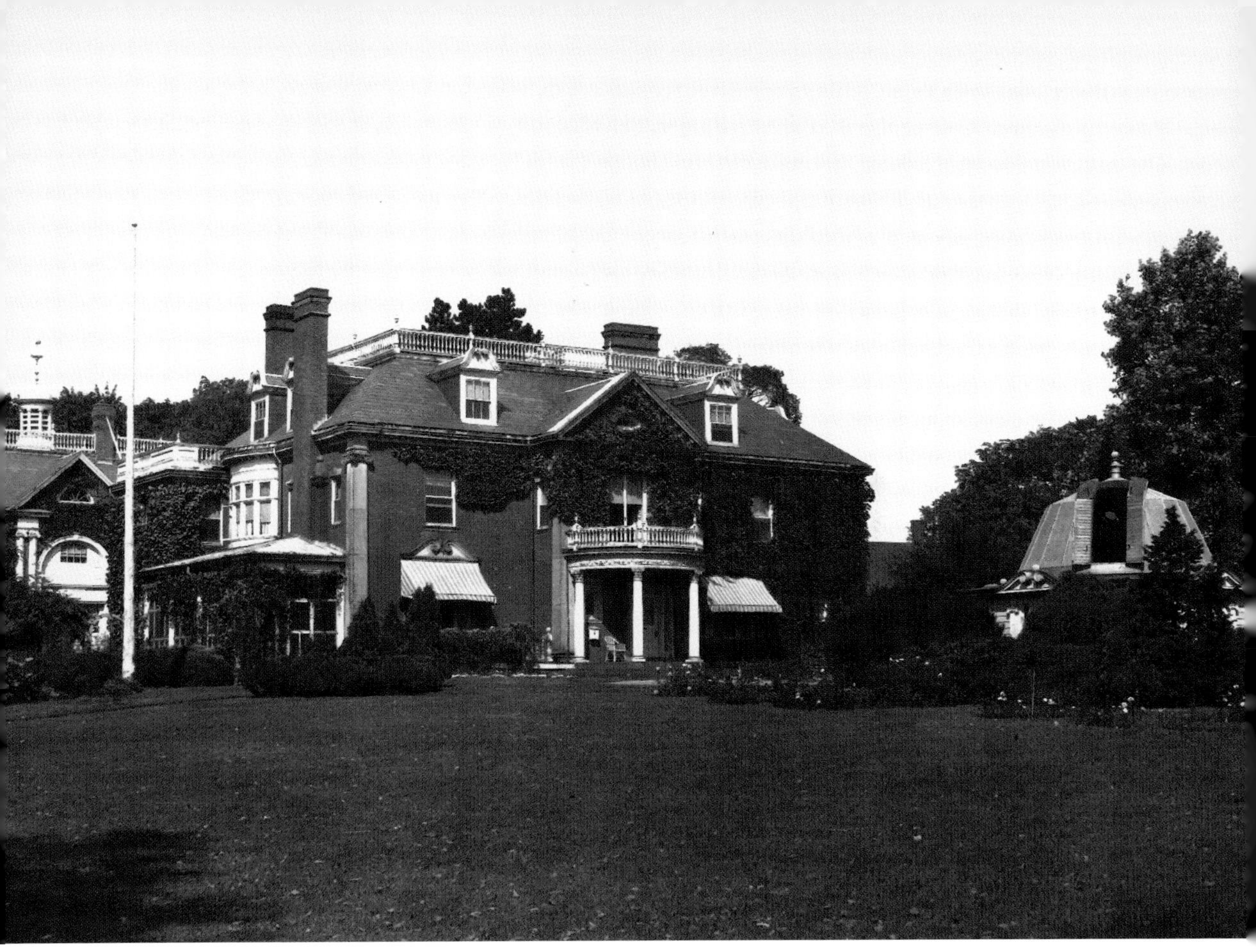

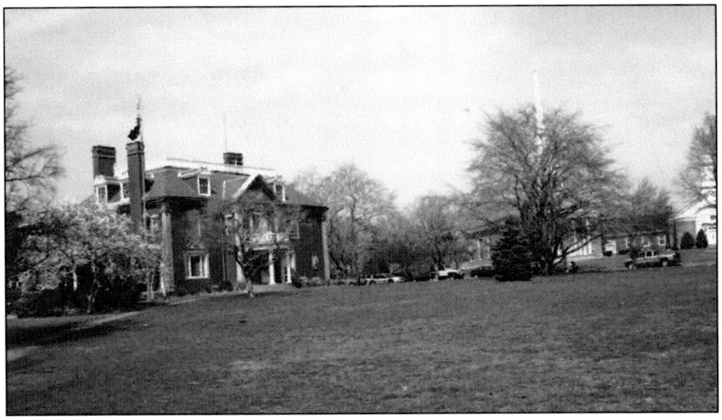

Before becoming known as the Elihu Thomson Administration Building, the red-brick mansion overlooking Monument Avenue was the home and workshop of Elihu Thomson himself. As cofounder of General Electric, Thomson tested many of his inventions in the workshop attached to the main house. A fancier of astronomy, Thomson also used his observatory and telescope to make regular studies of the heavens above. Today, the telescope is in the Franklin Institute in Philadelphia, and the whereabouts of the observatory building is unknown. (Courtesy Louis A. Gallo.)

An unidentified carriage driver pulls up to the front of the Thomson home in the early 1900s. On nearby Burrill Street, Philip Thrasher, a salesman from Marblehead, stops. In the background is the Mudge Estate. (Courtesy Louis A. Gallo.)

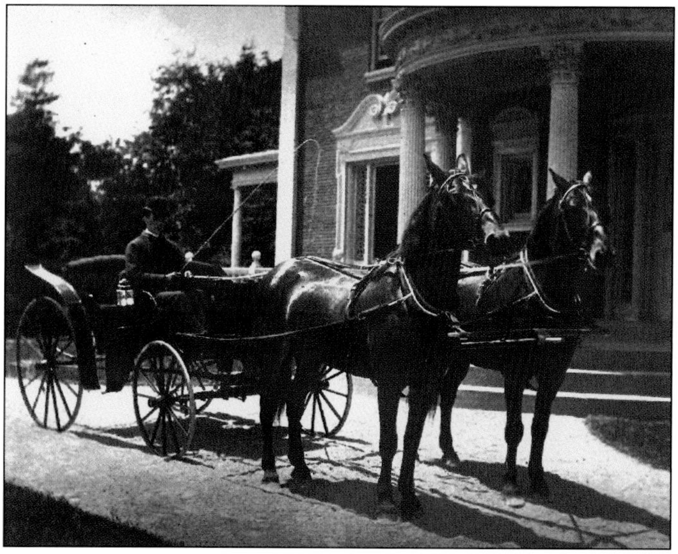

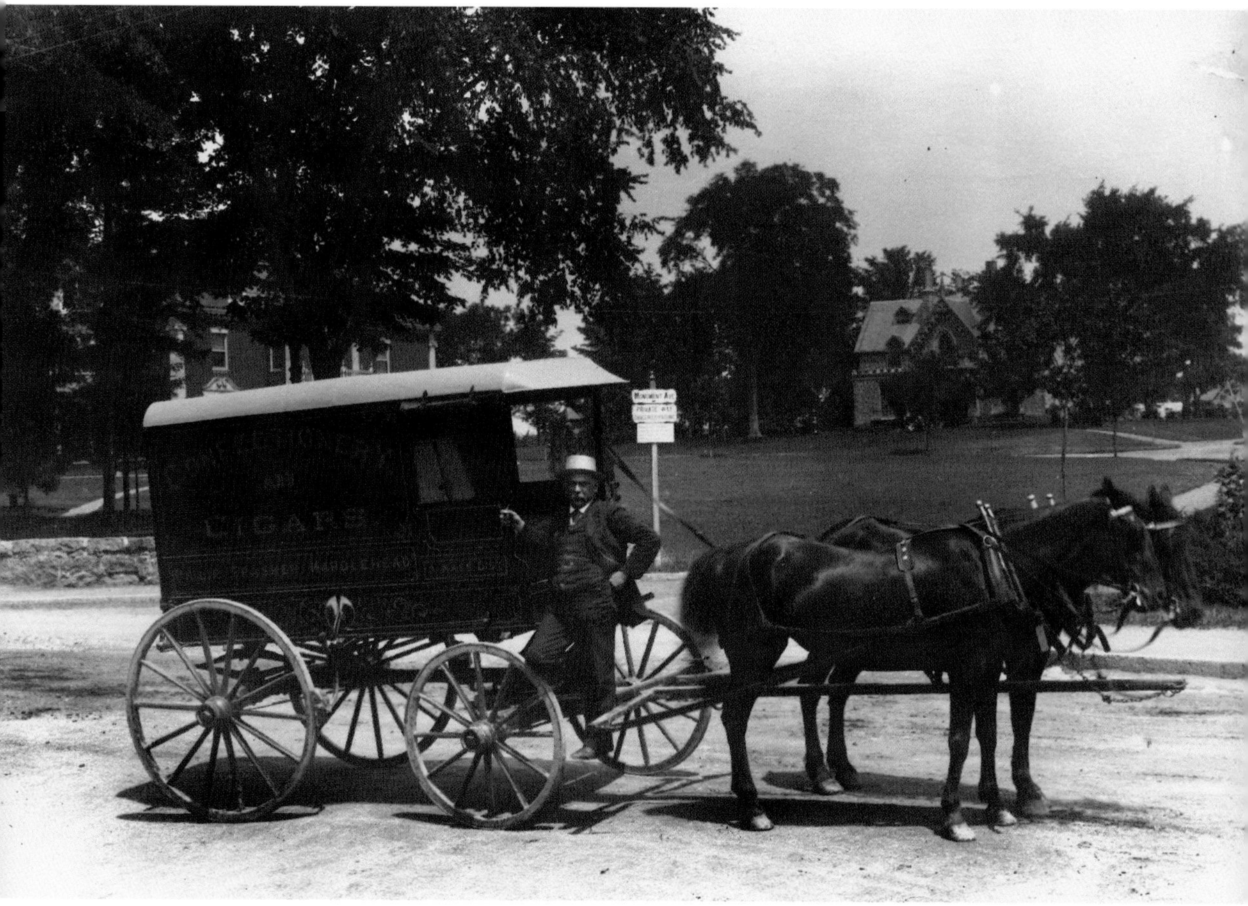

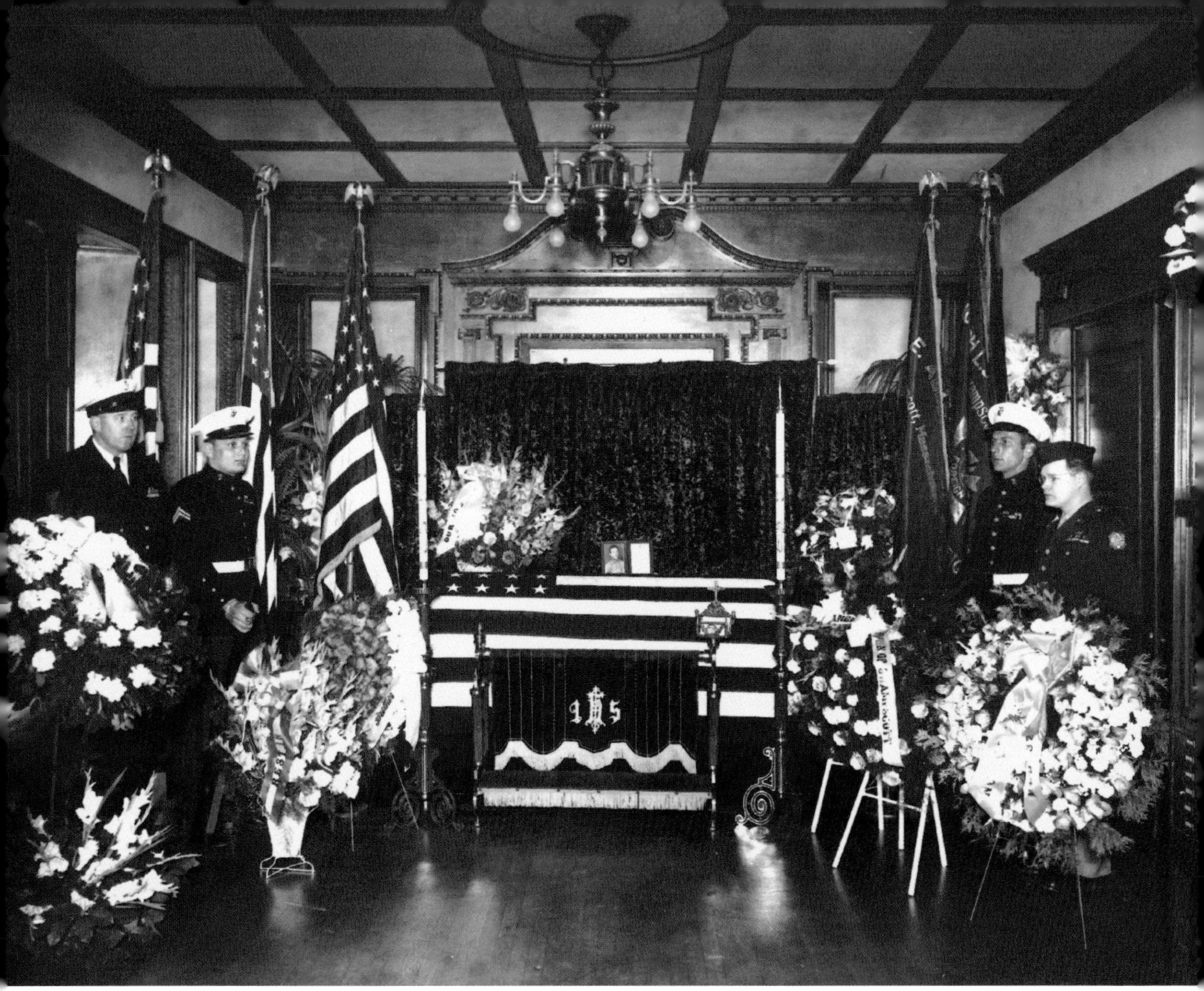

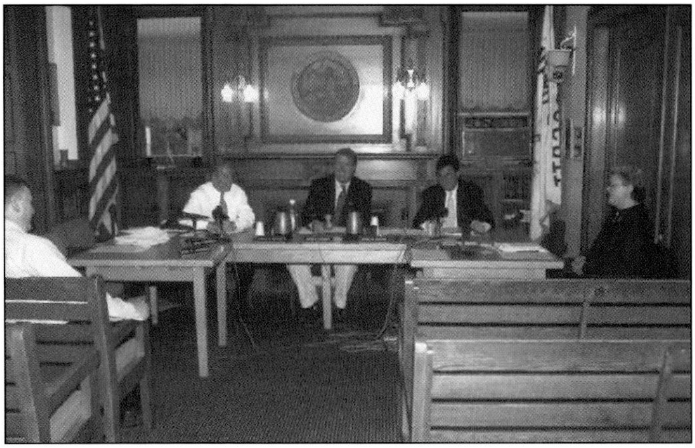

Before it became the selectmen's meeting room in town hall, this room served as Elihu Thomson's living room. According to Jim Cropley (far right), a wake was held for Harold Raymond in the room as part of the reburial project after World War II. Today, selectmen meet in the room regularly. From left to right are Kevin Goggin (building inspector); Dan Santanello, Reid Cassidy, and Marc Paster (selectmen); and Patricia George (executive secretary to the selectmen). Missing from the photograph are Carole Shutzer and Paul Levenson (selectmen). (Courtesy Louis A. Gallo.)

A Swampscott High School class gathers for a reunion photograph in front of the Willey House on Humphrey Street. The Willey House—also known as Kings Beach Inn and, later, as the Sea Breeze Inn—thrived and offered risqué entertainment until 1970, when it burned. (Courtesy Louis A. Gallo.)

Chapter 2
When We Were Young

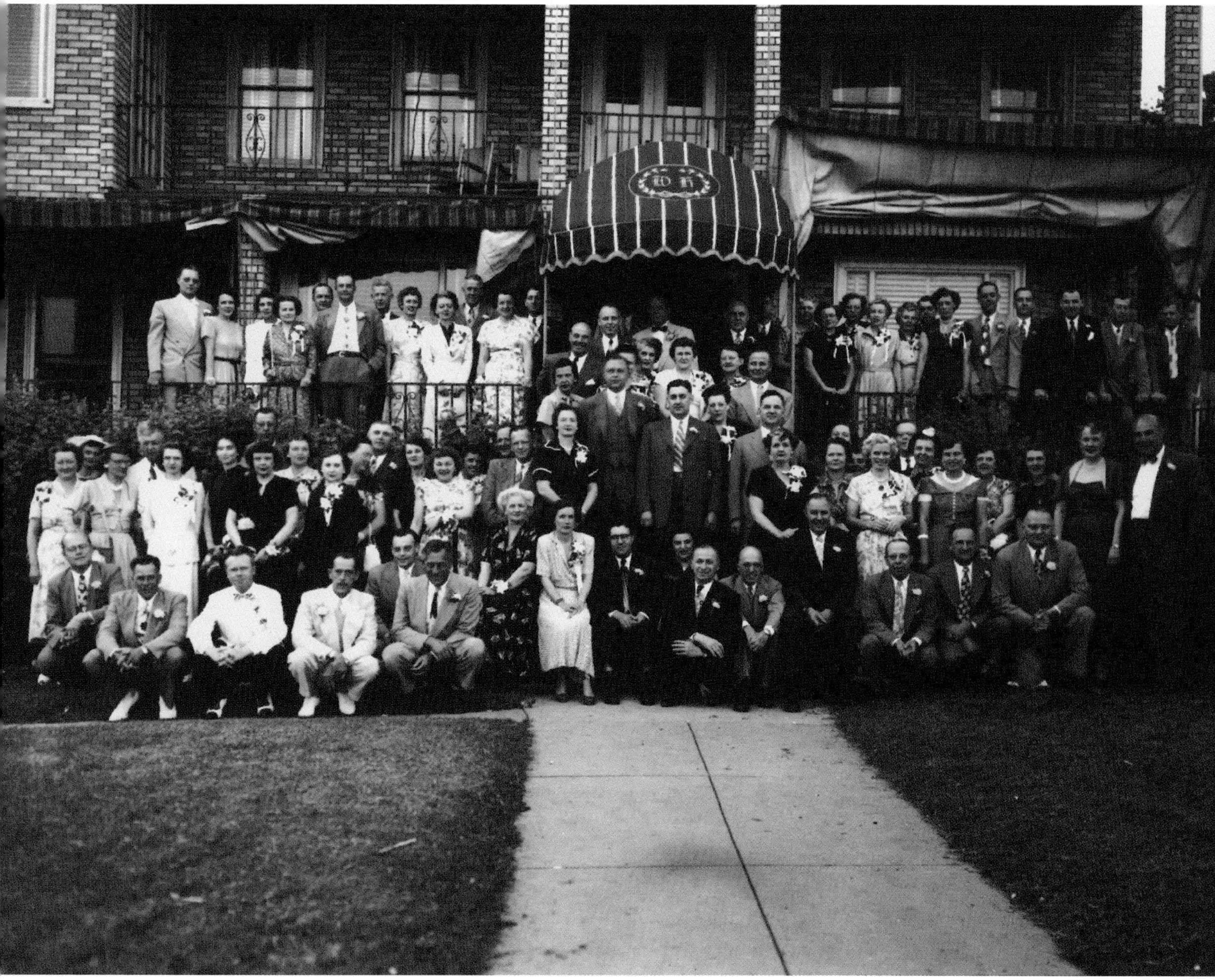

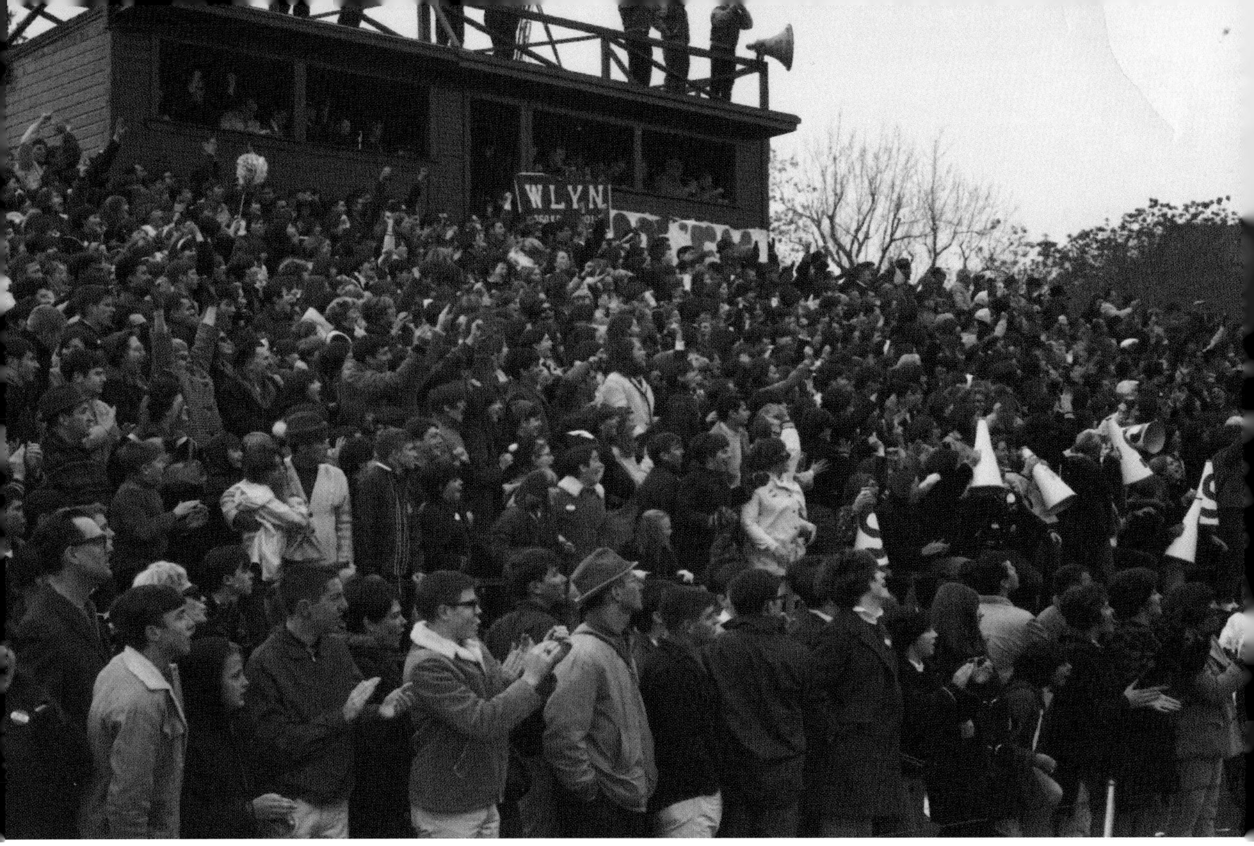

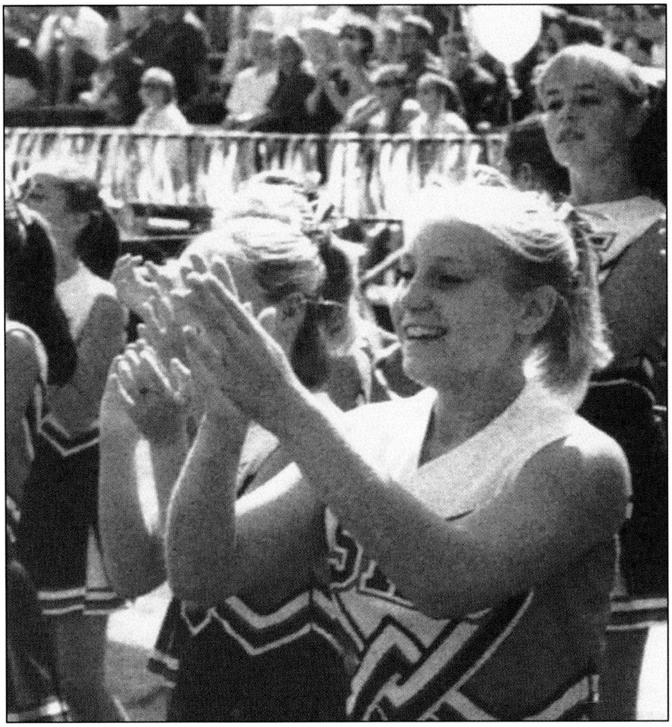

A 1960s football crowd goes wild for a Big Blue touchdown. Today, the stands at Blocksidge Field still pack a crowd, and cheerleaders still make sure the Big Blue fans cheer on the boys throwing the pigskin. (Courtesy Swampscott Historical Commission.)

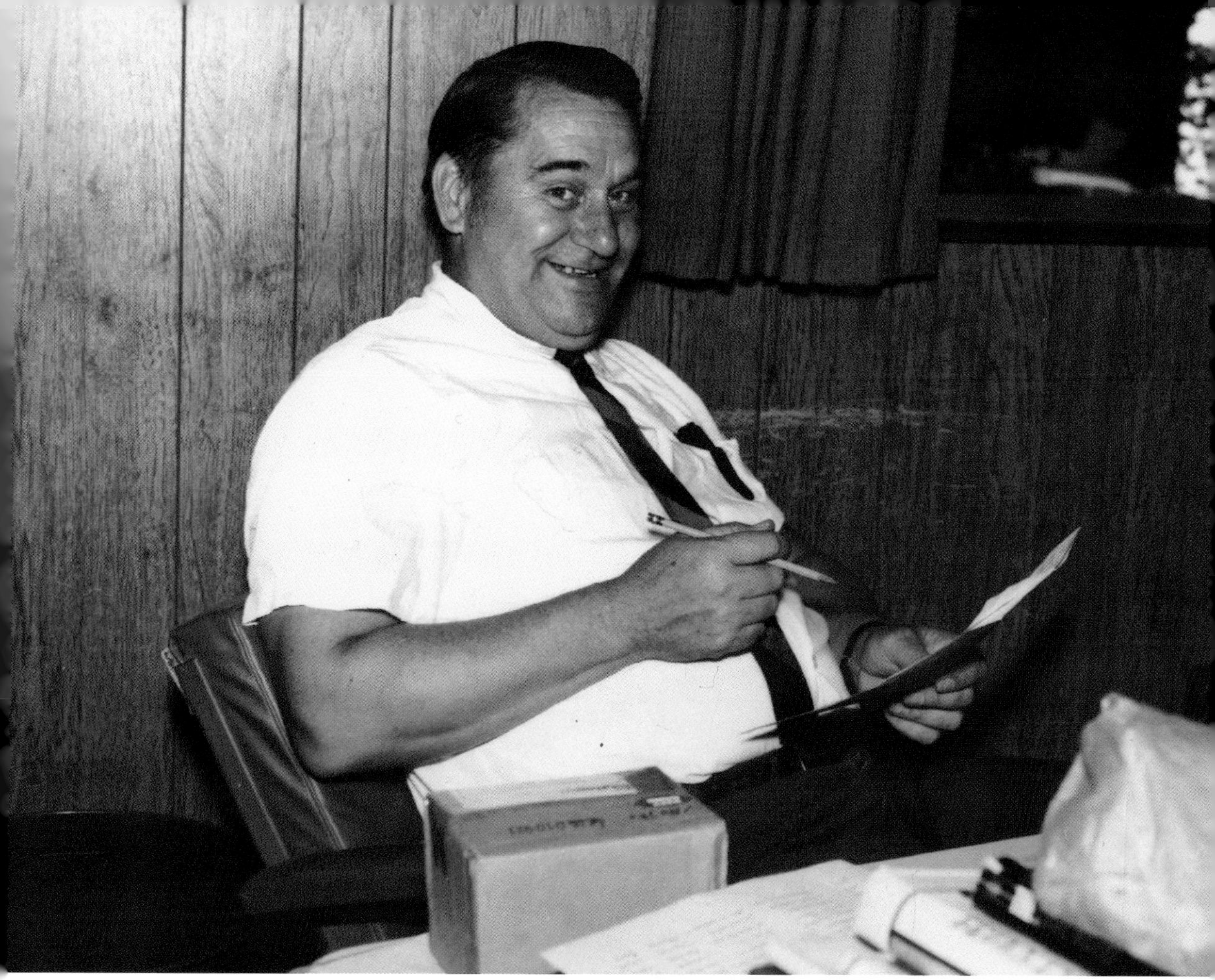

Stan Bondelevitch, shown here in 1970, is considered the best football coach the Big Blue ever had. "Bondi," who passed away in 2002 at the age of 83, will forever be remembered for his 42-year coaching career. From 1966 to 1972, his teams boasted 62 wins and only 3 losses. His 1967 team alone produced three players who went on to play in the National Football League: Dick Jauron for Detroit and Cincinnati, Billy Adams for the Buffalo Bills, and Tom Toner for the Green Bay Packers. (Courtesy Swampscott Historical Commission.)

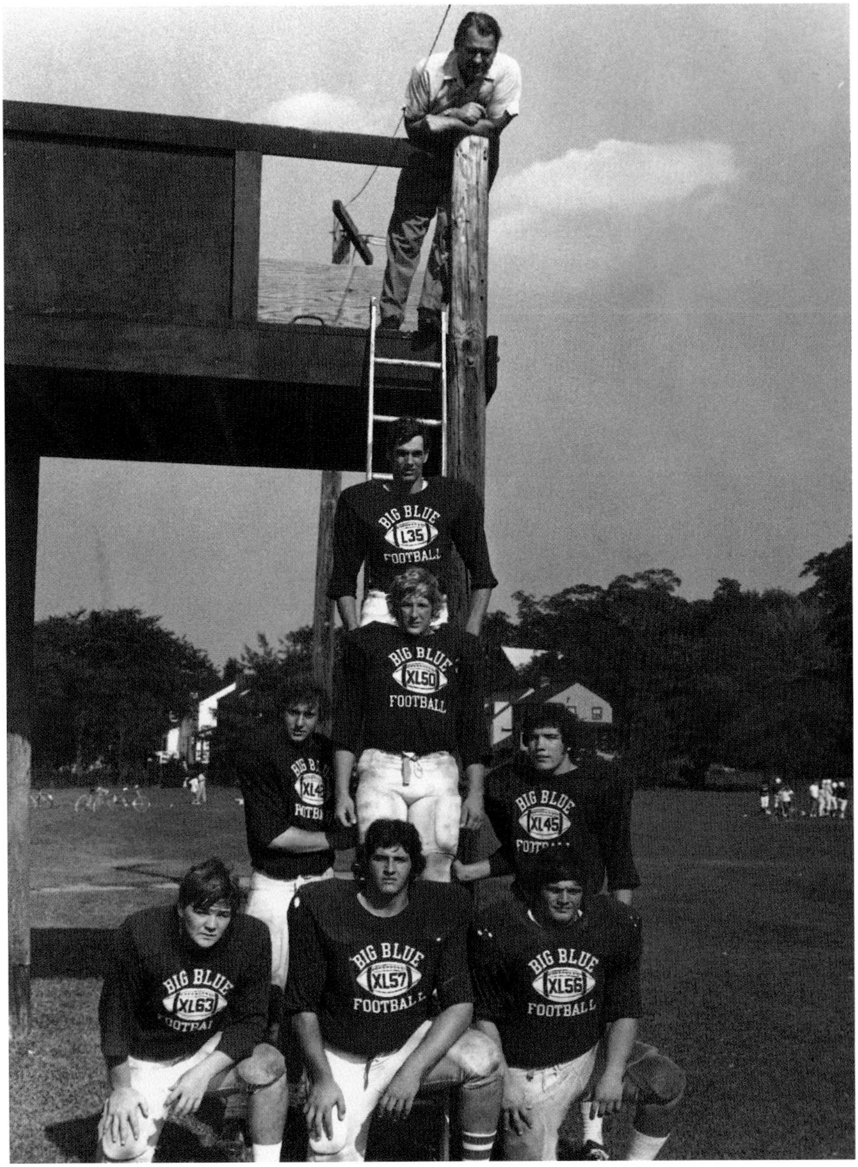

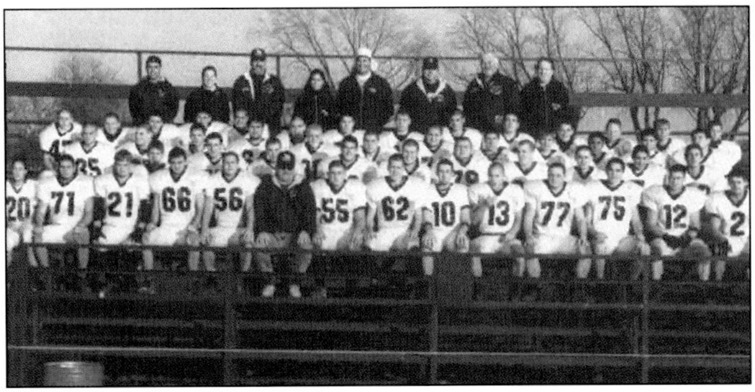

Football coach Stan Bondelevitch towers above the core of his 1972 team during a practice session at Blocksidge Field. Today's team still packs a punch, and several of today's coaches, including head coach Steve Dembowski, played for the same team while attending Swampscott High School. (Courtesy Swampscott Historical Commission.)

Before he became one of the best-known sports anchors on Boston television, Mike Lynch left his mark on Big Blue and Harvard football. Shown here in the 1969 Thanksgiving Day football game, Lynch kicked the final field goal against Marblehead with one minute left and won the game 15-13. (Courtesy Louis A. Gallo.)

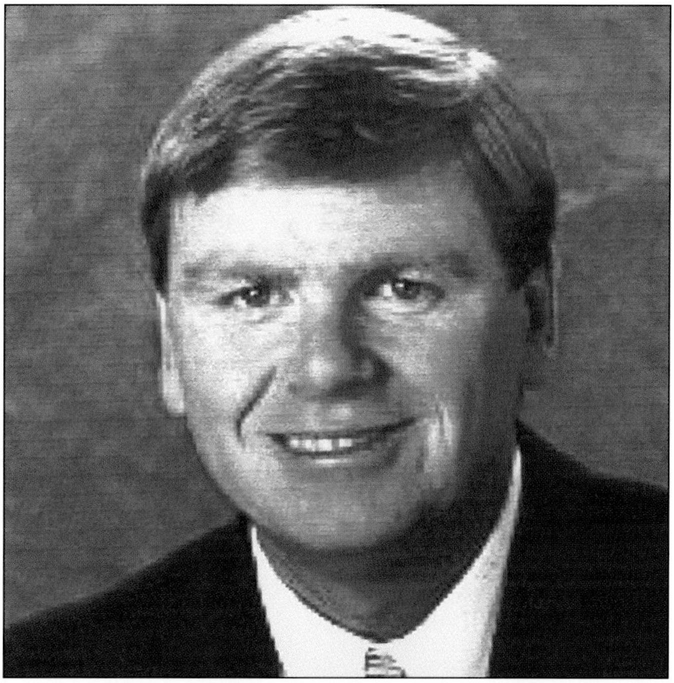

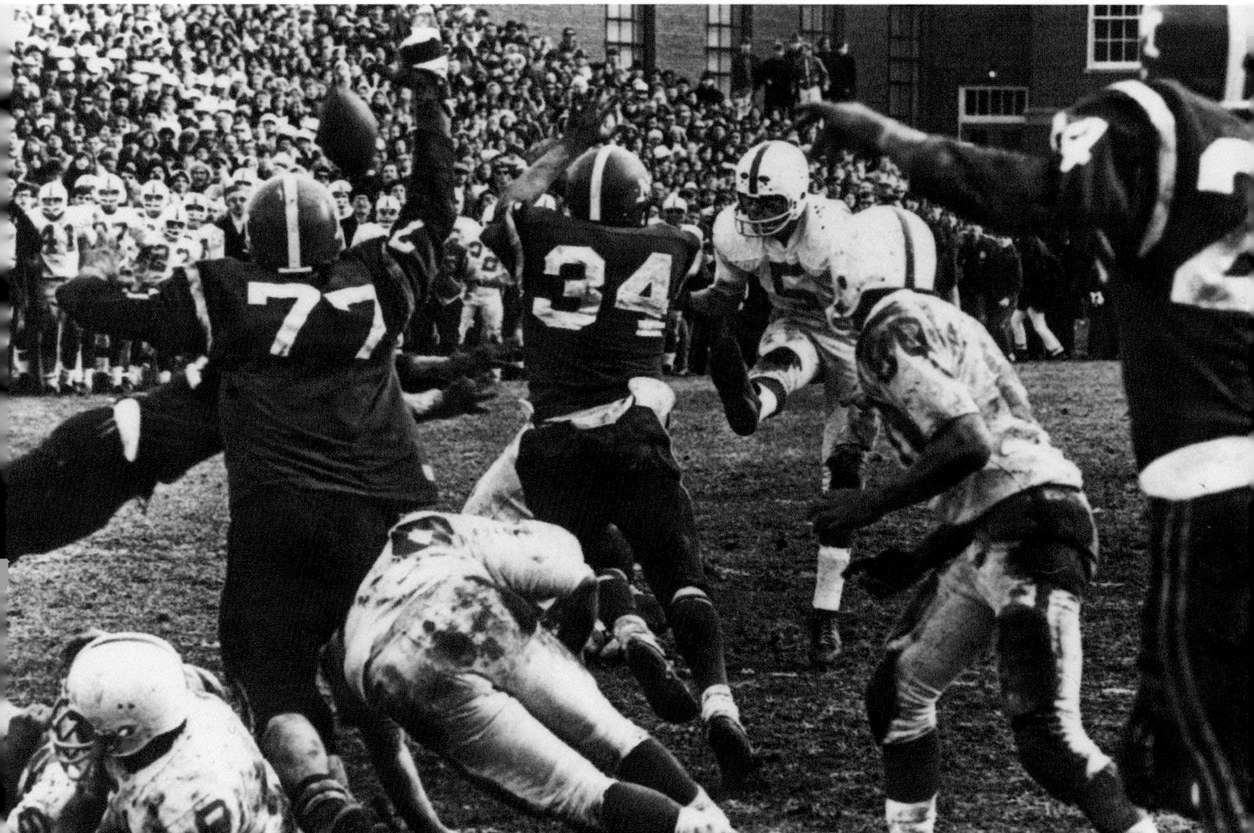

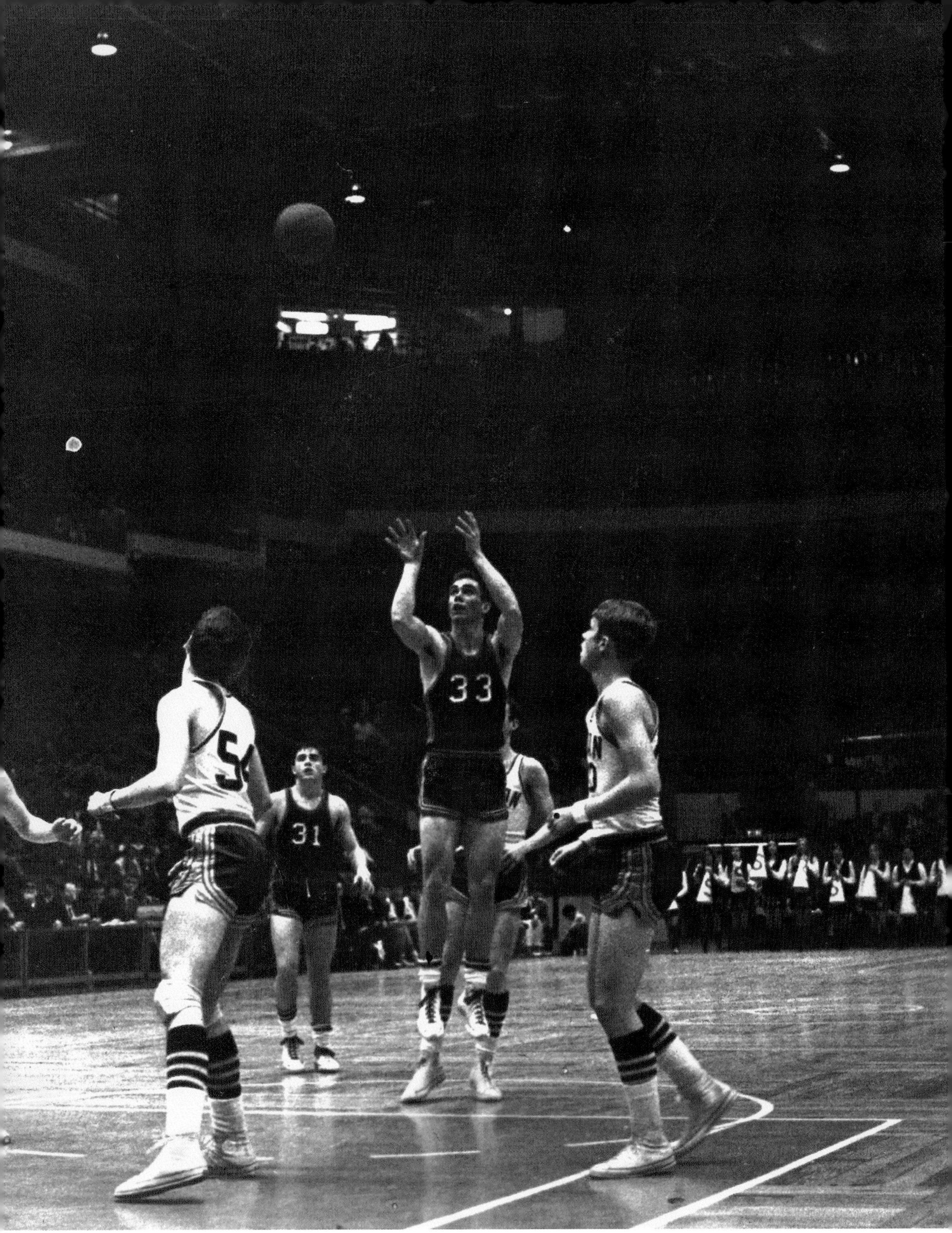
33
31

No matter what ball was put into play, Dick Jauron excelled. Known today as the winning coach of the Chicago Bears, Jauron is shown in 1969 (previous page), throwing a jump shot in the Boston Garden during the high school championships. In May 1969, before heading off to attend Yale, Jauron is recognized for his athletic and academic achievement with awards from Bertram Rodgers, school principal. (Courtesy Louis A. Gallo.)

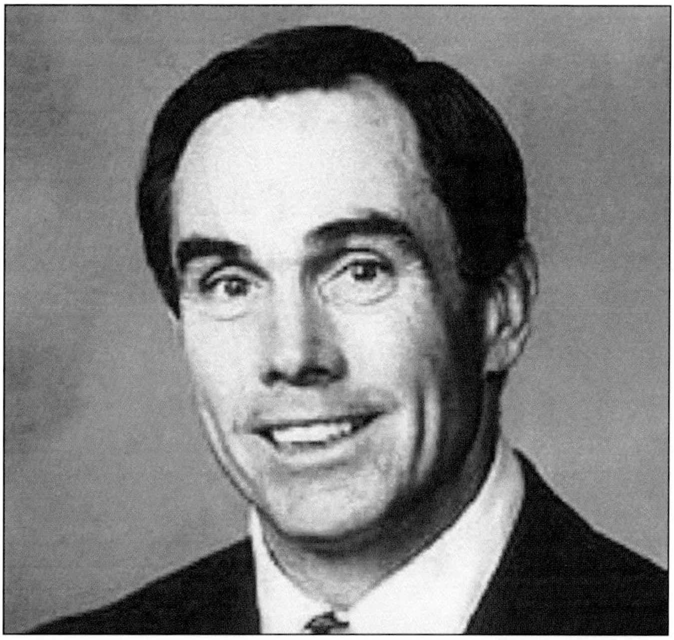

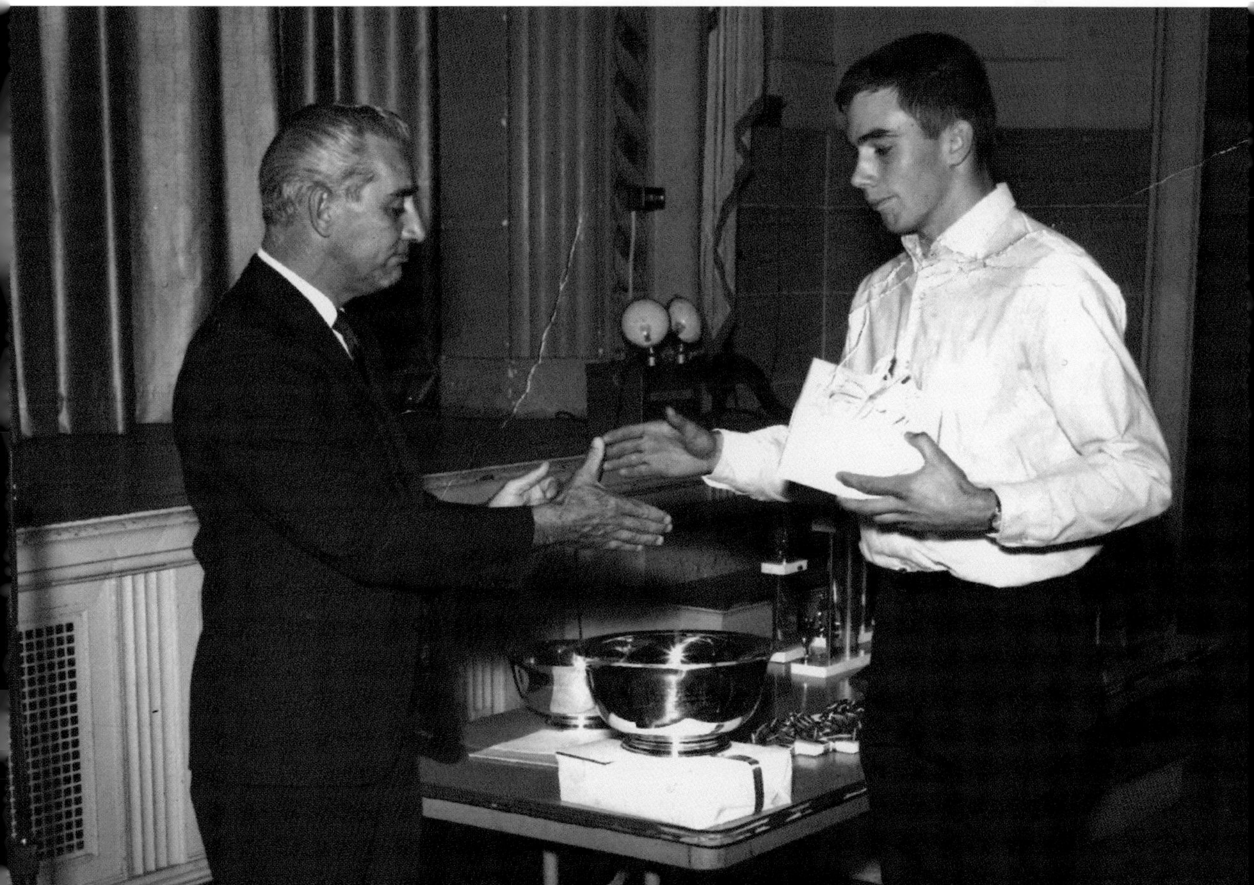

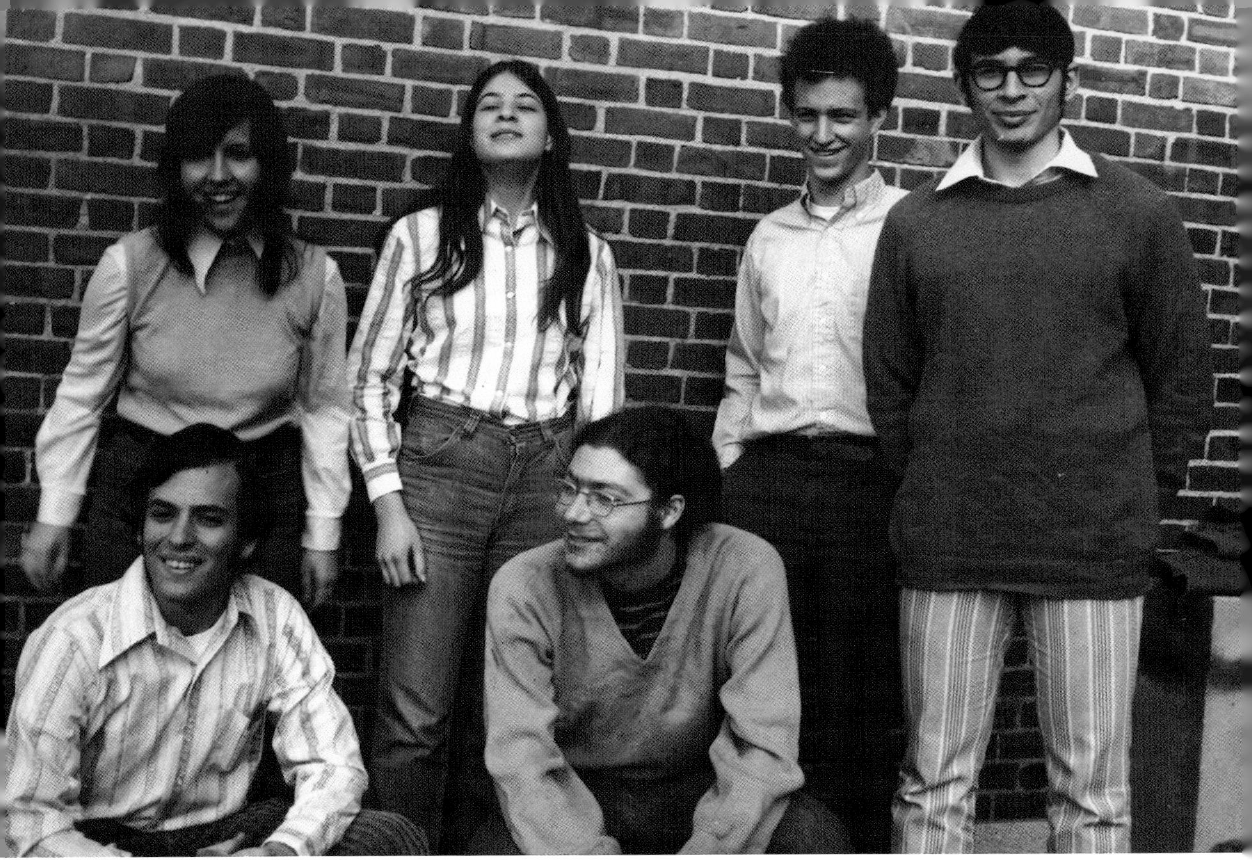

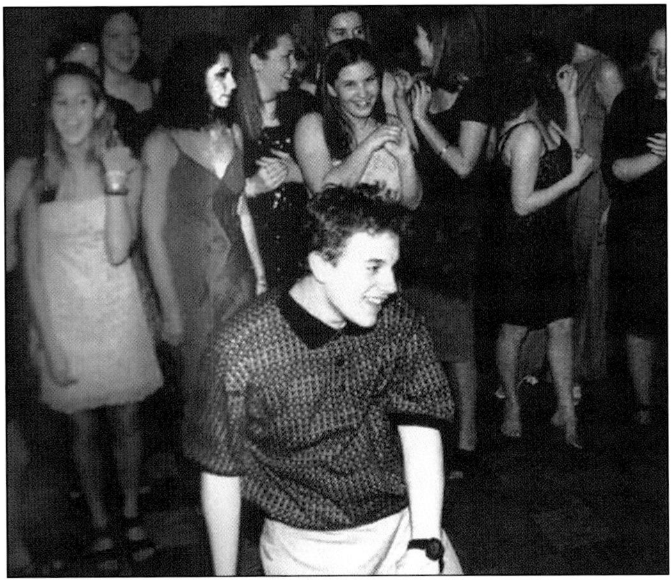

Good fashions never die; they just get recycled. Stripes, long hair, and long collars were the rage in the 1970s. Today, some of those fashions have returned, but the classic knit polo shirt has been added and clunky shoes are a must. (Courtesy Louis A. Gallo.)

High school would not be the same without the prom. In May 1960, the junior prom is held in the high school gymnasium with a *South Pacific* theme. The Class of 2000 took its senior prom to the Marriott. (Courtesy Louis A. Gallo.)

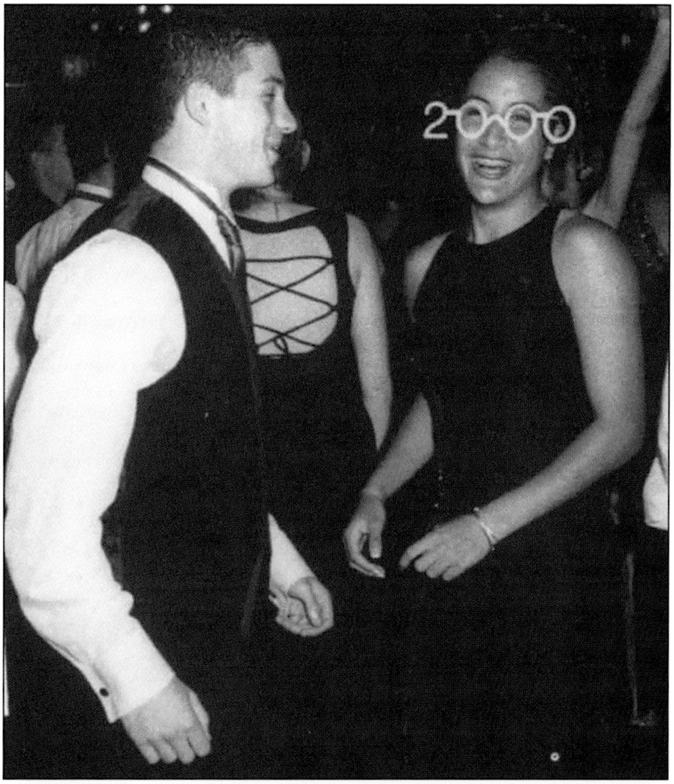

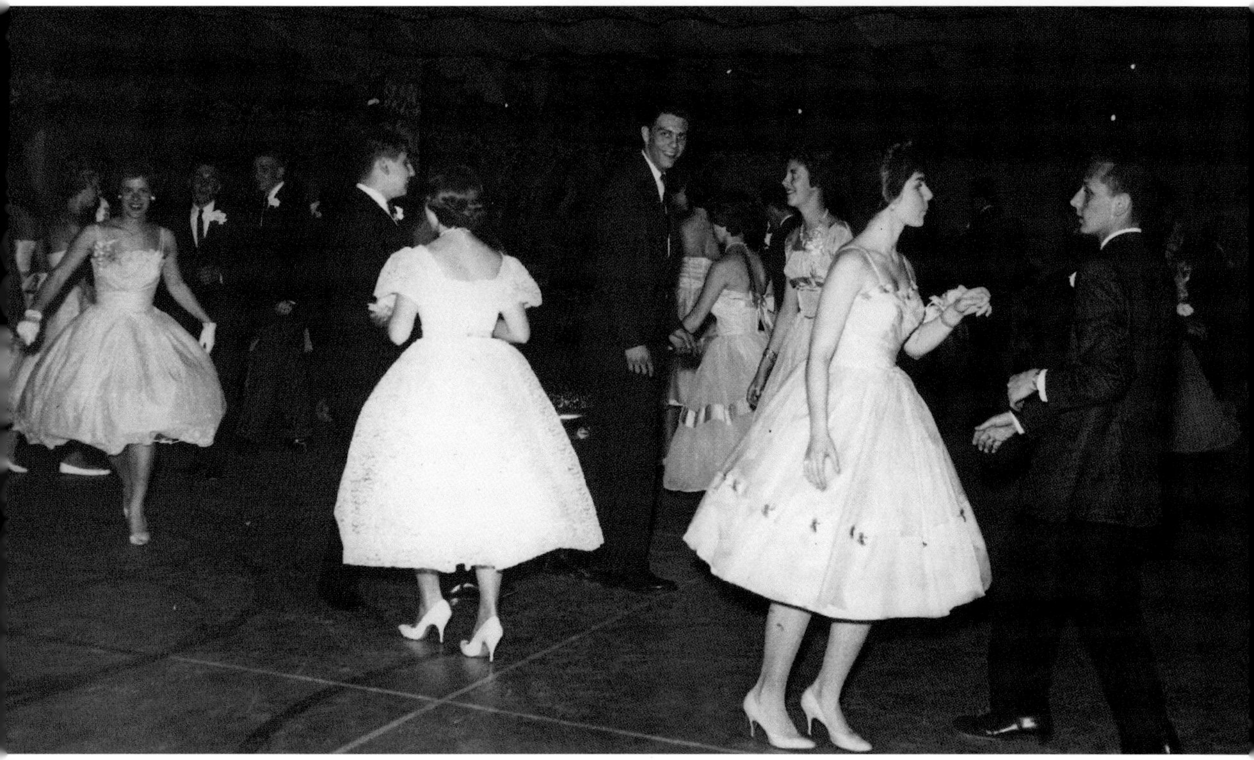

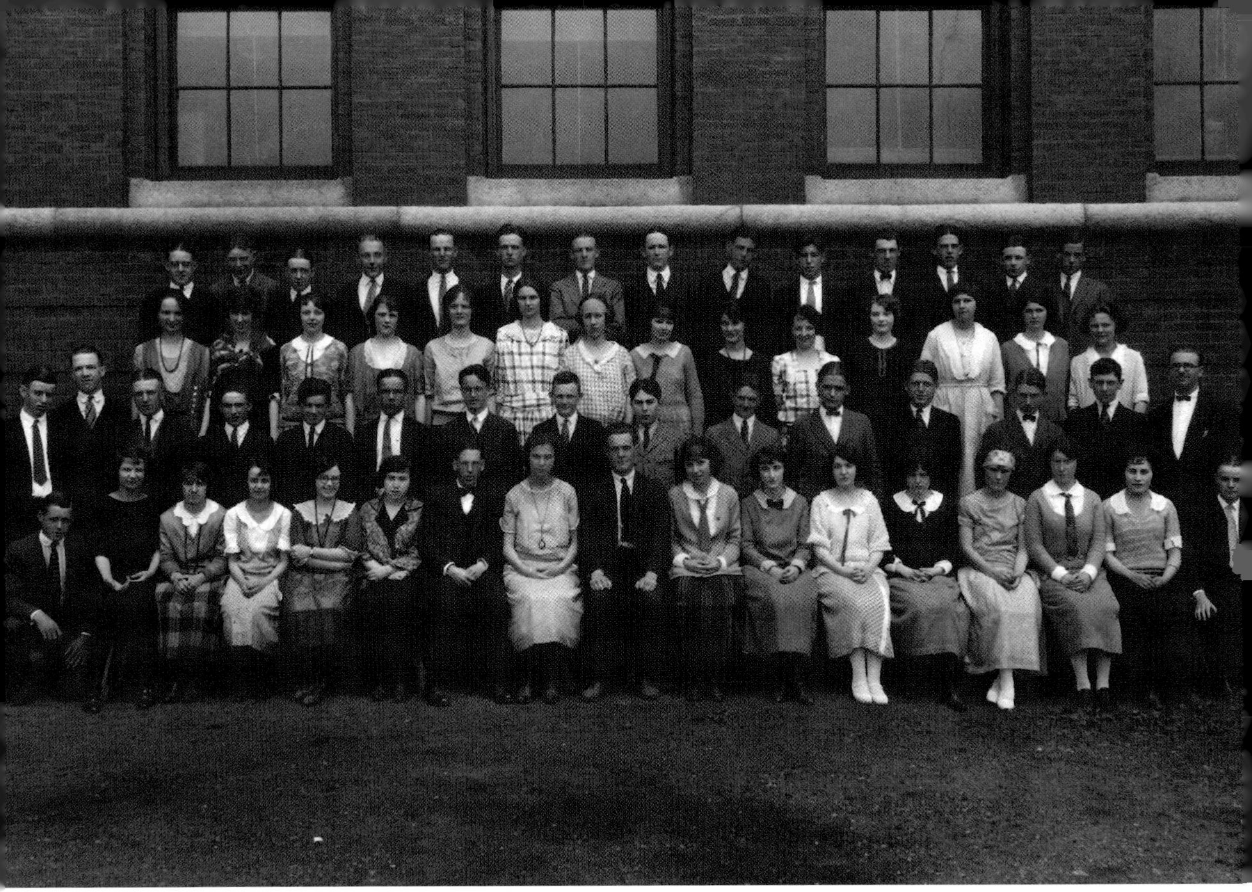

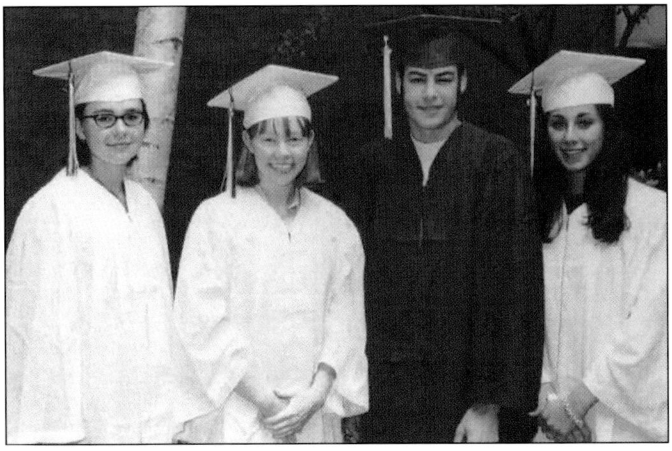

Students in the Class of 1923 pose for a class portrait in front of the school on Greenwood Avenue. Class of 2000 honor students, from left to right, Victoria Elman, Lindsay MacDonald, Gabriel Cooper, and Jillian Strasnick go for the traditional cap-and-gown look. (Courtesy Swampscott Public Library.)

Louise Stanley poses with her students in grades one through three at the Farm School in 1909. The one-room schoolhouse was located on Humphrey Street. Today, Clarke School students in the fifth-grade classroom of Pam Angelakis have their own sort of one-room schoolhouse, with class held in the "portables"—temporary purchased units, set up outside to ease a crowded school. (Courtesy Swampscott Historical Commission.)

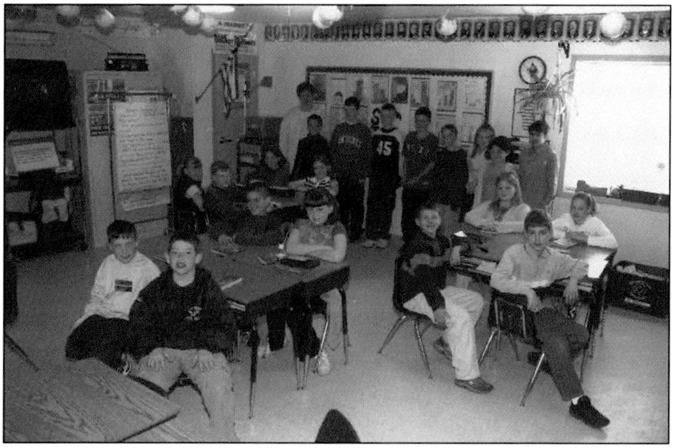

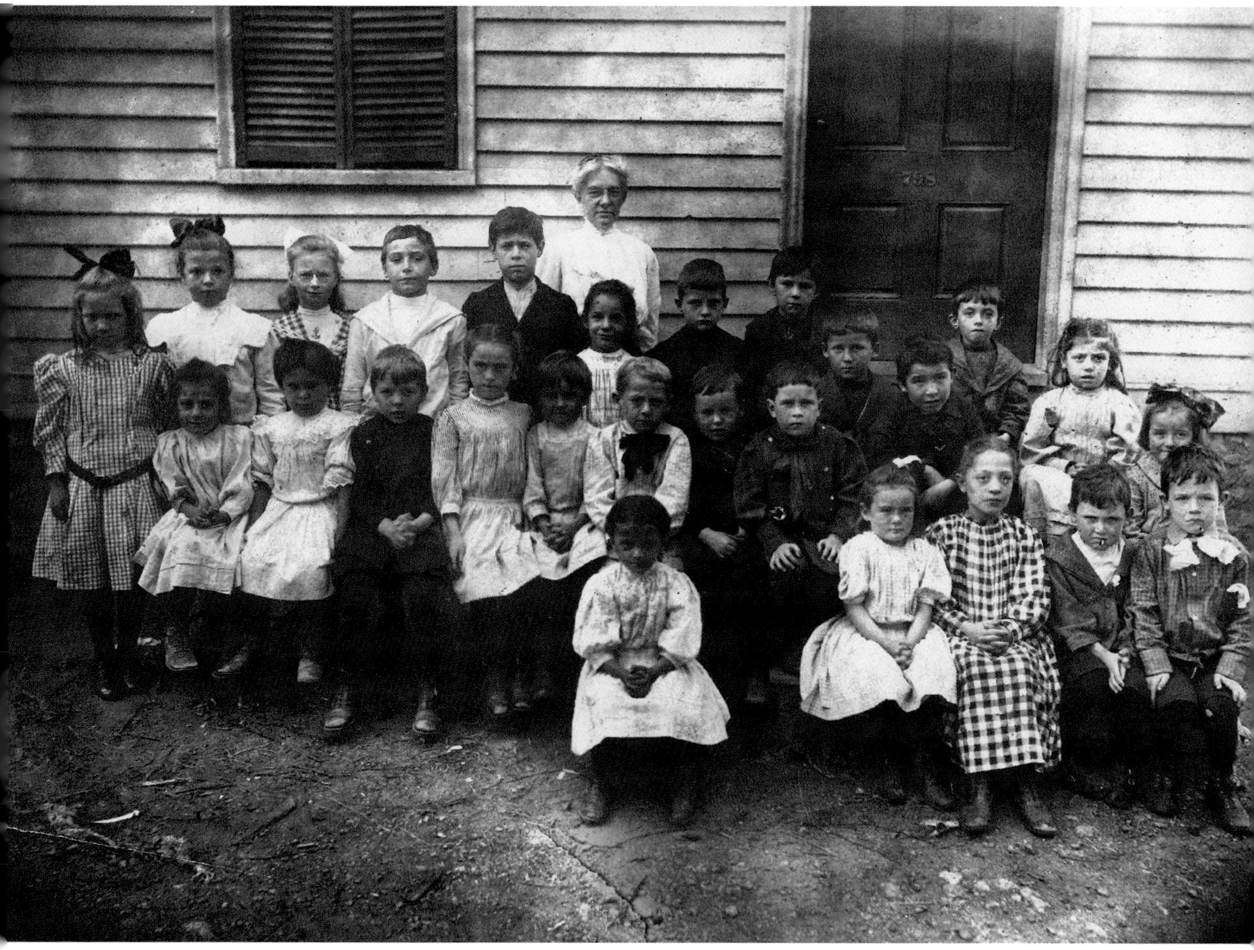

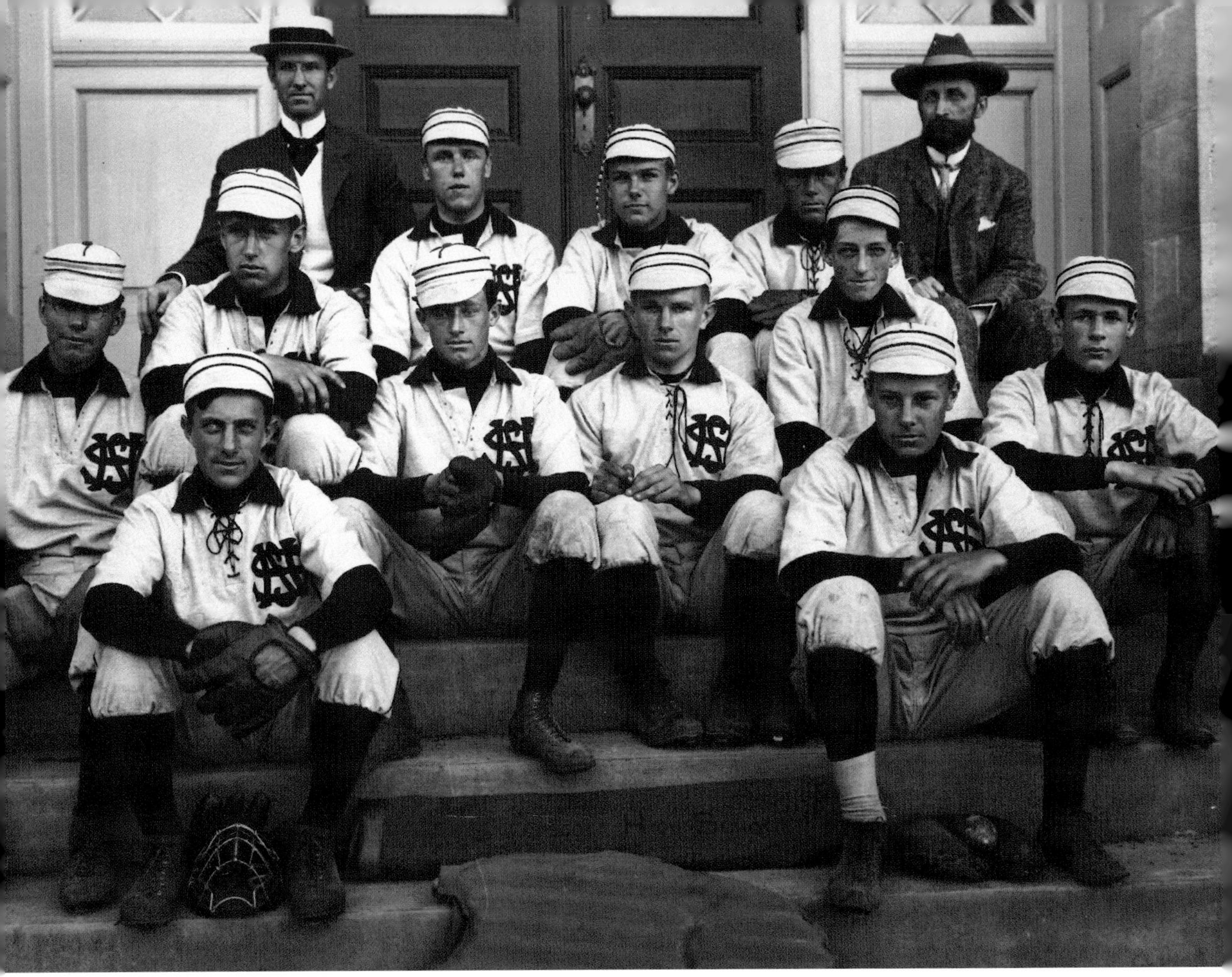

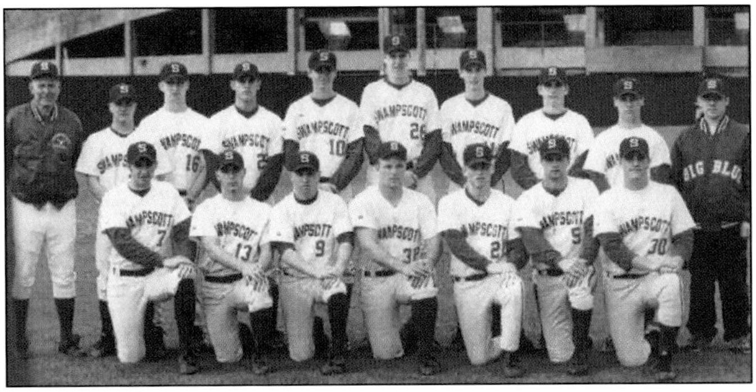

The first Swampscott High School baseball team was assembled in 1906. From left to right are the following: (front row) Lionel Melanson and Leonard Burdett; (middle row) Ed Nies, John Blaney, Bill Connors, Roland Barnes, John McNamara, and Theodore Haskell; (back row) coach Rev. Herbert Johnson, George Crowell, Edgar "Hap" Burdett, John Gounam, and ? Childs. The Big Blue baseball team of 2000 was coached by Frank DeFelice, one of the top coaches in the state. (Courtesy Swampscott Historical Society.)

The boys' basketball team of 2000 was coached by Brian Bagley. The early-20th-century Swampscott High School basketball team brought home the Northeast Conference trophy. (Courtesy Swampscott Public Library.)

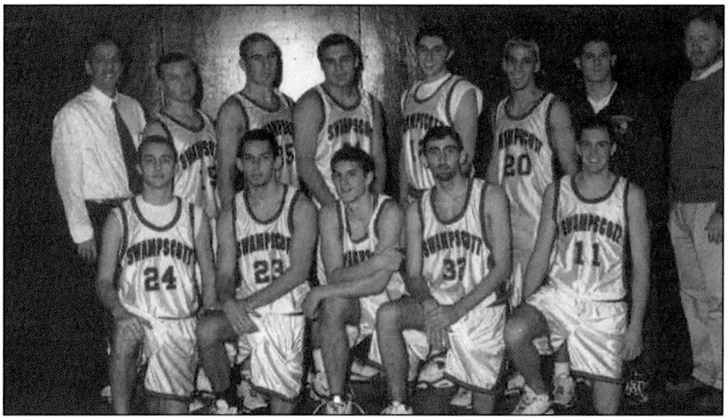

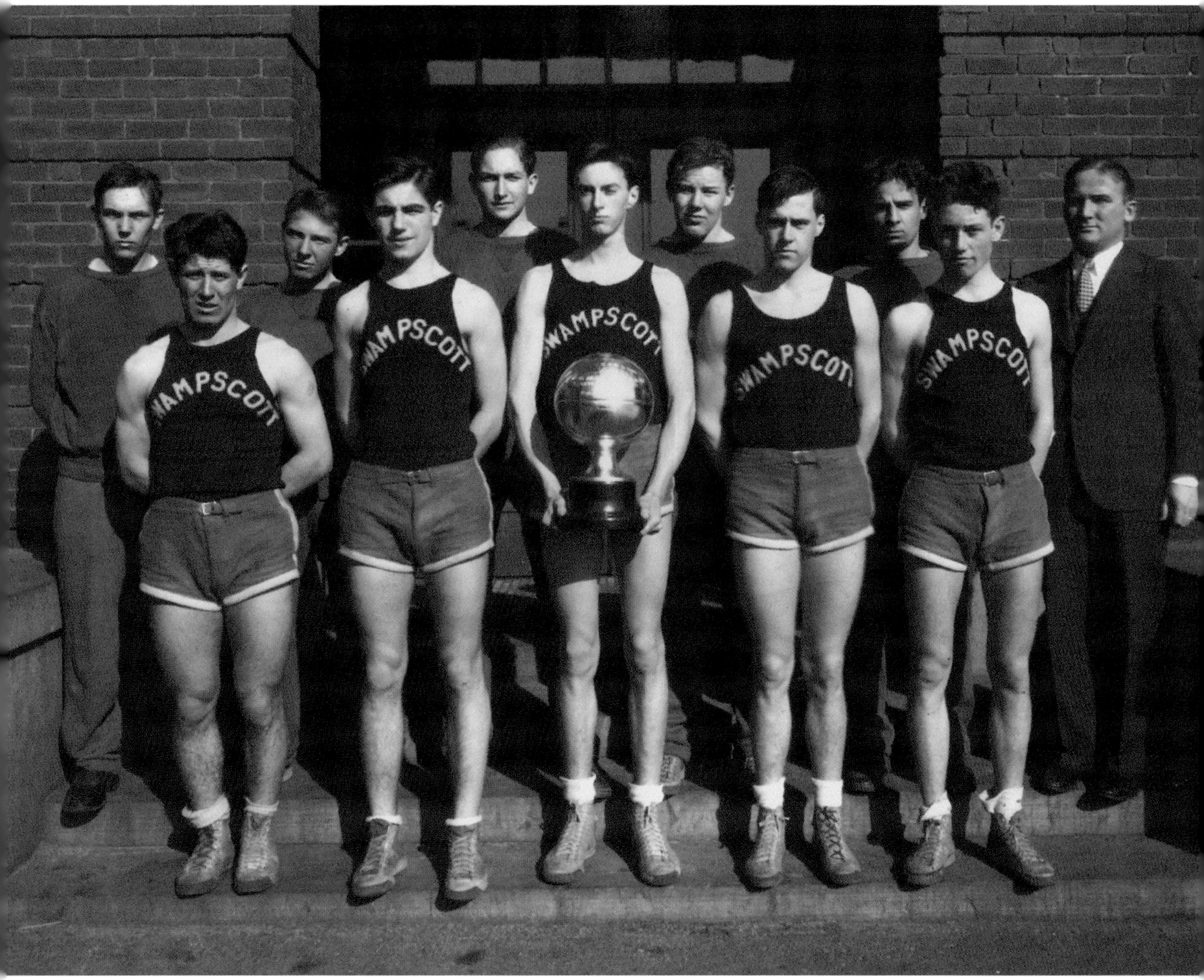

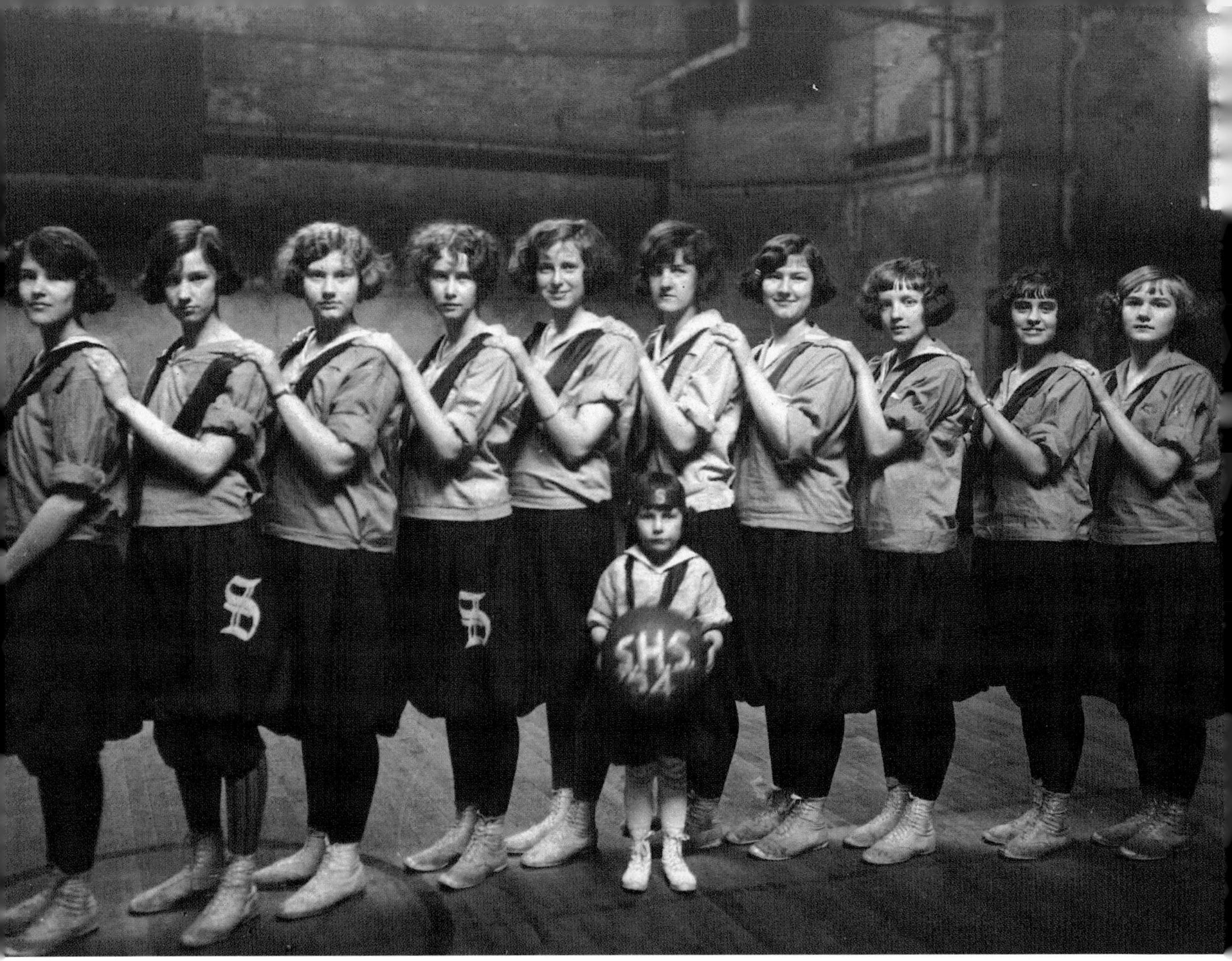

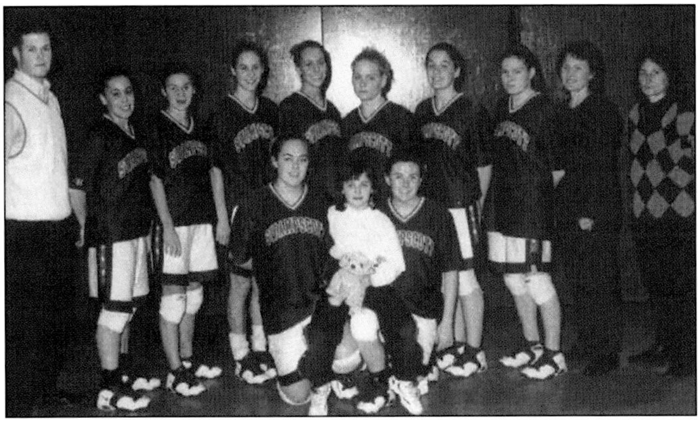

The first sport female high school students were allowed to play was girls' basketball. This 1924 team even included a mascot, little Wilma Legro. In back, from left to right, are team members Barbara Barley, Priscilla Newcomb, Marjorie Roswell, Mildred Ellis, Elizabeth Learned, Frances Kehoe, Laura Frye, Rita Farnsworth, Gladys Brown, and Dot Wilson. Notice the difference between the uniforms of 1924 and the ones worn today. (Courtesy Swampscott Historical Society.)

The Hadley School has been located on Redington Street since 1911. Back in either 1917 or 1918, students at the school had their portraits taken in front of the American flag. Vincent O'Brien, who later became a selectman and town moderator, is sixth from the left in the bottom row. (Courtesy Swampscott Historical Commission.)

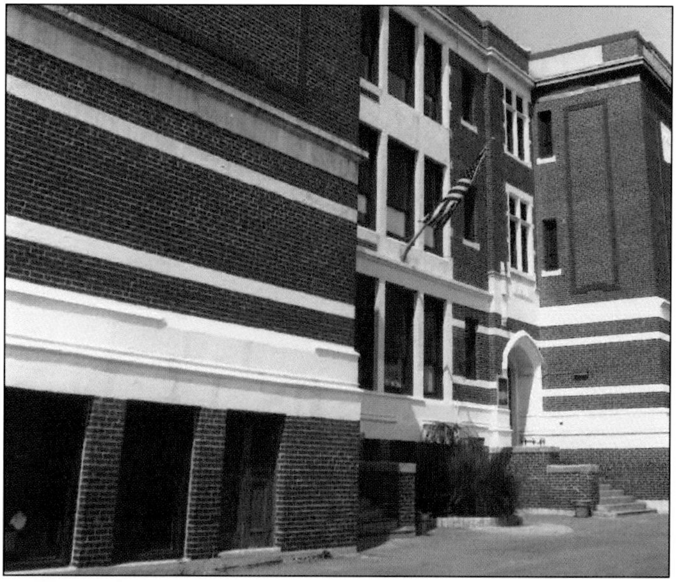

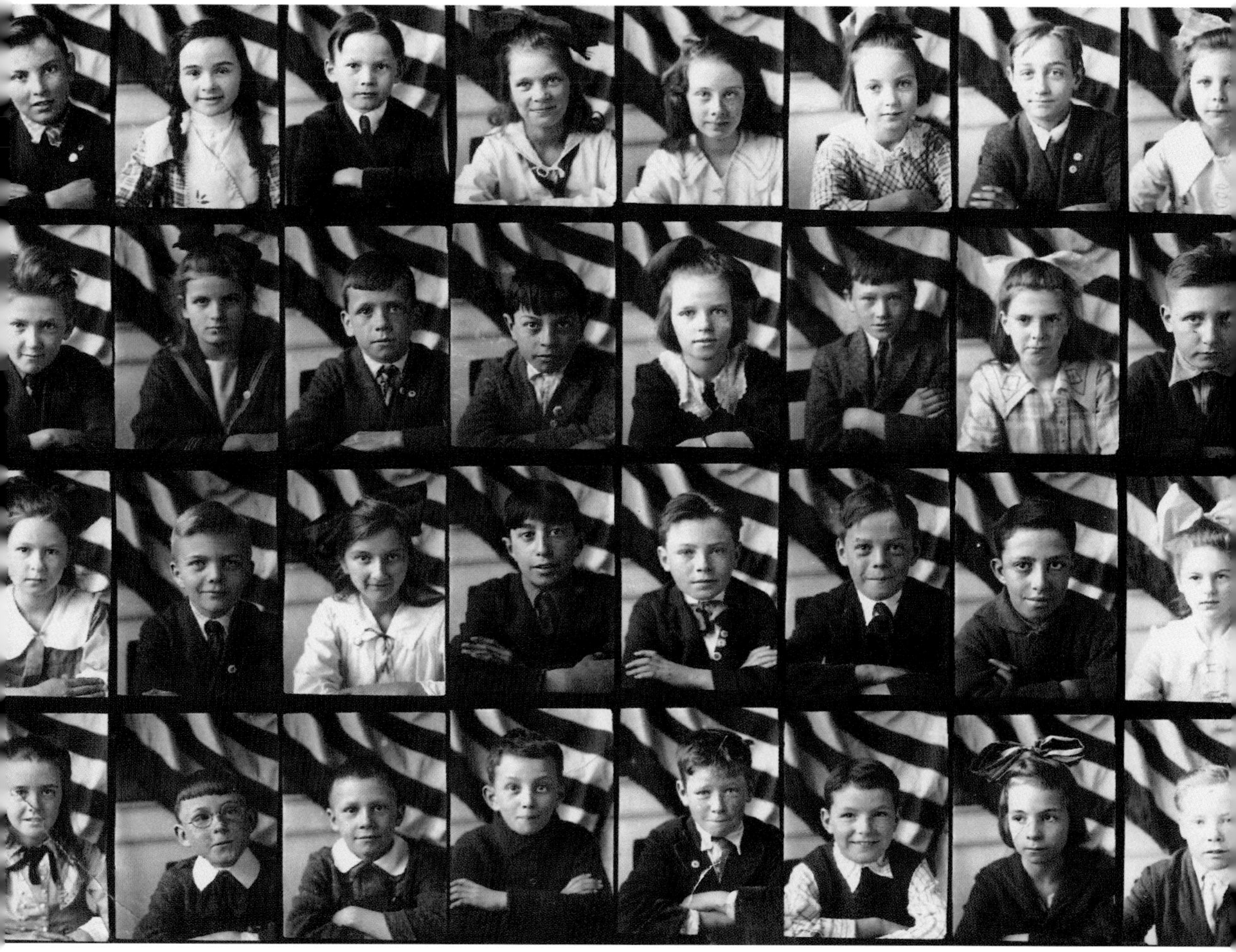

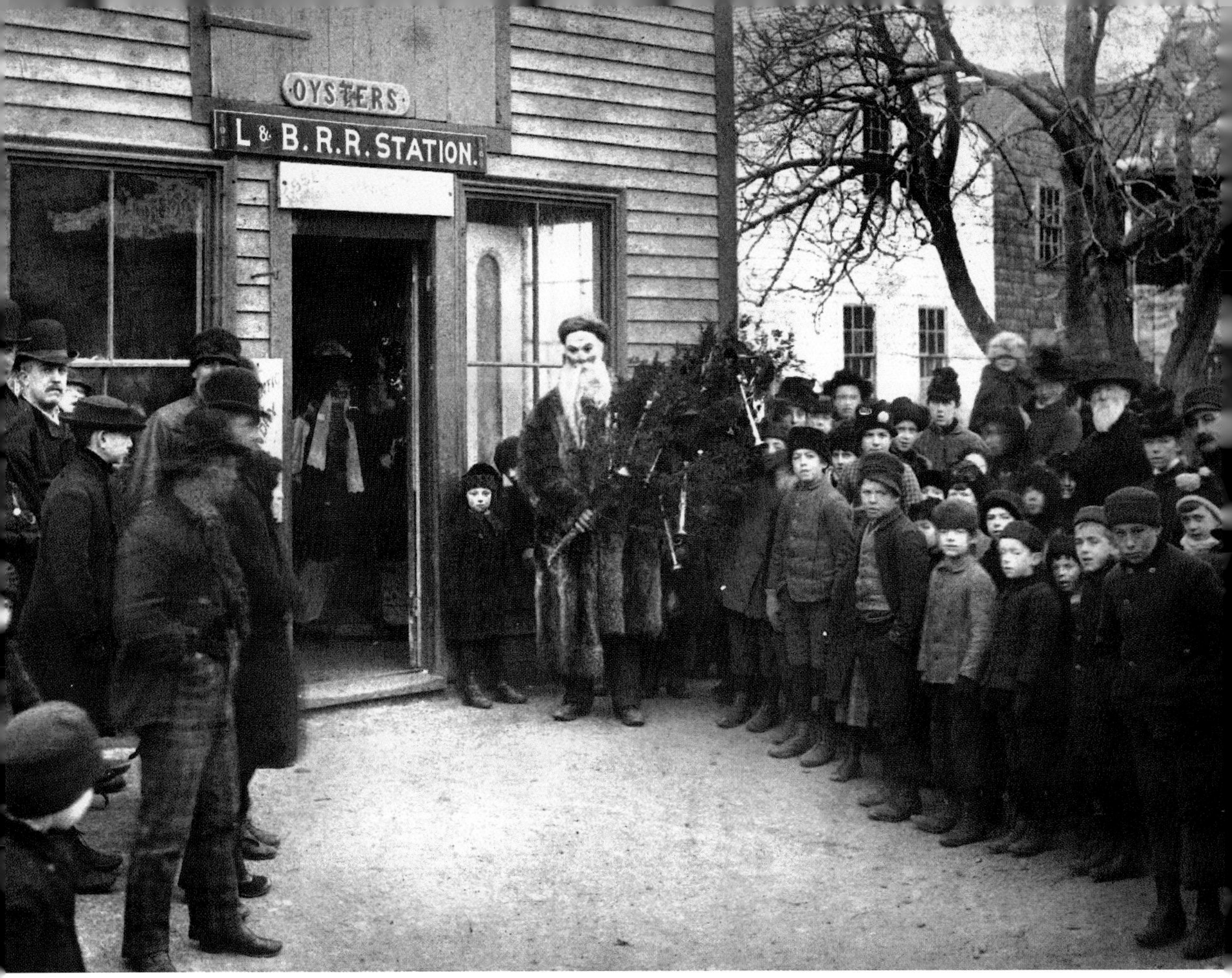

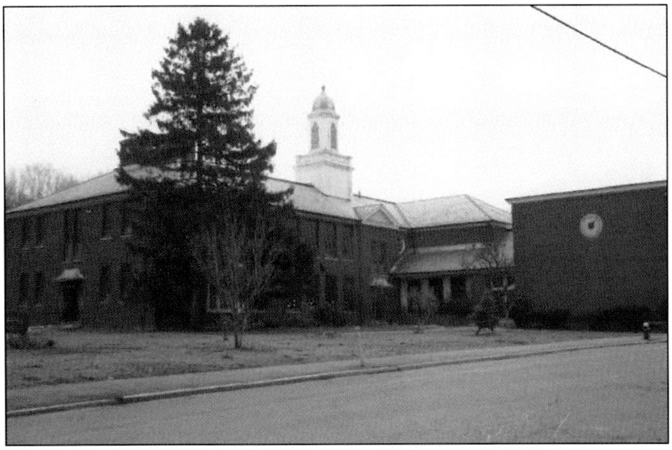

Looking like a fur trader from a faraway place, Dowdie Nesbeth (center, with beard) appears as St. Nicholas, visiting the children of the Beach School in front of the Essex Laundry Office and the L & B Railroad station in 1900. The school was once located on Puritan Road. The Stanley School later replaced the Beach and the Farm Schools. The Stanley School was named for Farm schoolteacher Louise Stanley. (Courtesy Swampscott Historical Commission.)

No matter how many years go by, some themes of school plays never change. Today's students from Sandy Budzinski's second-grade class at the Stanley School—from left to right, Gregory Dart, Sam Gold, Aidan Lang, Joe DeSalvo, and Alex Sneirson—practice for their performance of *Sounds a Little Fishy to Me* on the same stage used by students in 1930 who performed a play based on the sea. (Courtesy Swampscott Public Library.)

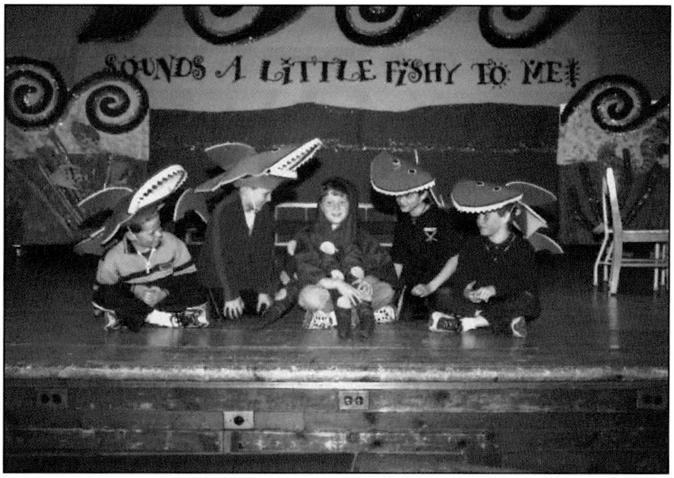

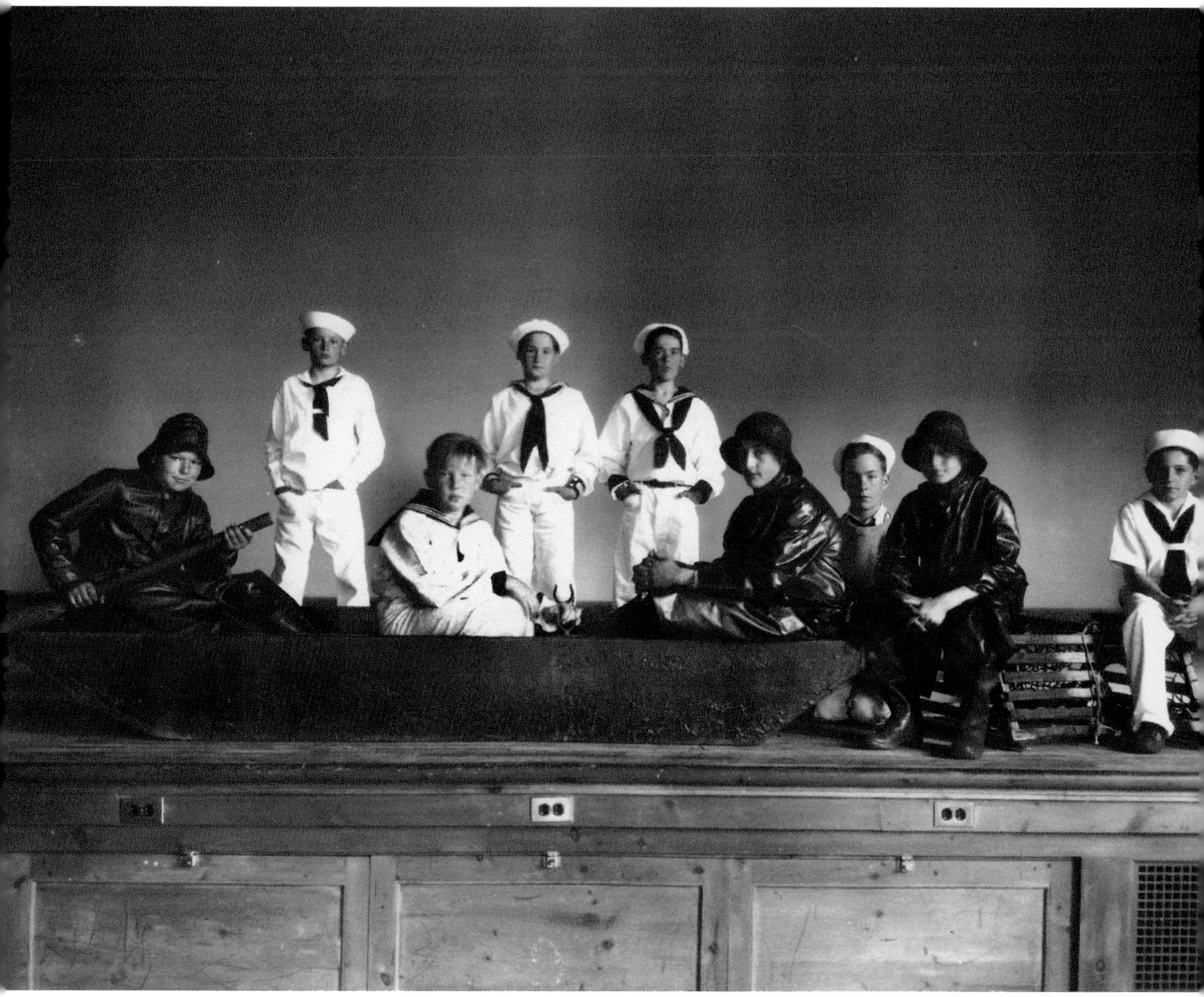

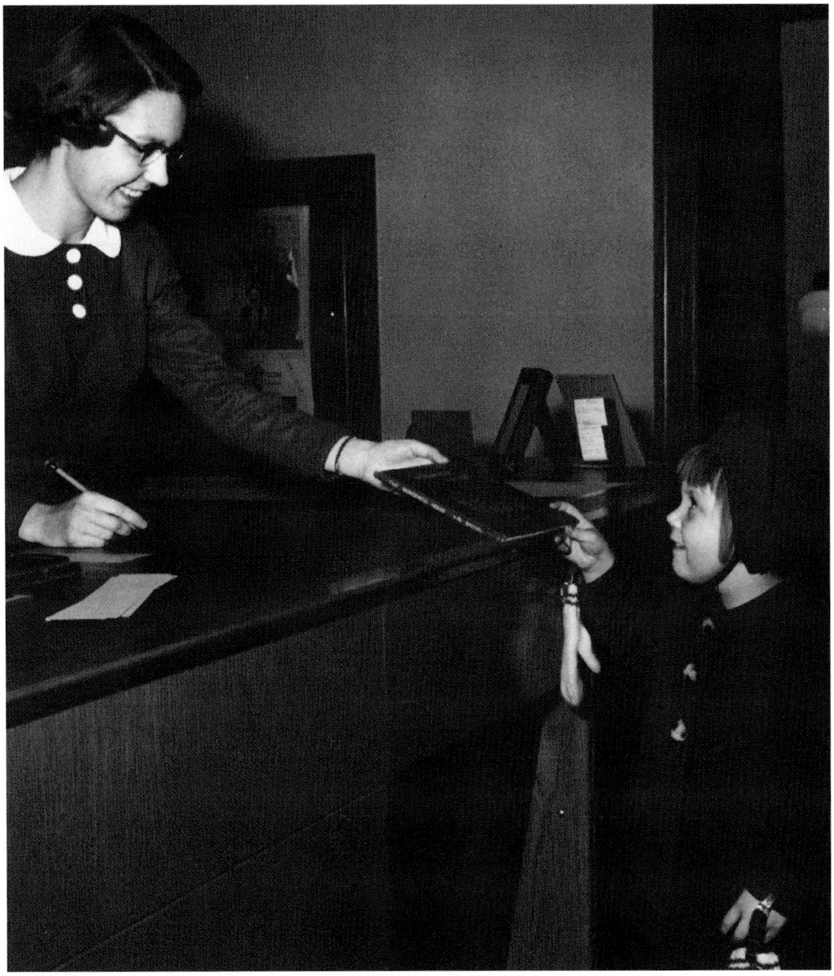

The early days at the Swampscott Public Library were not as exciting as times are today. Back in the 1950s, this little girl borrowed her mother's library card until she was old enough (age seven) to get one of her own. Today, head reference librarian Vicky Coffin works with patron German Gorovodsky on the computer. (Courtesy Swampscott Public Library.)

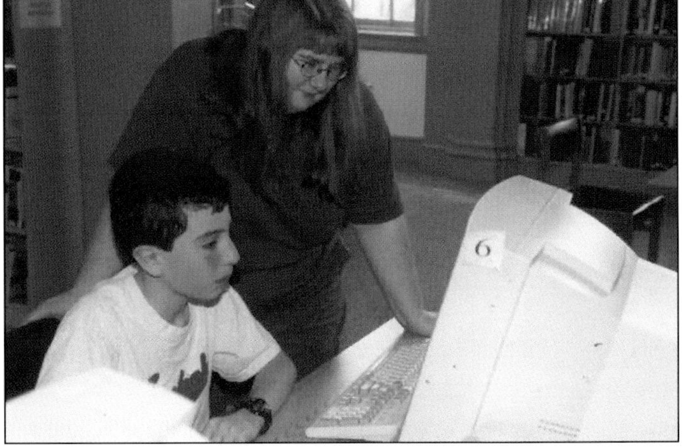

Young people in Swampscott gladly donned elegant attire from another time during the town's 50th anniversary in 1902. These youngsters showed off their flair on the Women's Club parade float. From left to right are the following: (front row) Blanche Pitman Bicknell, Edna Stocker Spence, and Ruth Shattuck; (back row) Myra Southworth, Pedrick Irwin, Percy Norcross, and George Crowell. (Courtesy Swampscott Public Library.)

Chapter 3

FOUNDATIONS OF OUR FOREFATHERS

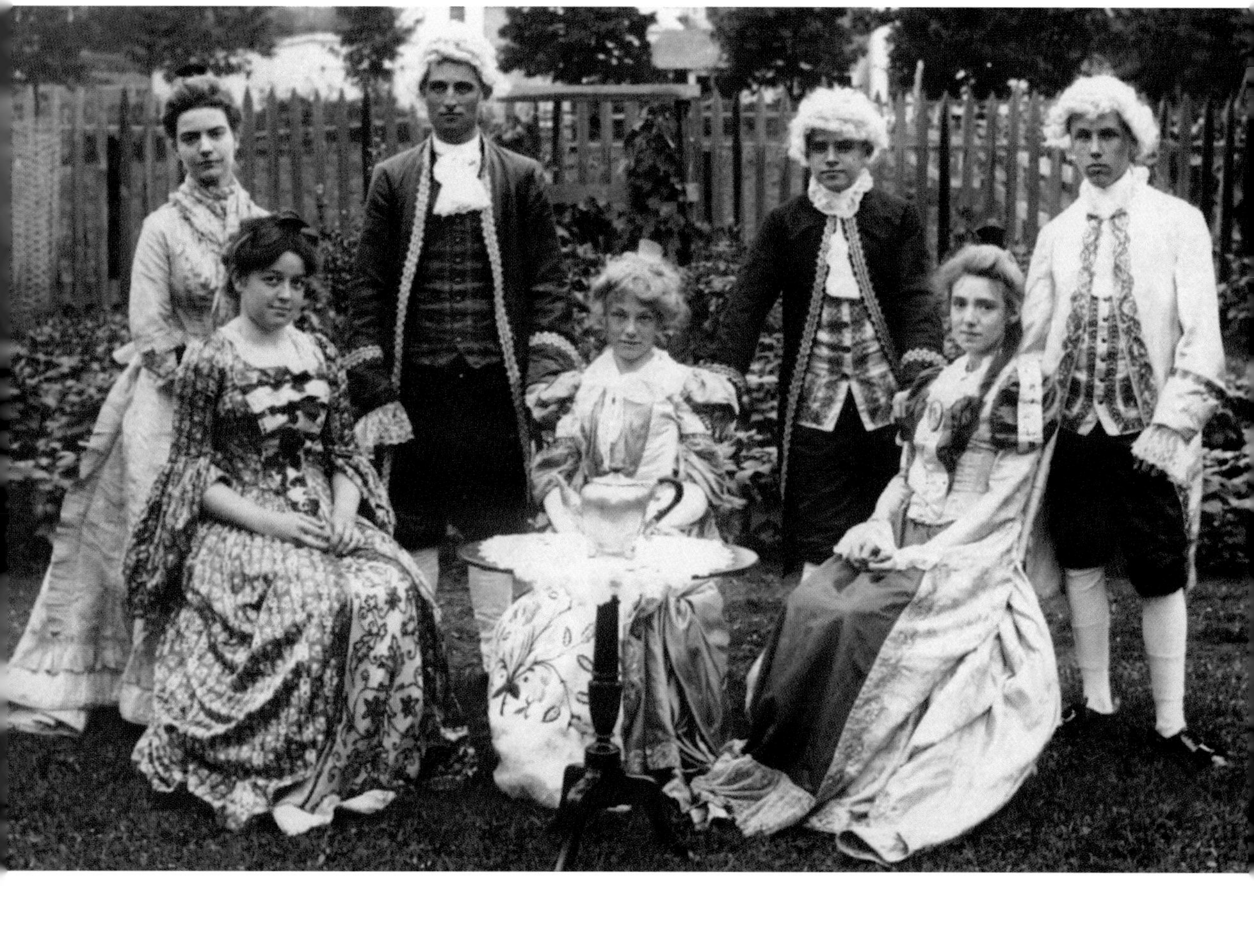

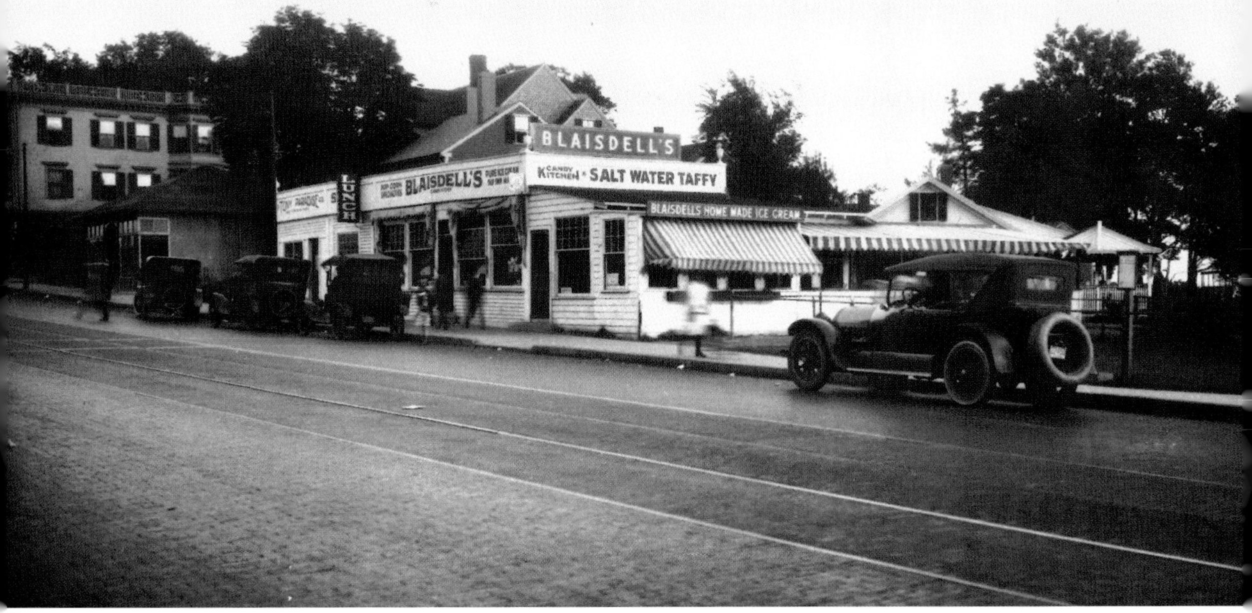

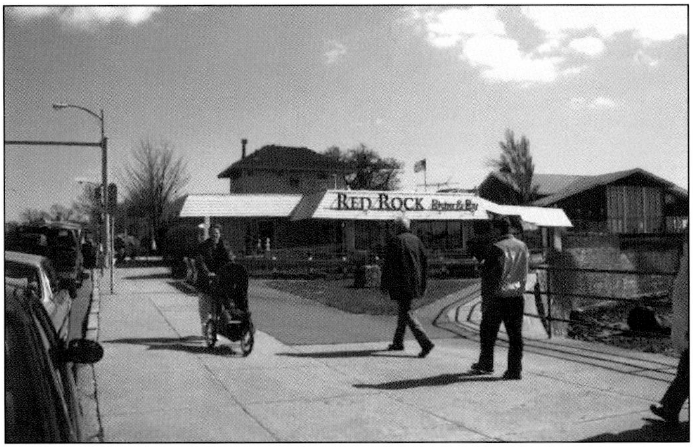

This restaurant and ice-cream shop has been known by several names over the years and, today, is called the Red Rock Bistro & Bar. At the beginning of the 20th century, it was the popular spot Blaisdell's, which later became Doane's and then Dale's. The area behind Blaisdell's, Cliff Terrace, became the Hawthorne Restaurant. (Courtesy Swampscott Historical Commission.)

The Swampscott Post Office used to have more of a front-and-center appearance when it was located at 454 Humphrey Street (lower right), as shown in 1929. Today, the post office is located in a residential area on Elmwood Road. (Courtesy Swampscott Public Library.)

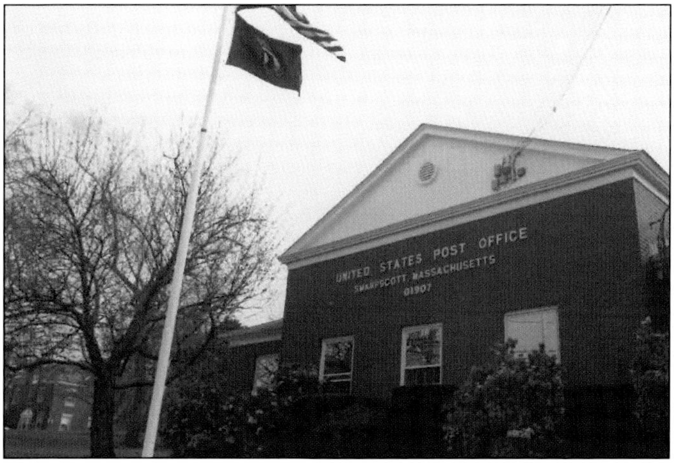

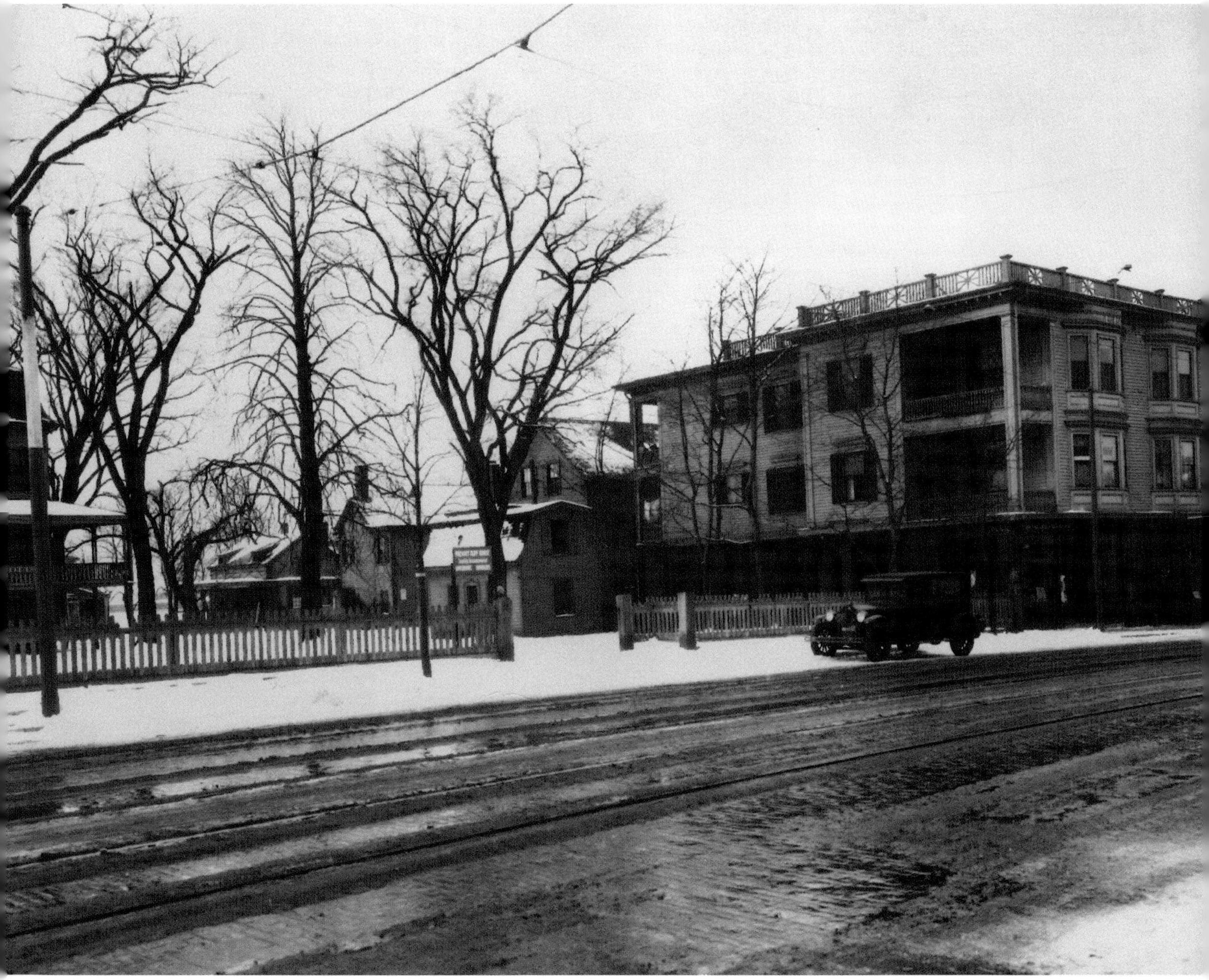

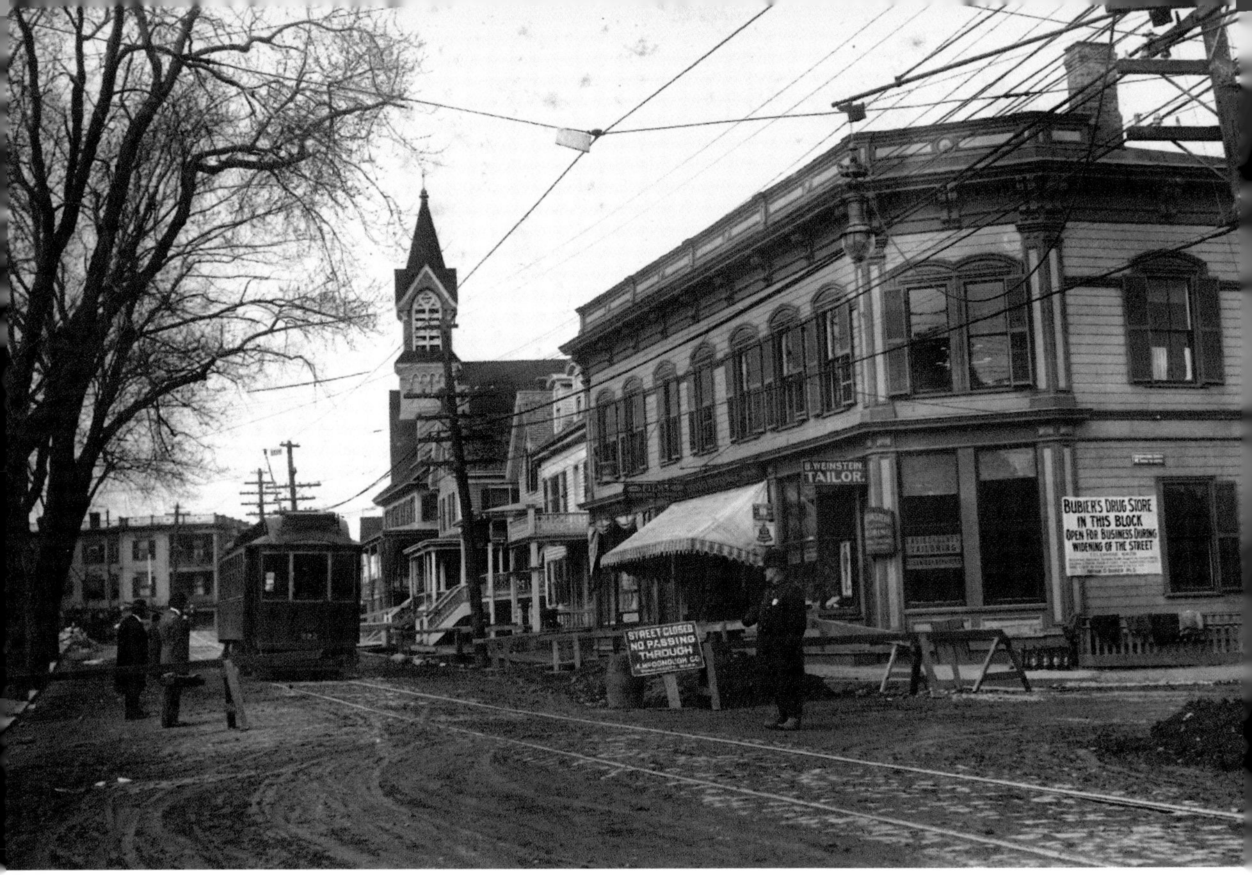

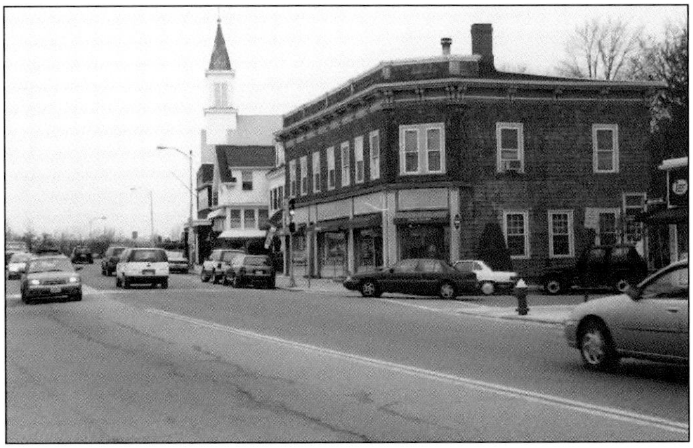

Swampscott photographer Stuart Ellis captured this image of Humphrey and Blaney Streets during the widening of Humphrey in 1917. Today, the wider street is a challenge to cross and invites drivers to pick up speed. In recent years, there has even been discussion of narrowing the street. (Courtesy Louis A. Gallo.)

Before there was a bank and before there was today's insurance company, this site on Humphrey Street was the location of the Blaney House, built in 1641 by Capt. Ralph King. (Courtesy Swampscott Historical Commission.)

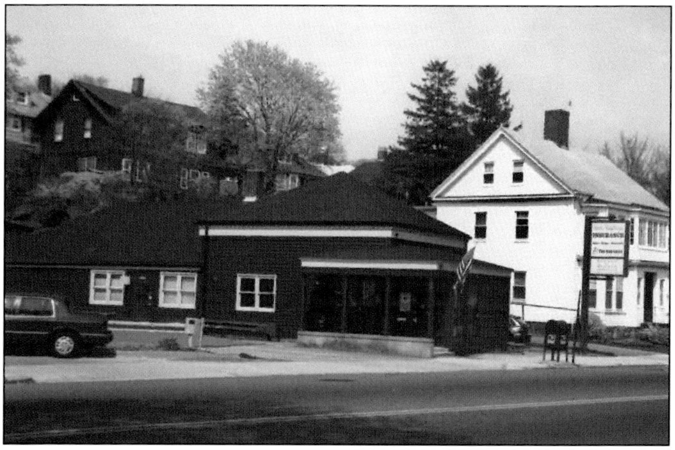

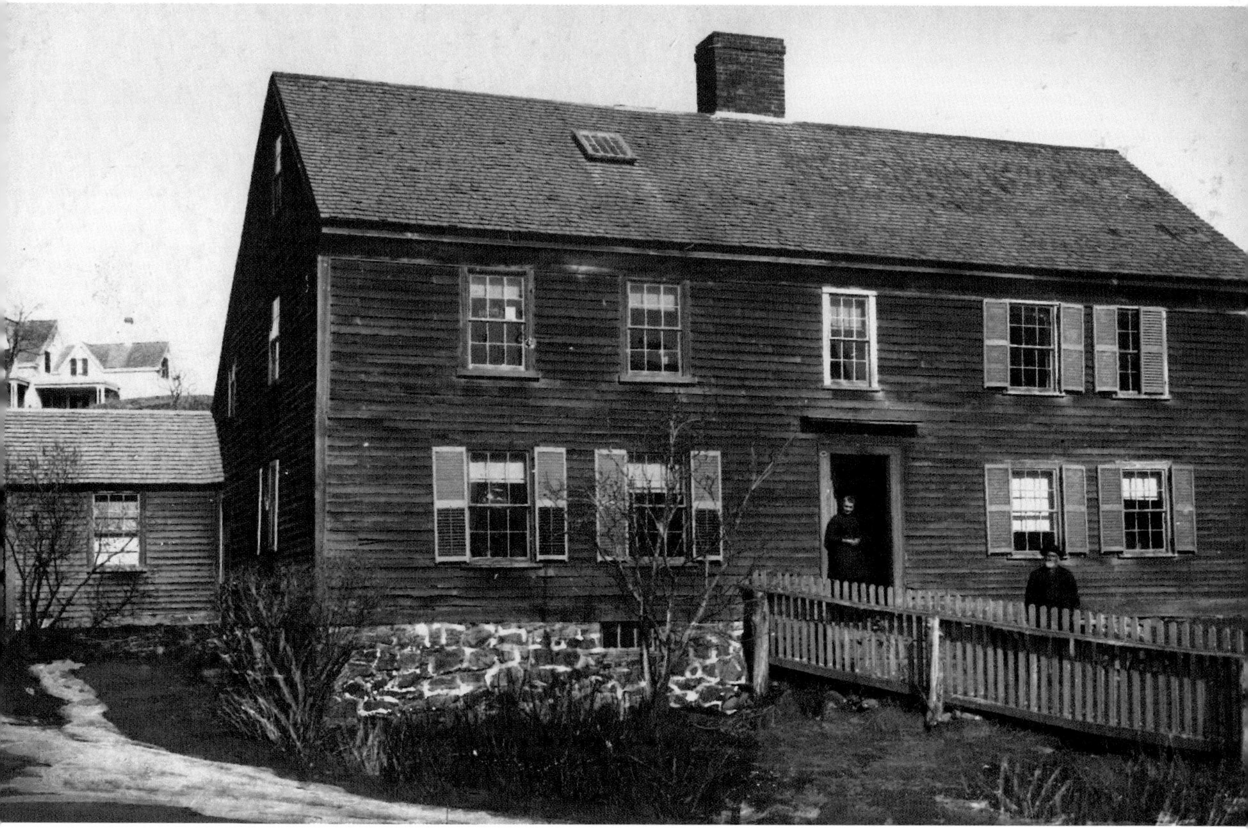

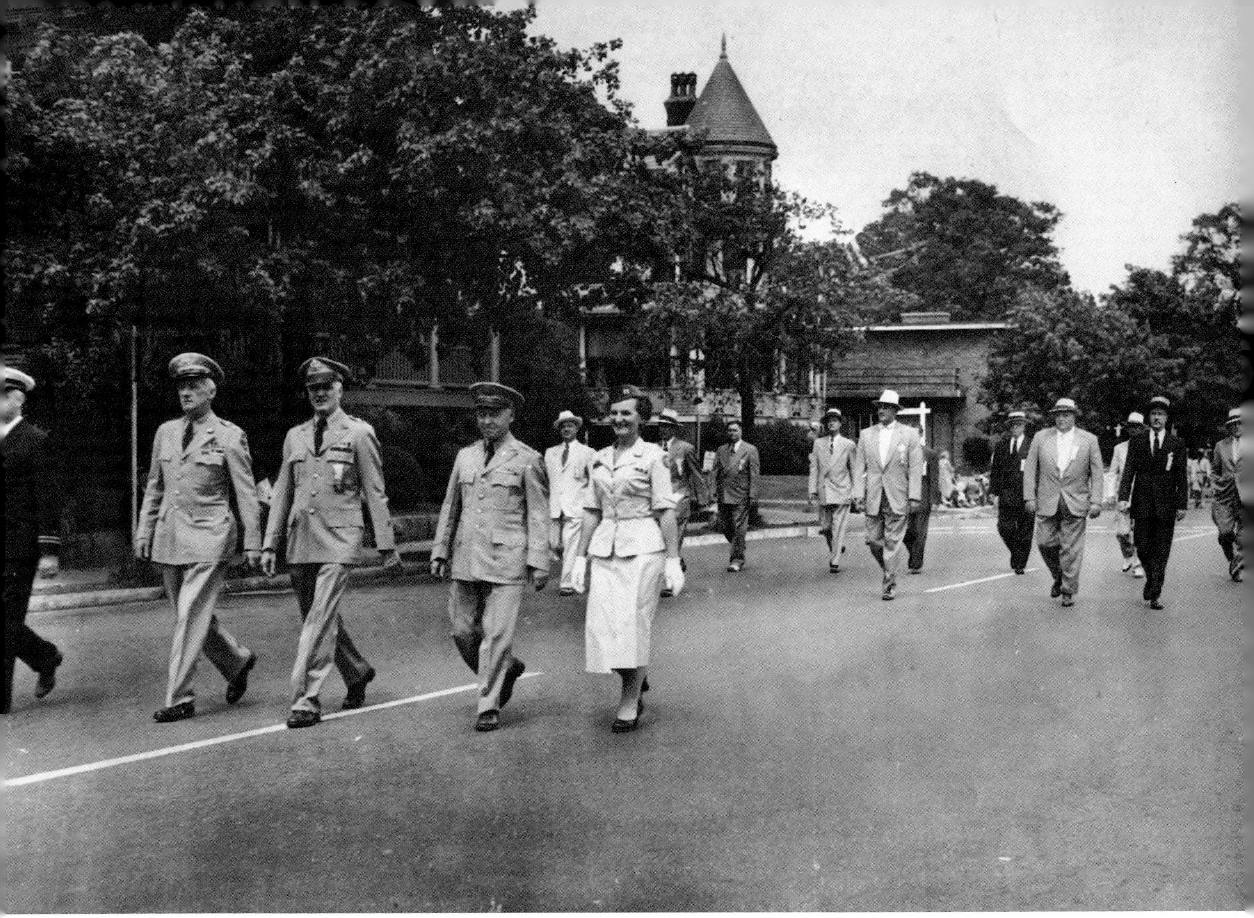

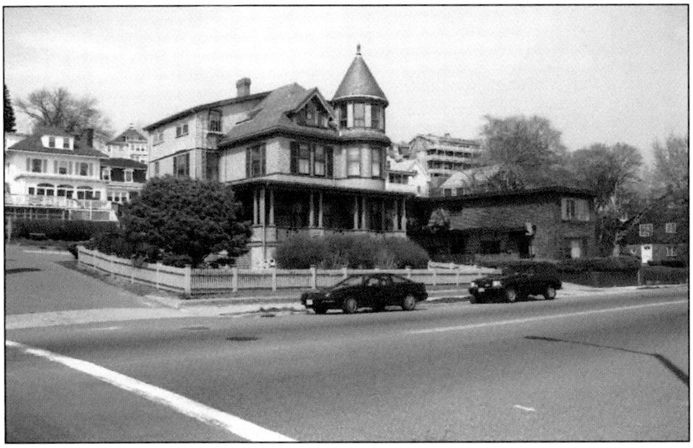

Humphrey Street has always been included on the local parade route. During the town's 100th anniversary celebration, members of the military and local officials marched toward town hall. The buildings in the background remain true to form today. (Courtesy Swampscott Historical Commission.)

A bit of a conflict exists as to when the Swampscott Club was founded. The chimney says 1750, but other records indicate 1789. No matter, the club survives today with members such as, from left to right, Bob Grimes, Bob Snow (club historian), and Arthur McGovern. Back in July 1919, the club was decked out for a celebration. (Courtesy Swampscott Historical Society.)

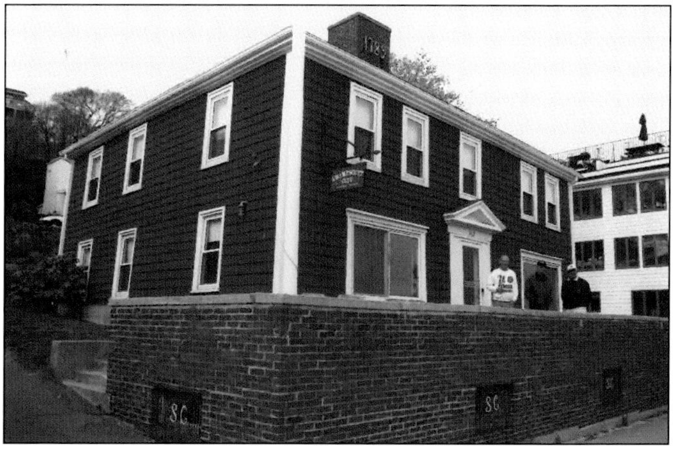

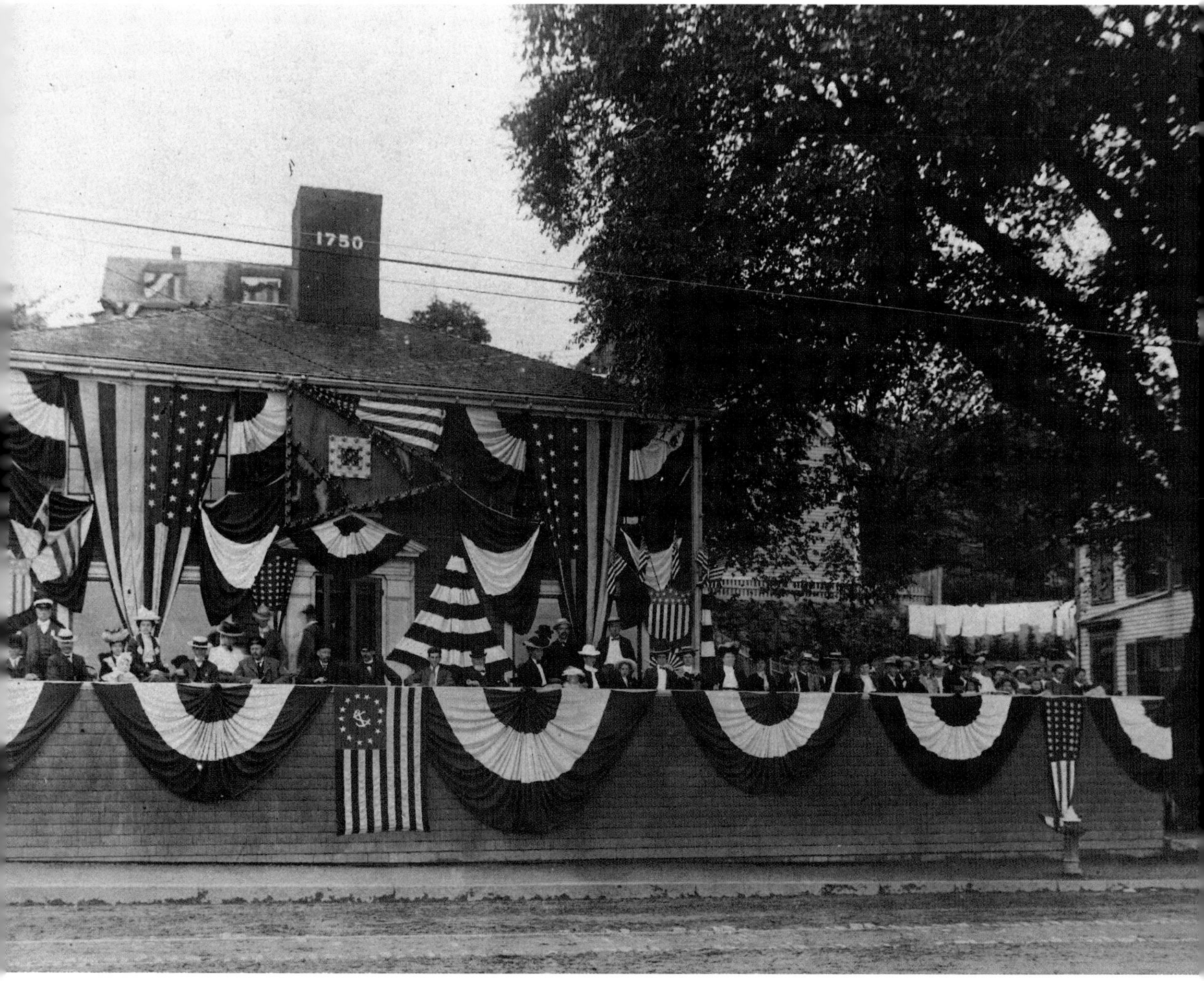

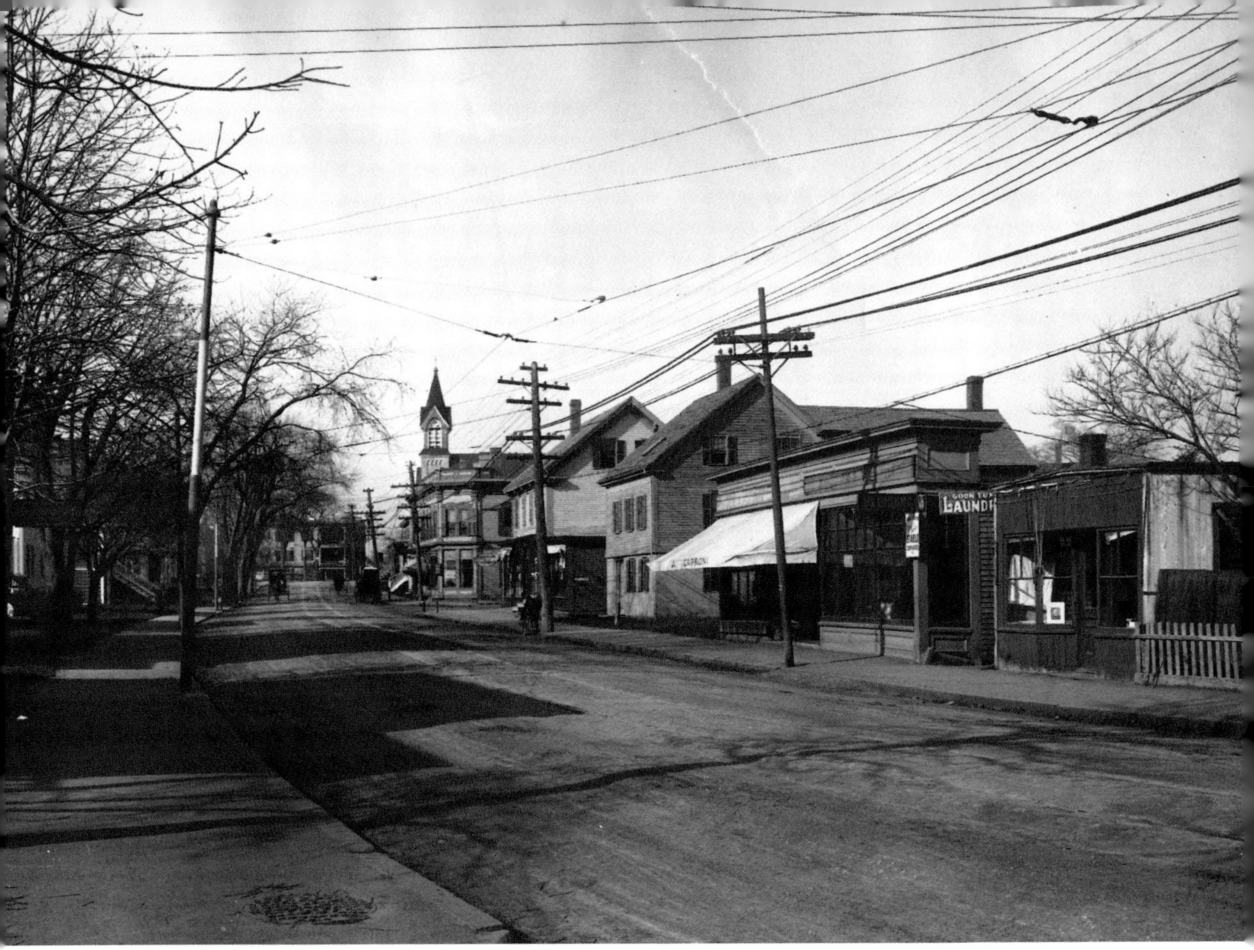

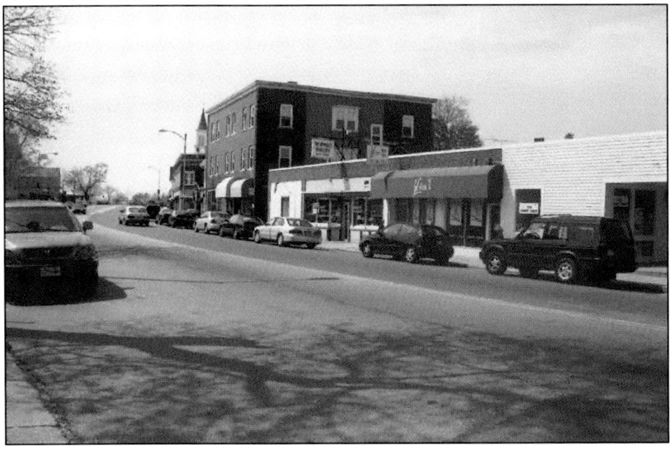

Humphrey Street in 1912 was a wonderful dirt road, suitable for the trolley, which ran on tracks in the center, and horse-drawn buggies, which kept to the side. (Courtesy Swampscott Historical Commission.)

Today, two homes have a commanding view of Fisherman's Beach from their perch on Humphrey Street. However, back in 1922, the American Legion post made its home at 380 Humphrey Street and all pitched in for a renovation of the building. (Courtesy Swampscott Public Library.)

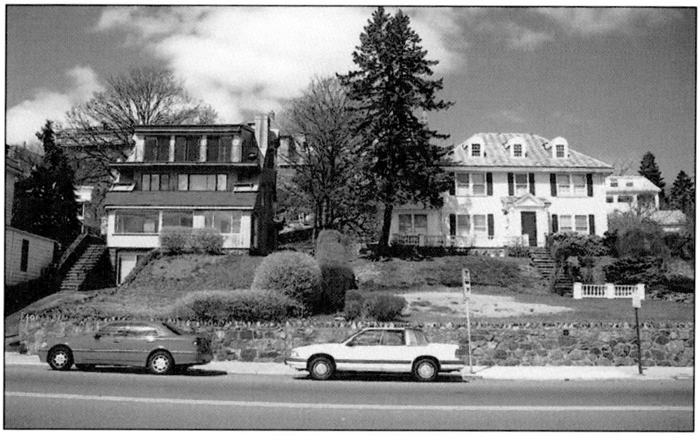

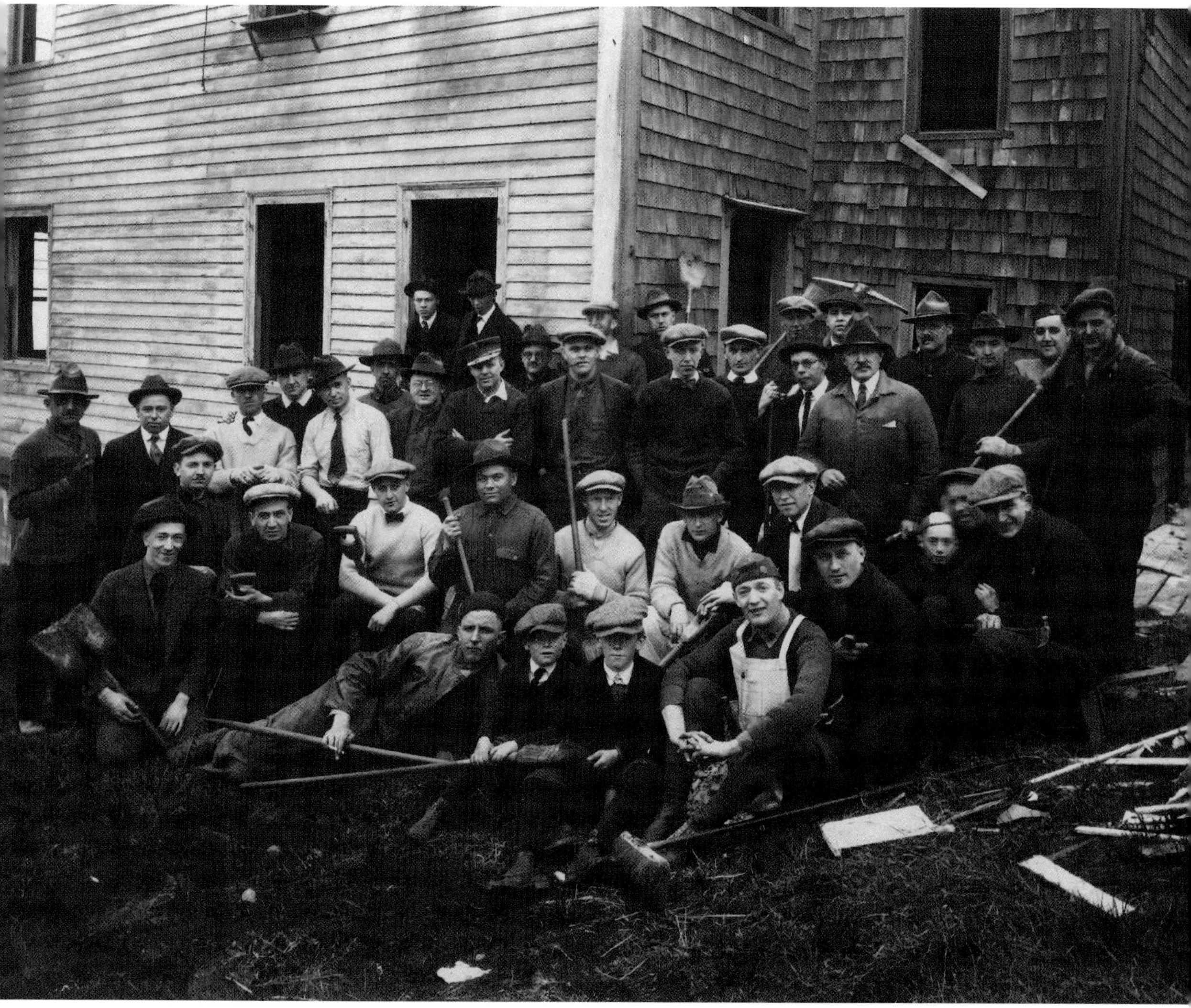

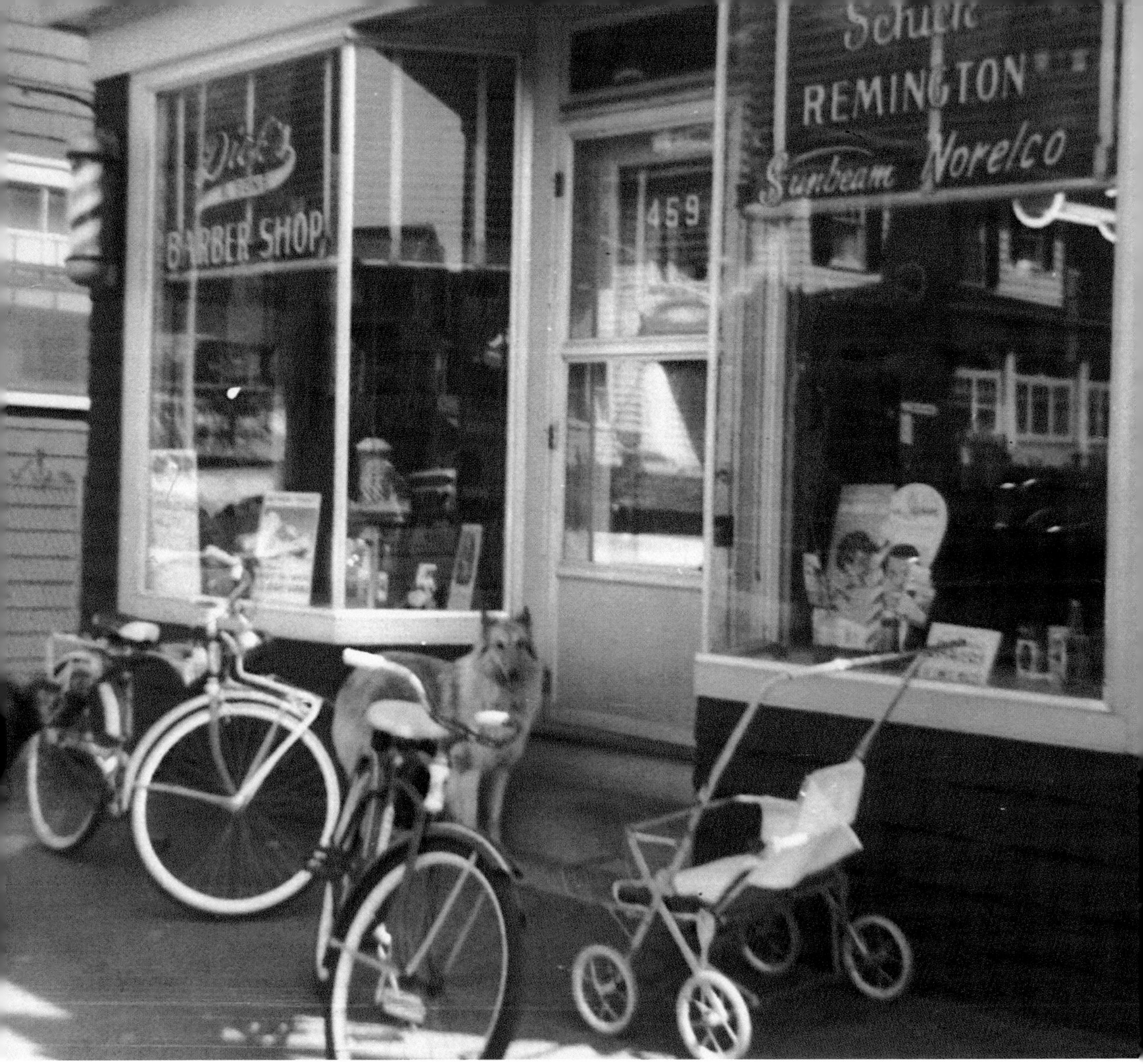

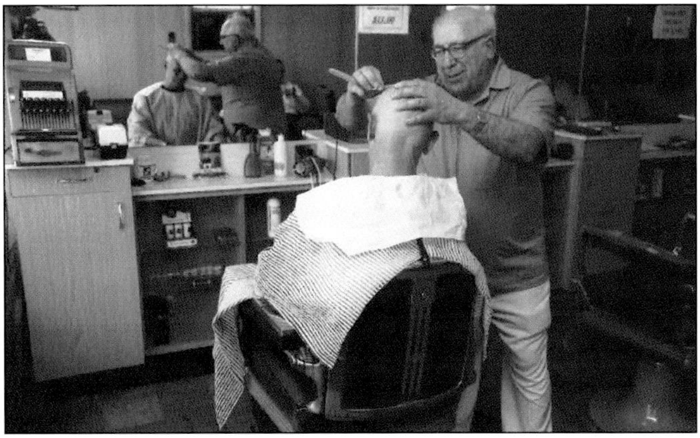

The window at Dick & Sons Barber Shop has changed very little over the years. Built on Humphrey Street in 1941 by Dick Maniglia, the barbershop is now owned by sons Richard (opposite page) and Tony (left) Maniglia. One of the rare breeds of true barbershop, it has all the styles, from ducktails to ponytails and crewcuts to flattops. (Courtesy Swampscott Historical Commission.)

The barber chair has not changed much over the years either (except for the ashtray attached to the arm). Some clients have been getting clipped at Dick & Sons Barber Shop since they were young boys. Richard Maniglia puts the final touches on a client. An unidentified barber (below) who worked for the original owner is ready for the next cut. (Courtesy Swampscott Historical Commission.)

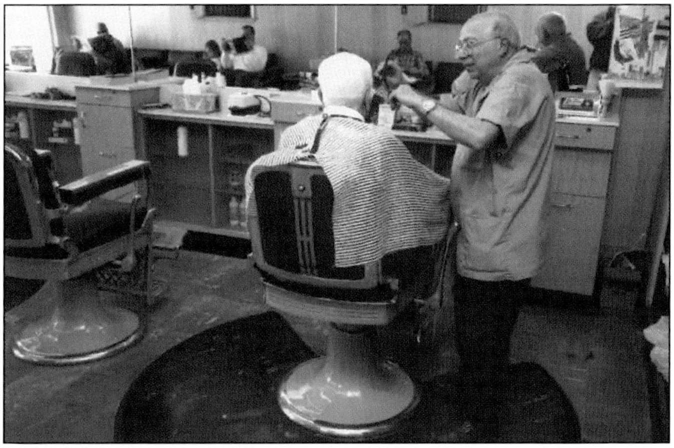

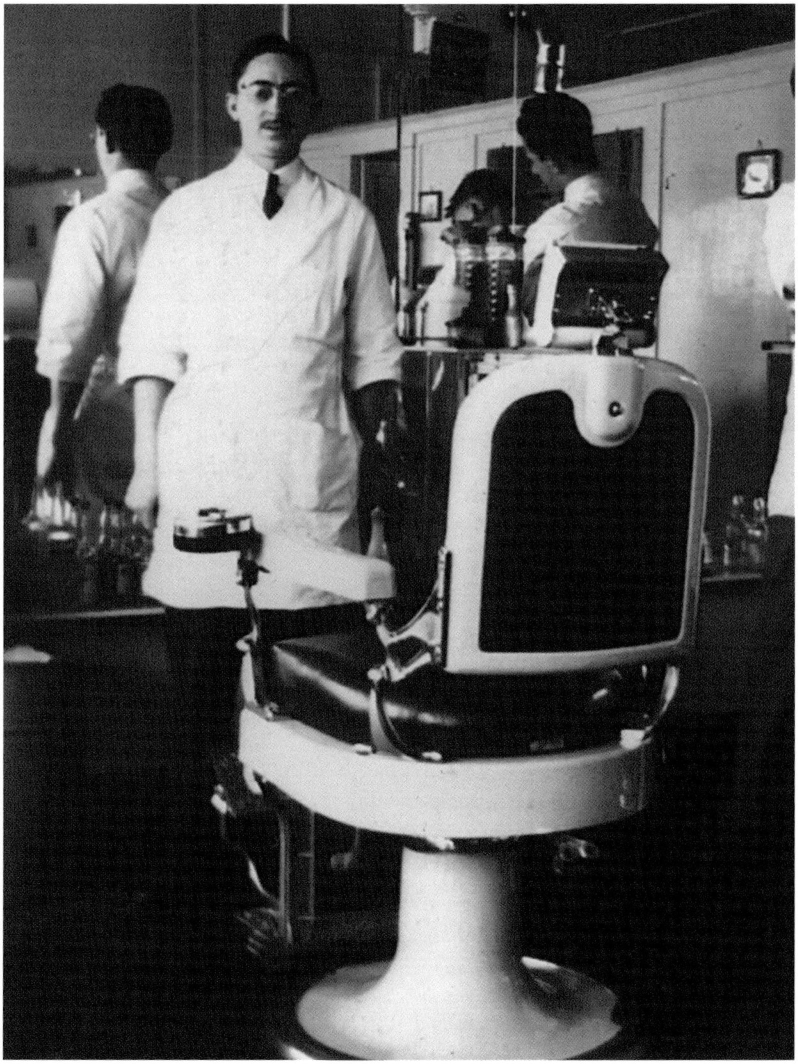

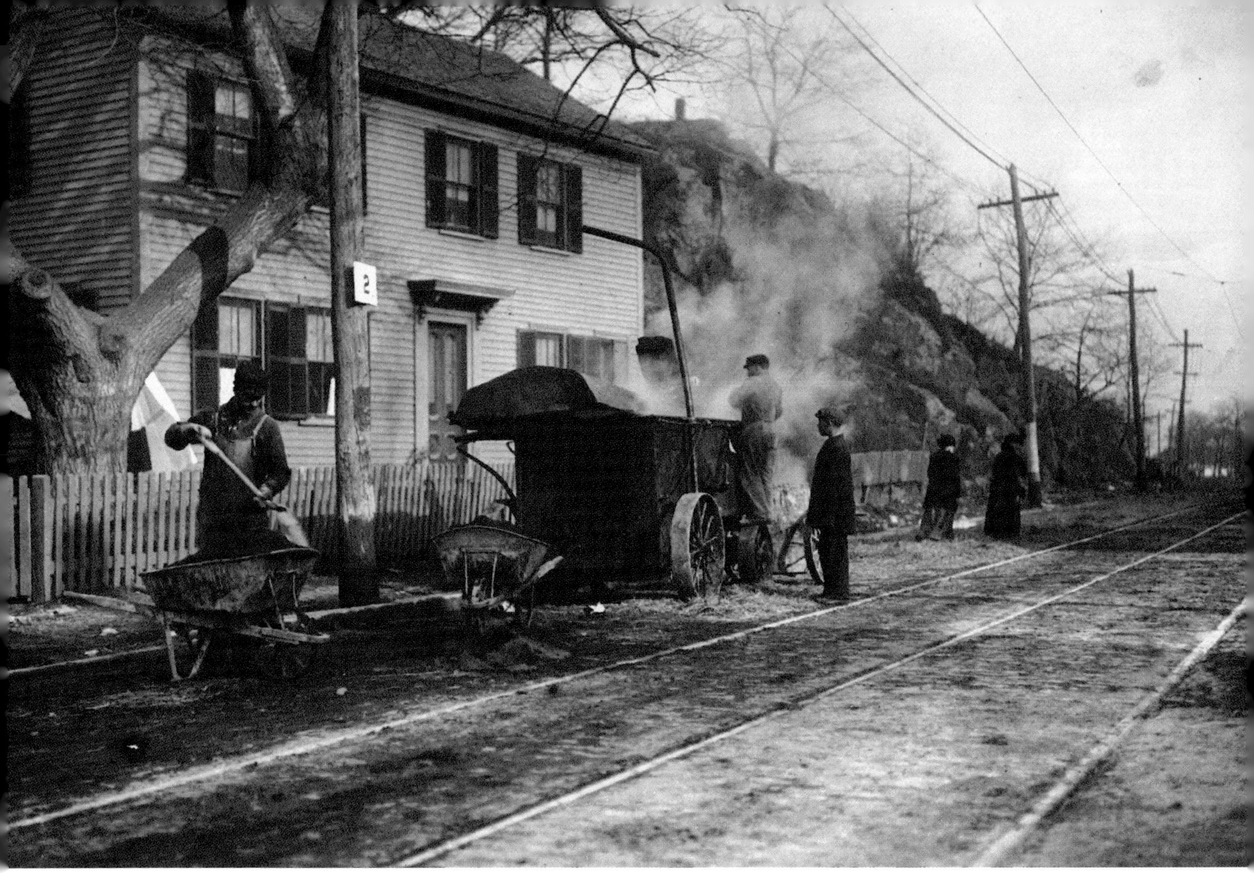

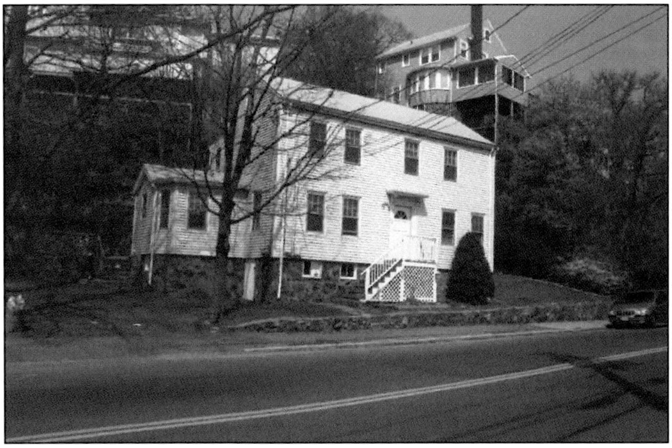

Crews work on the widening of Humphrey Street near the No. 500 area of the street. The home pictured in the early-1900s photograph still stands today. (Courtesy Louis A. Gallo.)

Men work in front of the old post office on Humphrey Street during the street-widening project. Today, the same spot is a parking lot for Anthony's Pier 4 Café, formerly known as Hawthorne by the Sea, owned by famed Boston restaurateur and Swampscott resident Anthony Athanas. (Courtesy Swampscott Historical Commission.)

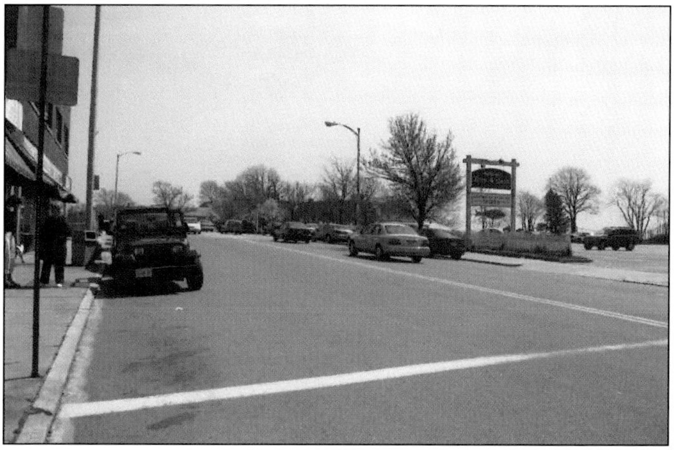

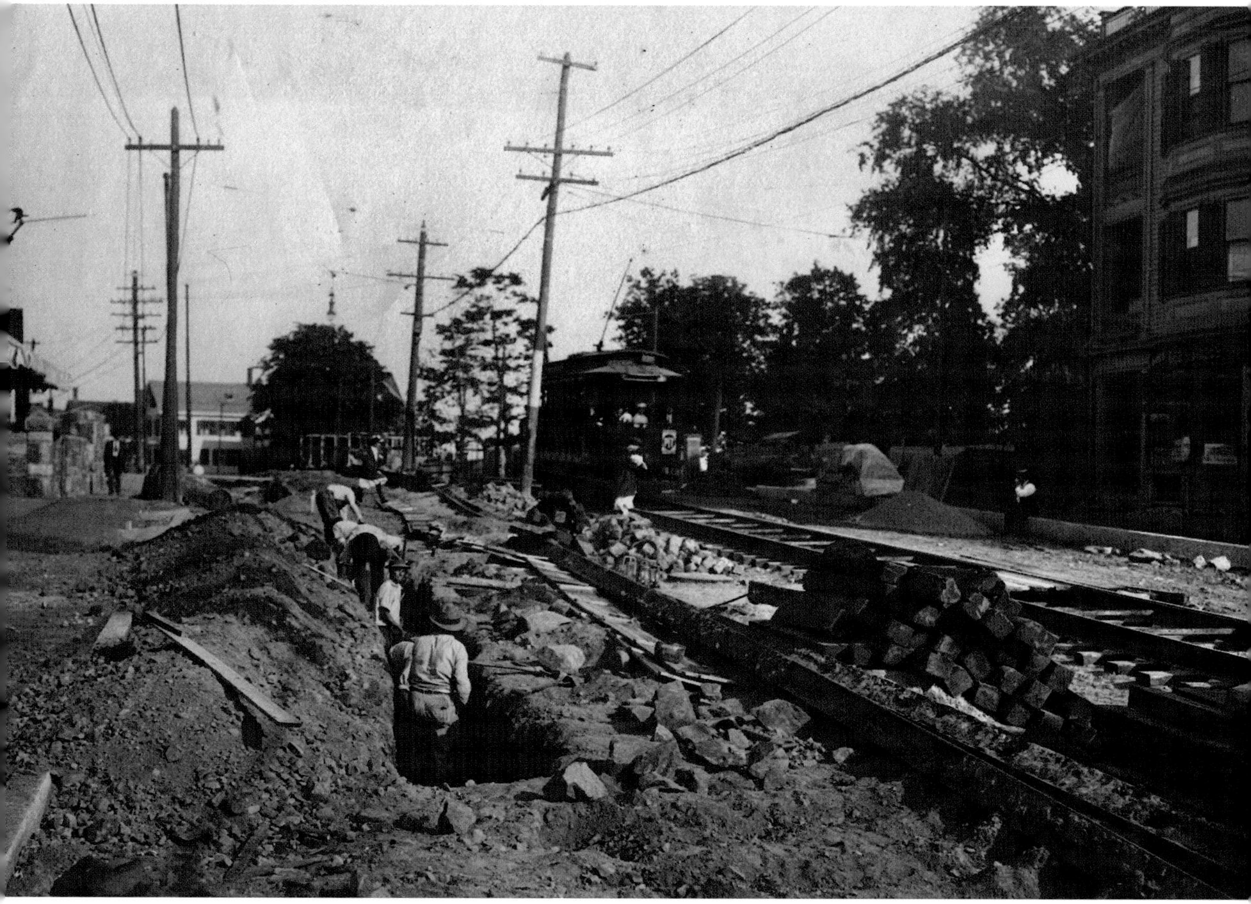

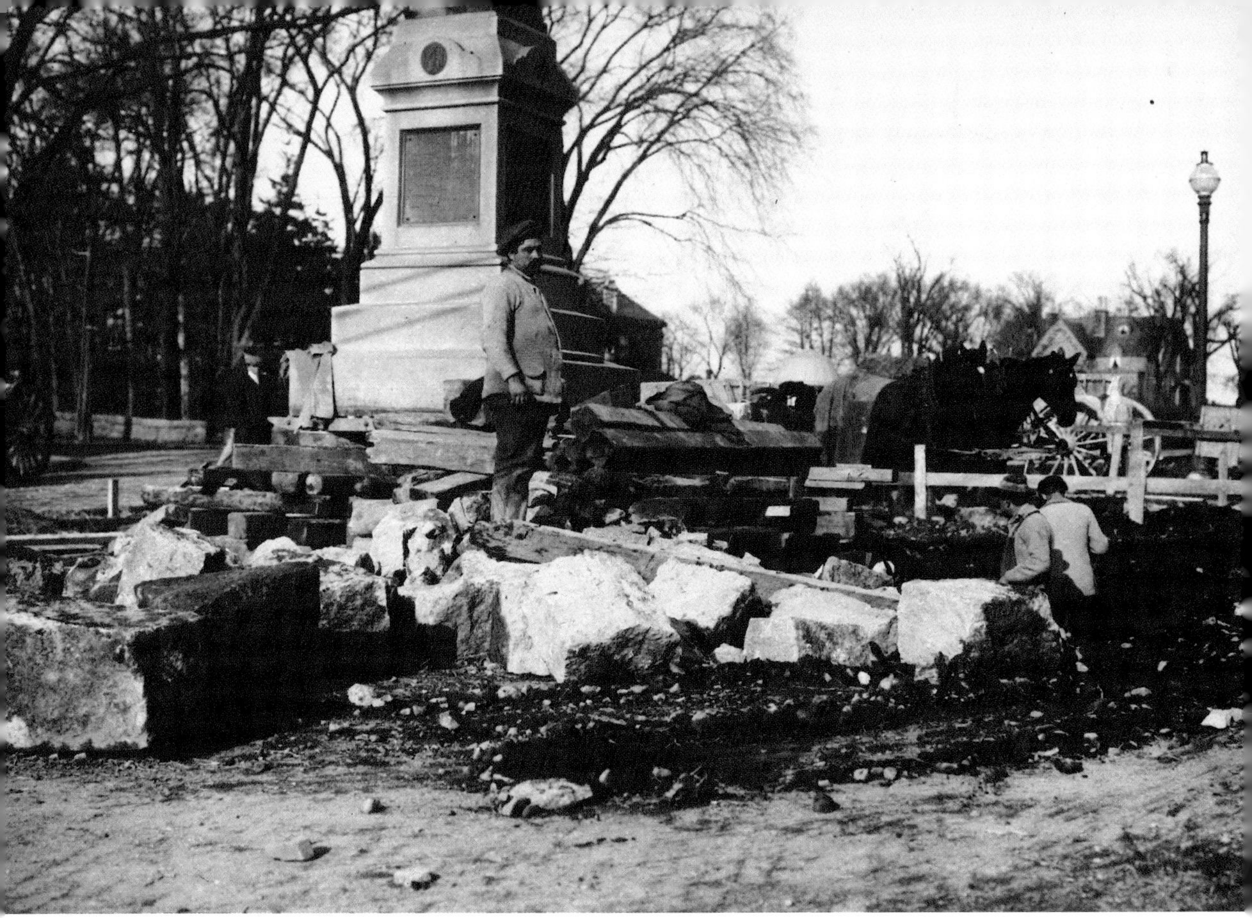

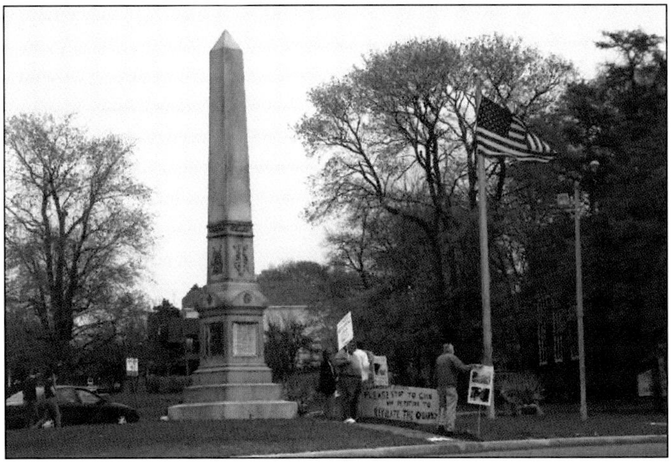

One of the first landmarks when arriving in Swampscott, this could be the most moved monument in town. The Soldiers and Sailors Monument was built in 1883 and has been moved twice since then, once for the widening of Humphrey Street in 1914 and once again in 1923. (Courtesy Louis A. Gallo.)

The widening of Humphrey Street in 1914 was one of the largest public works ventures undertaken at the time. In April of that year, crews waste no time after the winter thaw to get to work. (Courtesy Louis A. Gallo.)

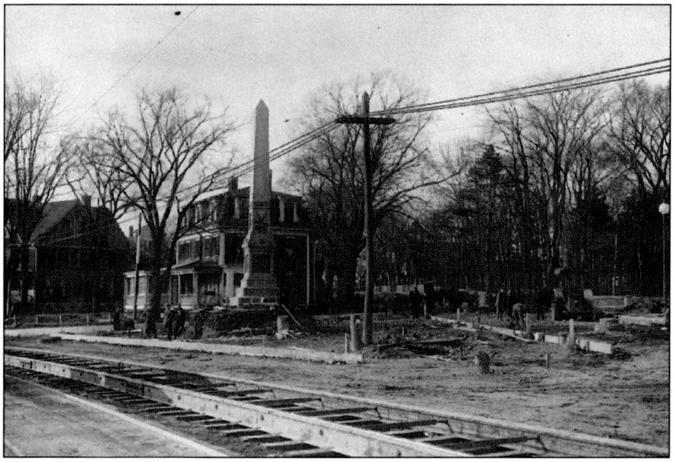

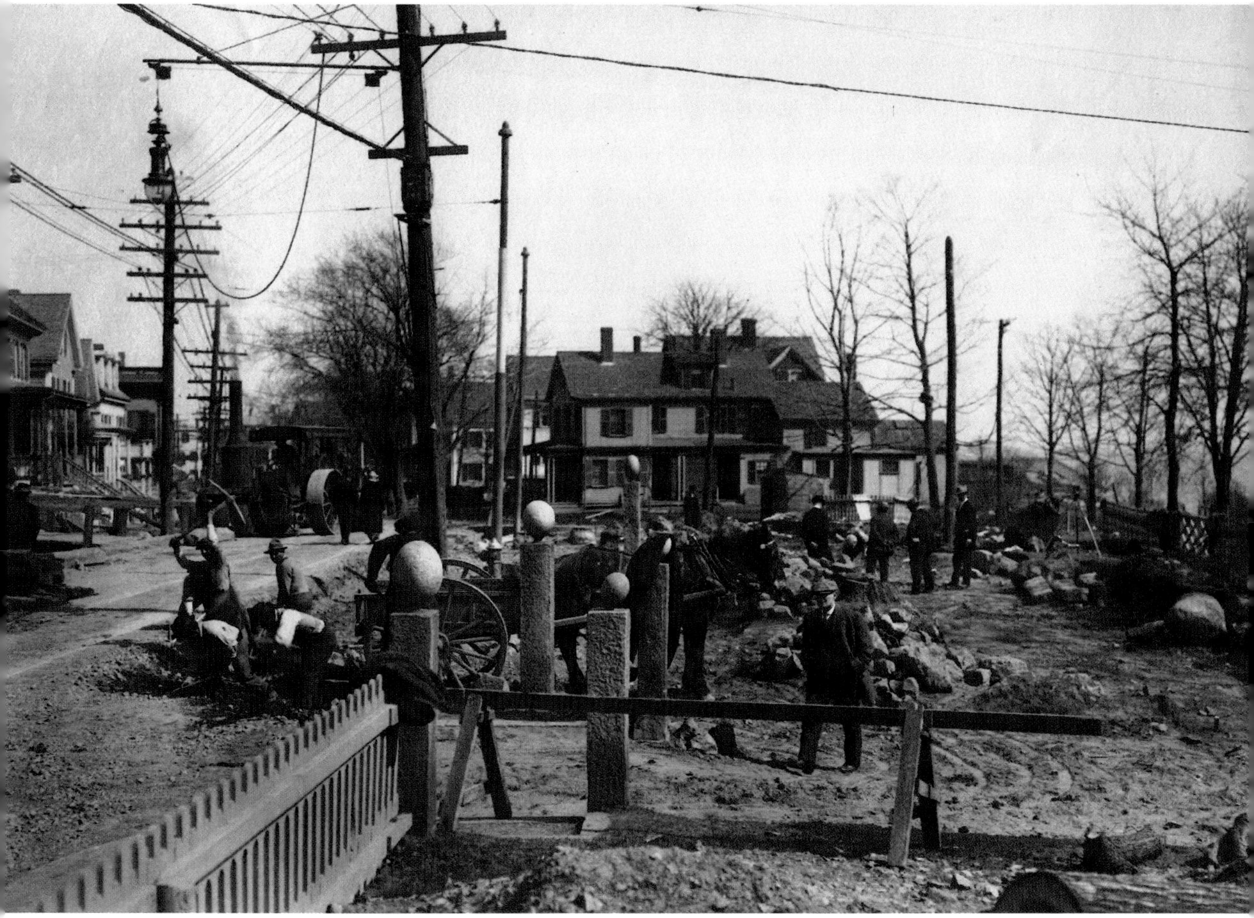

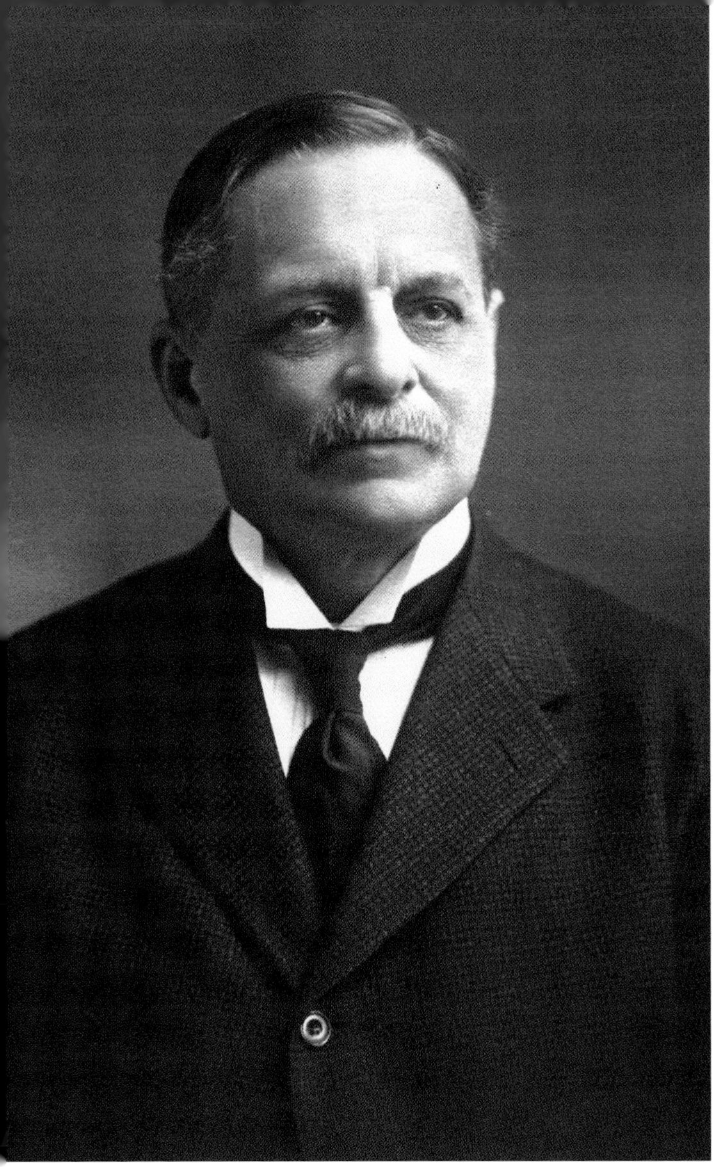

Where would we be today without Elihu Thomson? The cofounder of General Electric made his home in Swampscott from 1889 until his death in 1937. Today, his home on Monument Avenue is the town's administration building, acquired in 1945. (Courtesy Swampscott Historical Commission.)

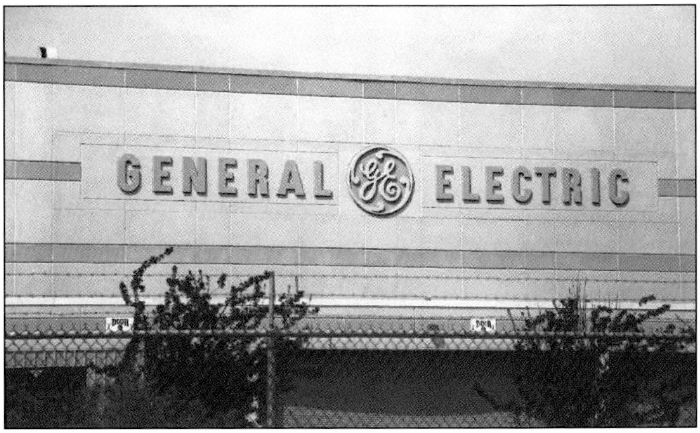

The cornerstone for the Machon School on Burpee Road was placed in during this grand ceremony in 1921. The town had appropriated $90,000 for the construction in 1919. (Courtesy Swampscott Historical Commission.)

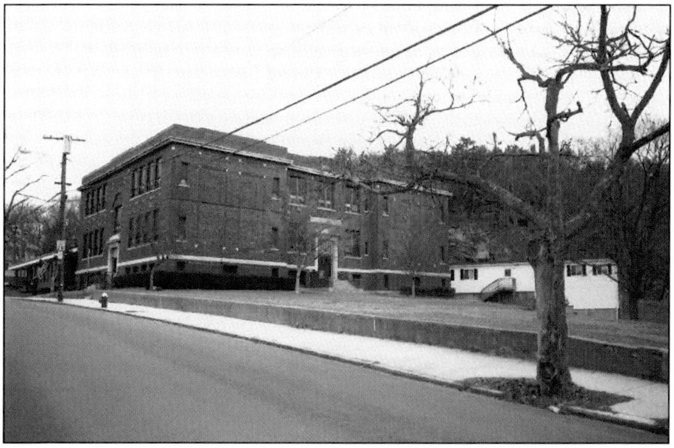

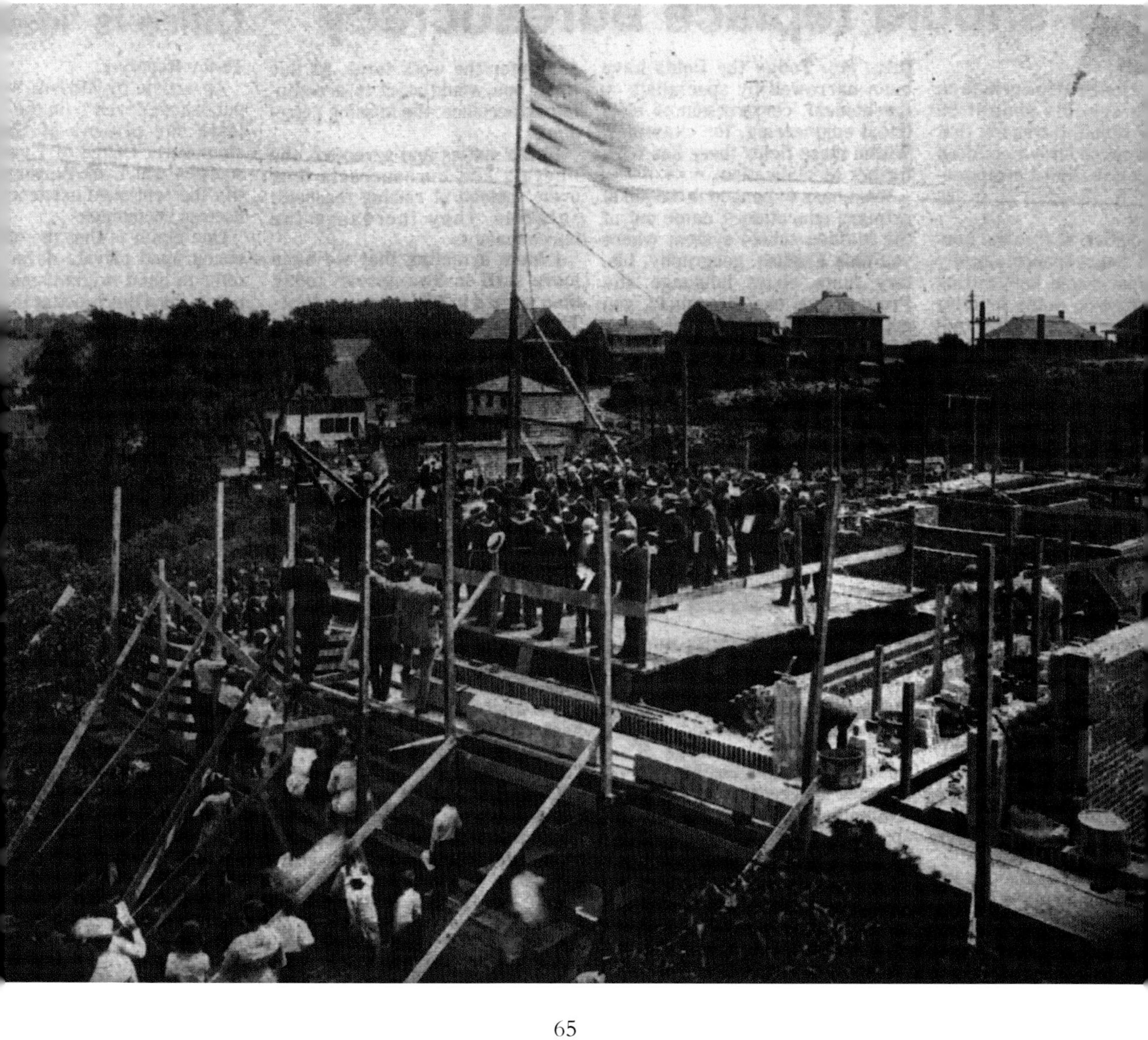

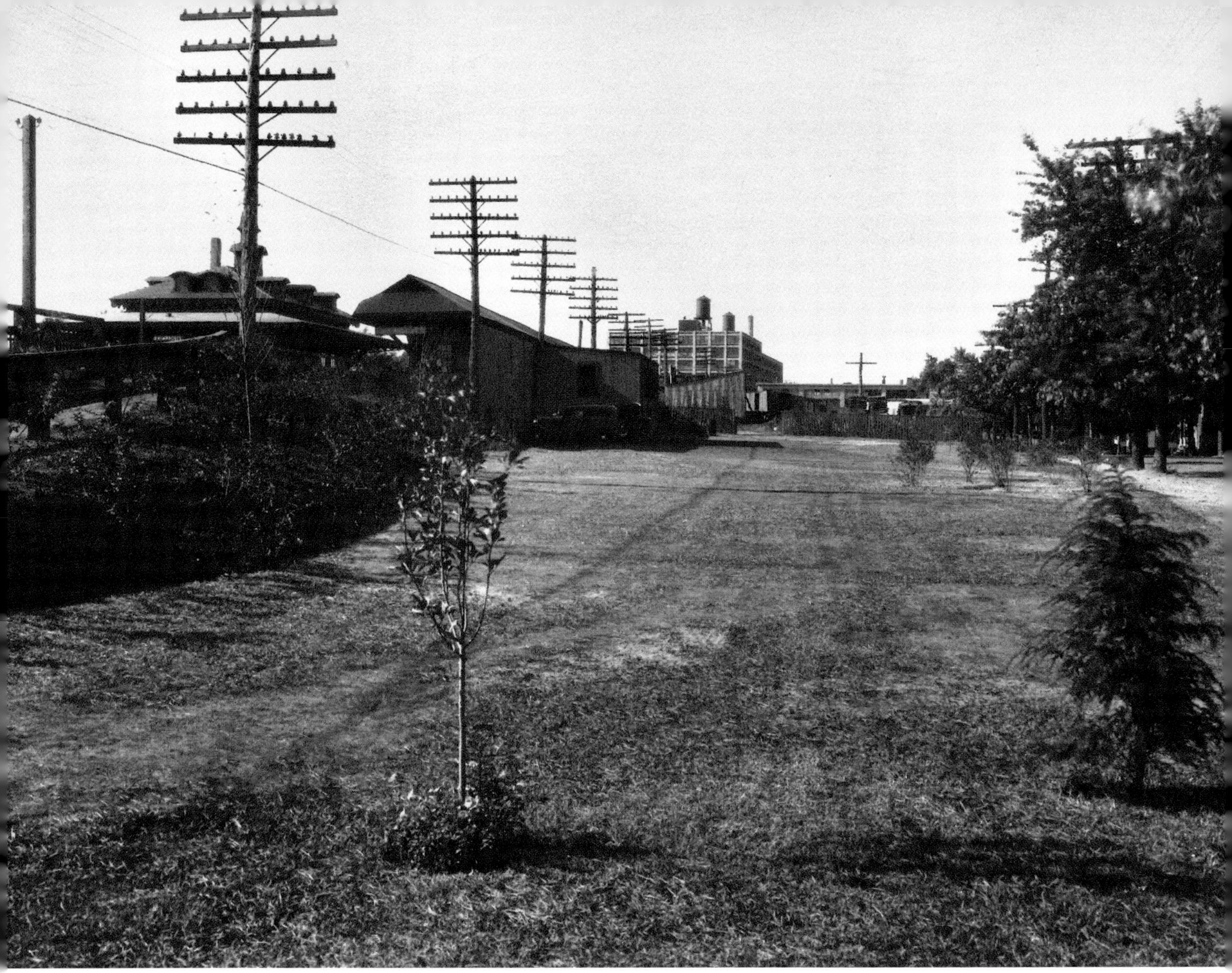

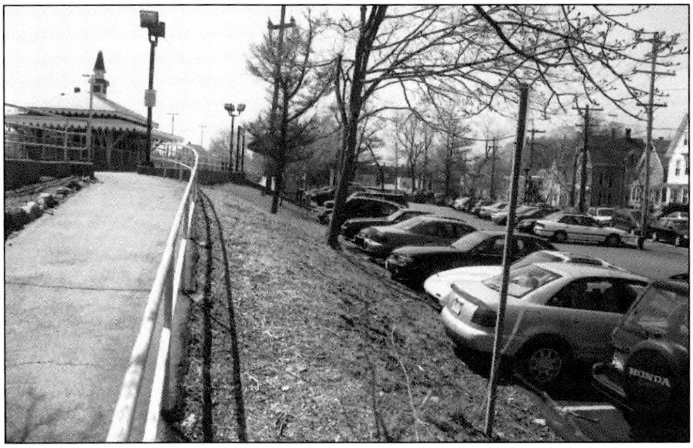

Grass has been replaced by asphalt at the Columbia Street side of the railroad depot, inbound to Boston. Shown here in 1933, the area almost looks pristine compared to the asphalt of today. (Courtesy Swampscott Public Library.)

It was in Swampscott in 1865–1866 that Mary Baker Eddy created the Christian Science Church, after spiritual healing was credited with her recuperation from a fall. In September 1921, the grounds at the Paradise Road home had simple gardens. The home still exists today. (Courtesy Swampscott Public Library.)

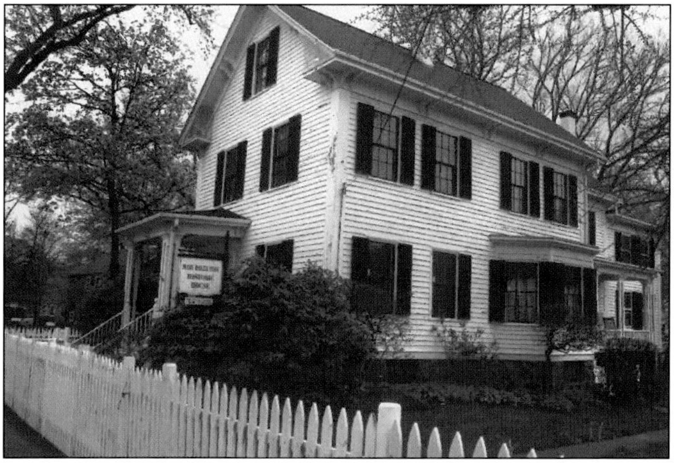

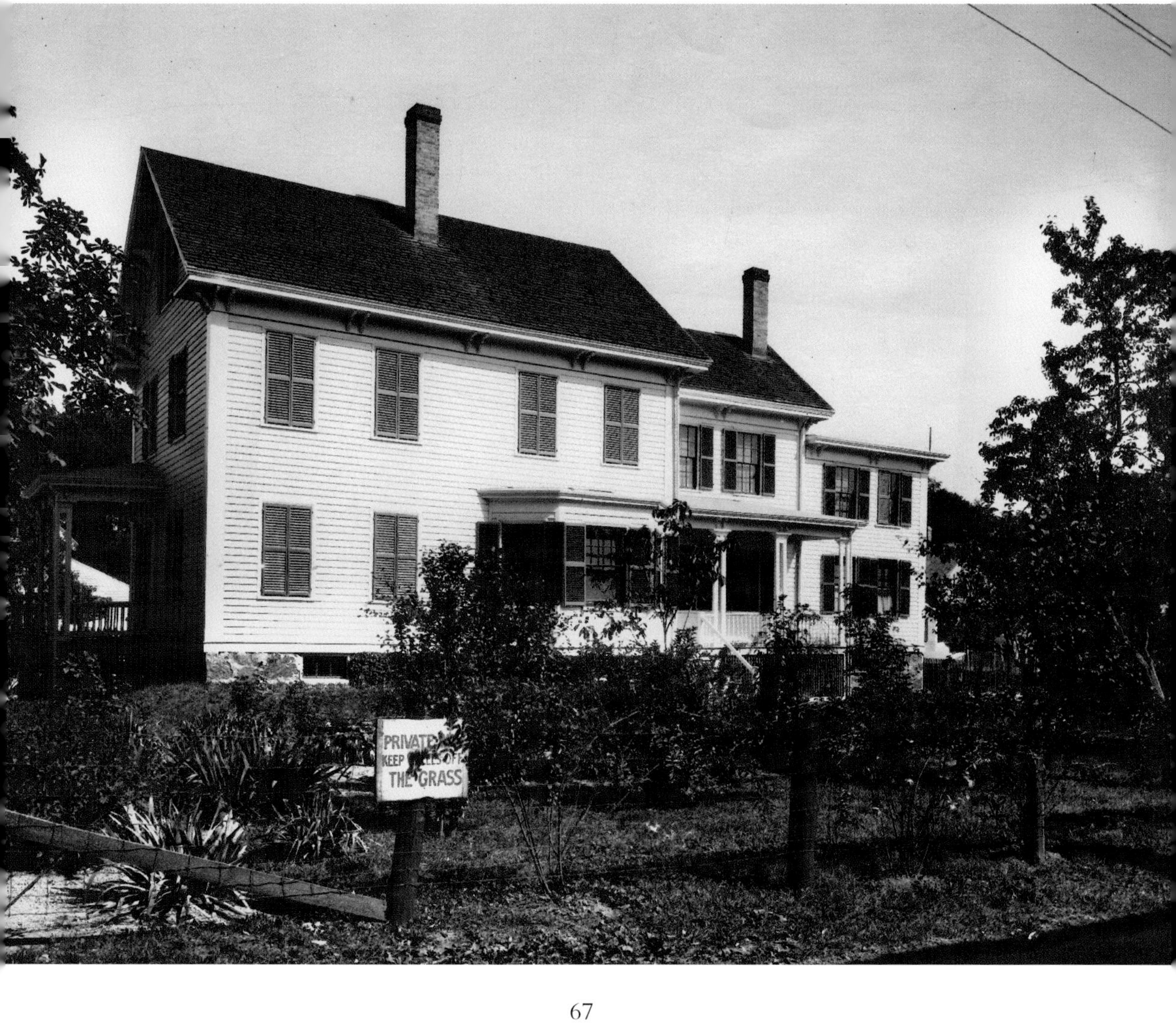

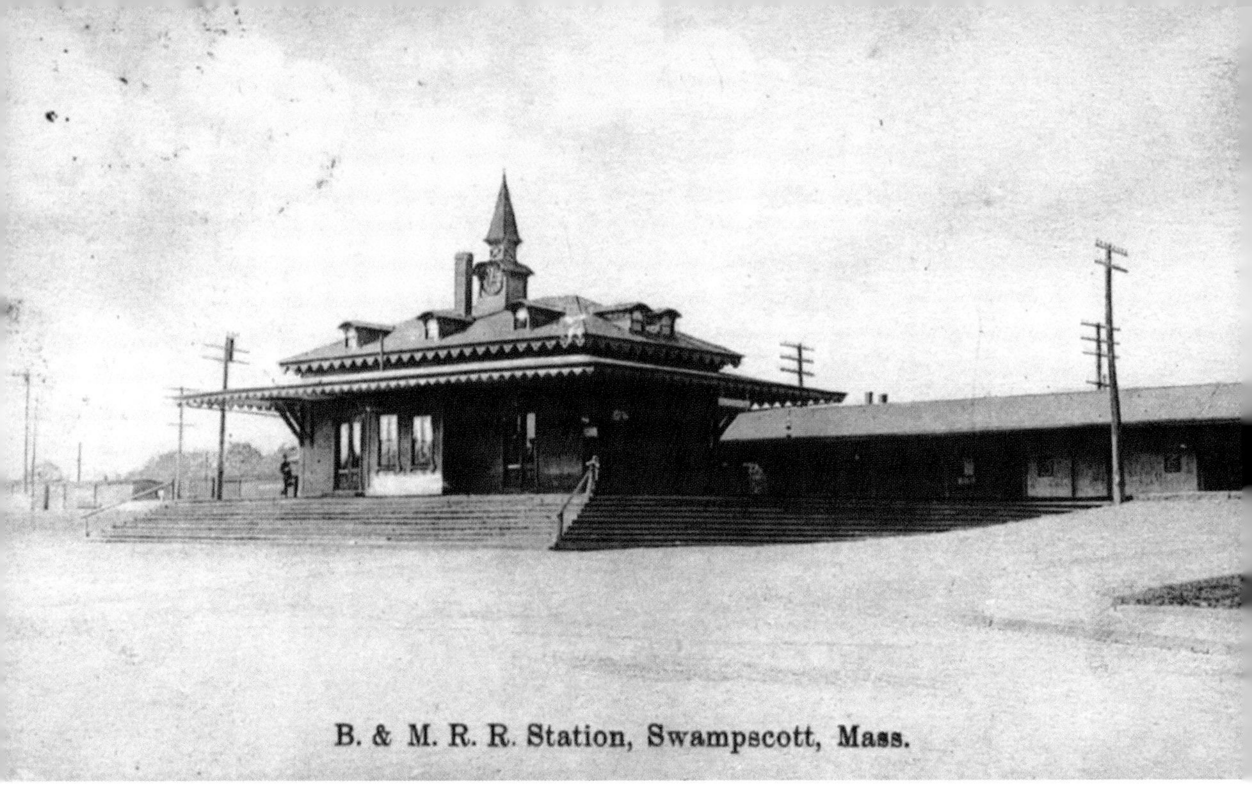

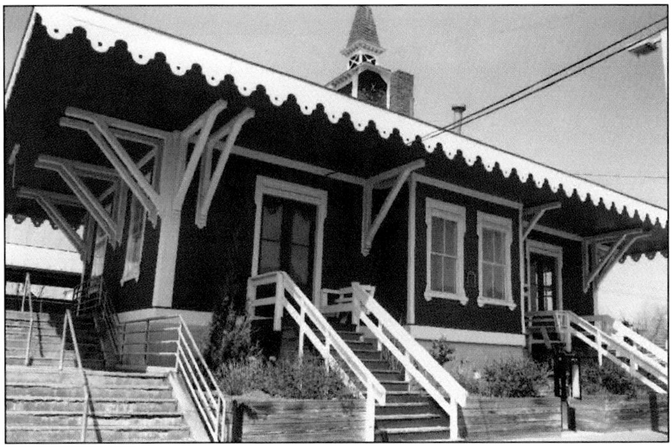

The Boston & Maine Railroad station, on Railroad Avenue, was built in 1868 and has been the backdrop for several events: young men going to war, summer residents arriving for vacation, and businesspeople traveling to Boston. These men (opposite page) traveled from Boston on the train to participate in a local parade. (Courtesy Swampscott Historical Society.)

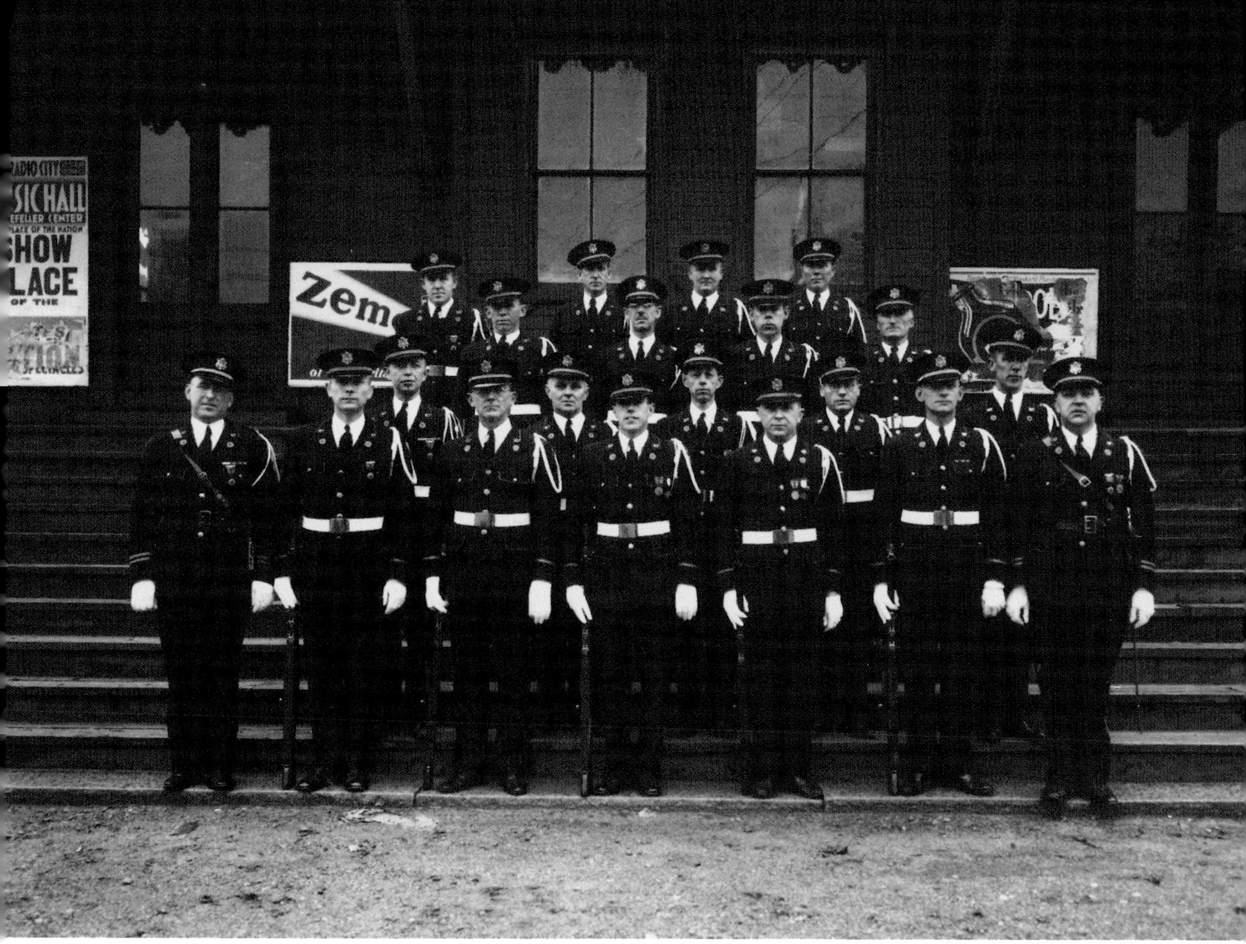
RADIO CITY
SICHALL
EFELLER CENTER
SHOW
LACE
OF THE
Zem

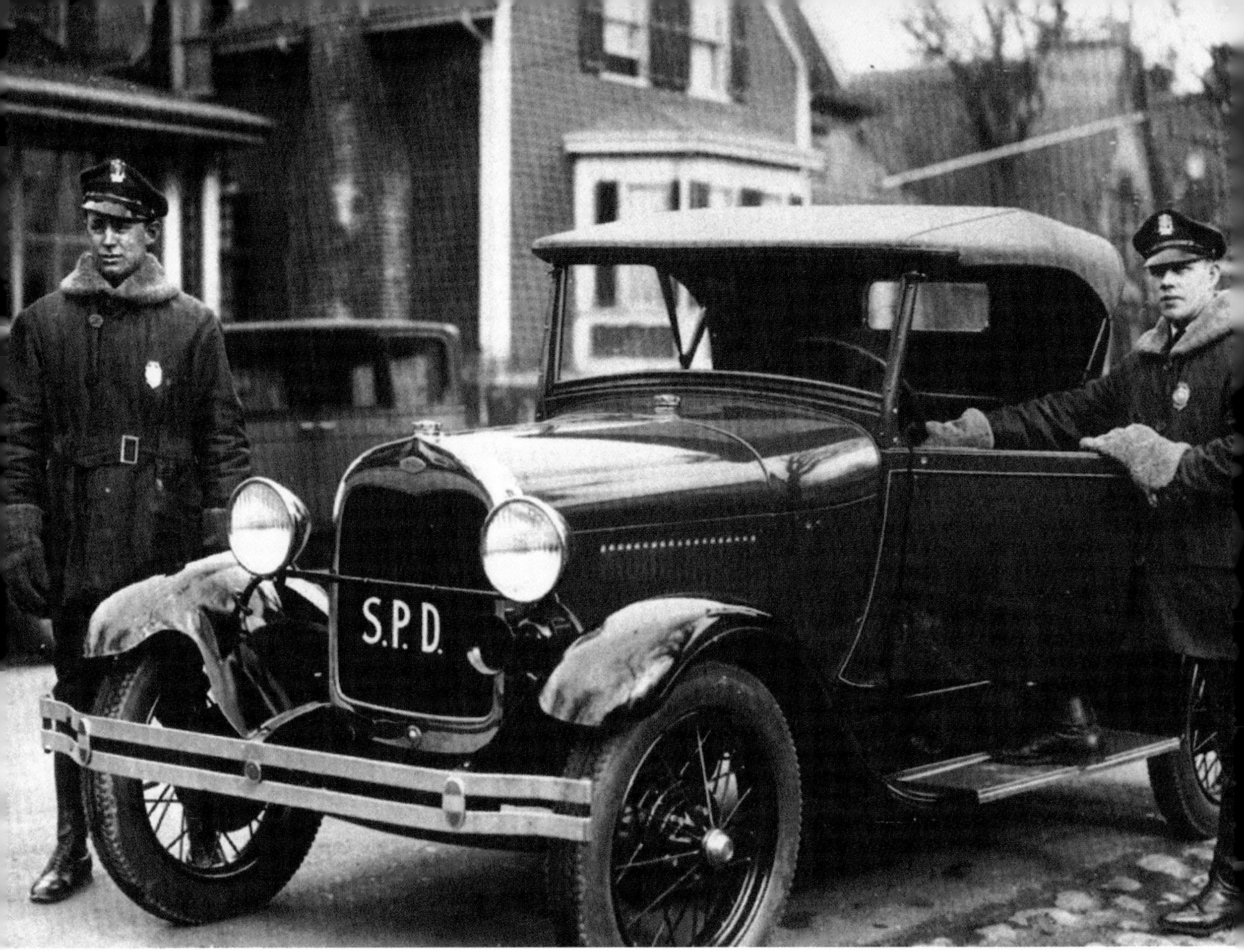

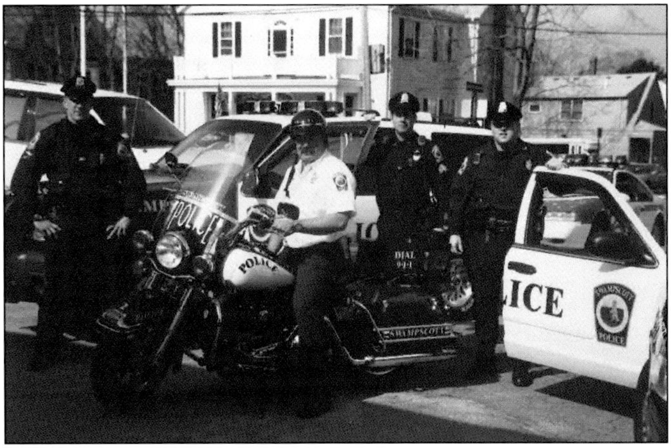

The Swampscott Police Department has always been fond of Ford vehicles, even in the early days. No doubt this early convertible was loved in the summer but required the wearing of extra clothing in the winter. Today, officers use Ford sedans, Ford sport utility vehicles, and Harley Davidson motorcycles to get around, as shown by current policemen, from left to right, Officer Savy Caruso, Lt. Peter Cassidy, Sgt. Rick McCarriston, and Officer Jay Locke. Over the years, reserve officers and special officers have been used to support the regular police force. The 1905 specials (opposite page) included, from left to right, Fred McNamara, Alfred Frazier, John Thomas, Dick Gilley, Frank Griffin, John Bryson, Lemuel Pickard, John Doherty, and Eben Martin. (Courtesy Louis A. Gallo and Swampscott Public Library.)

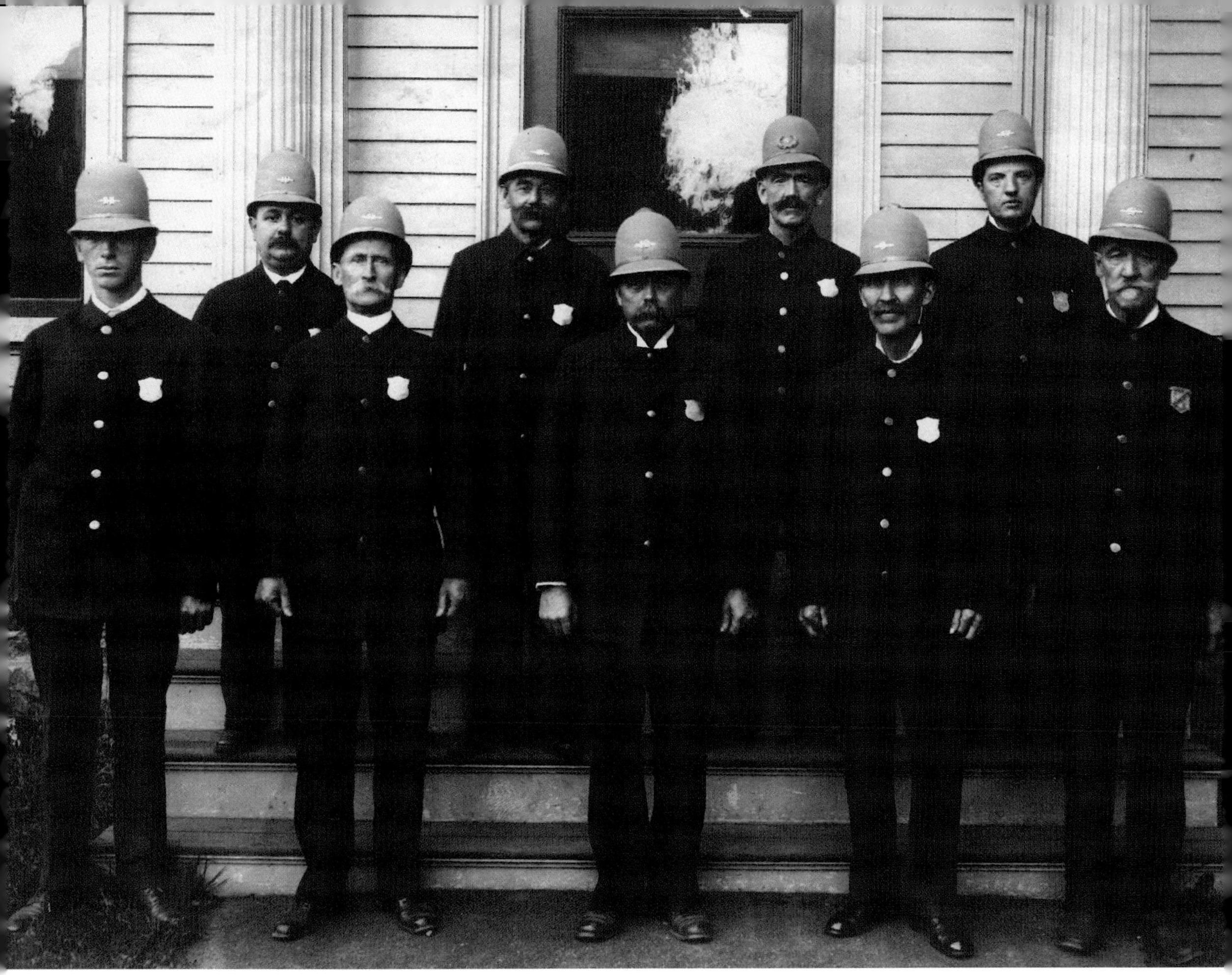

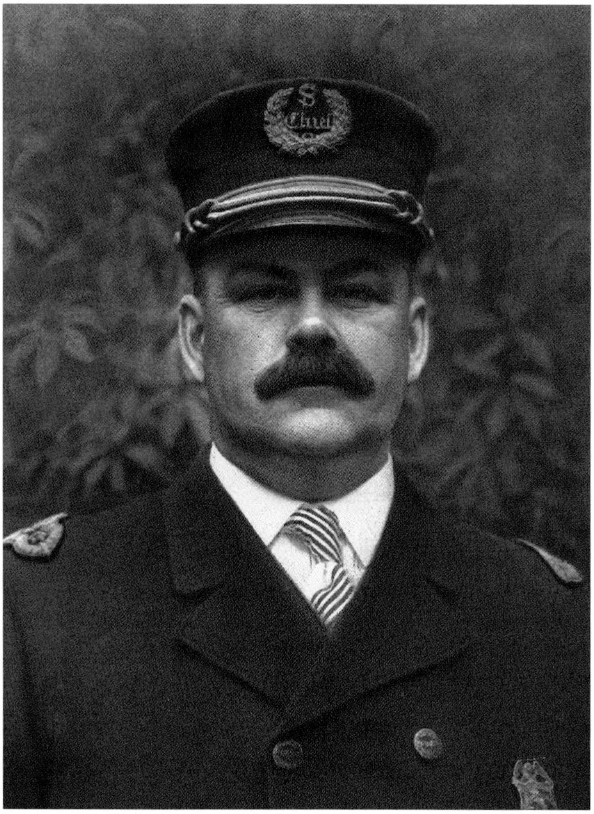

An 1882 photograph of the first police chief, Joseph Symonds, was not available; however, this view shows Ulysses Corson, one of the town's early chiefs. Today, Ronald Madigan (below) is at the helm, having worked his way up through the department. (Courtesy Swampscott Police Department.)

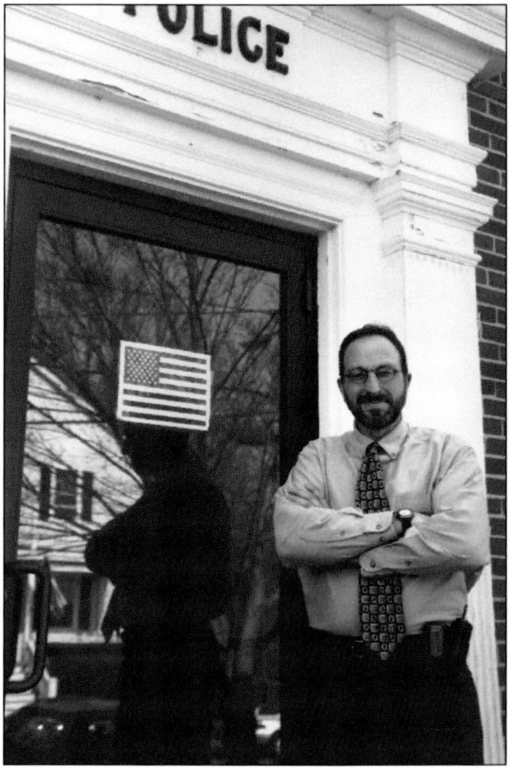

Members of the fire department and town officials in the early part of the 20th century show off a new fire truck for the Swampscott Fire Department. Today, Lawrence Galante is chief of the fire department. (Courtesy Swampscott Historical Commission.)

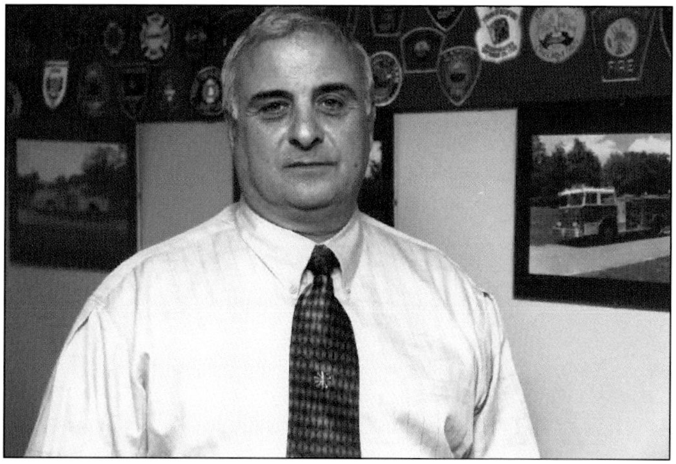

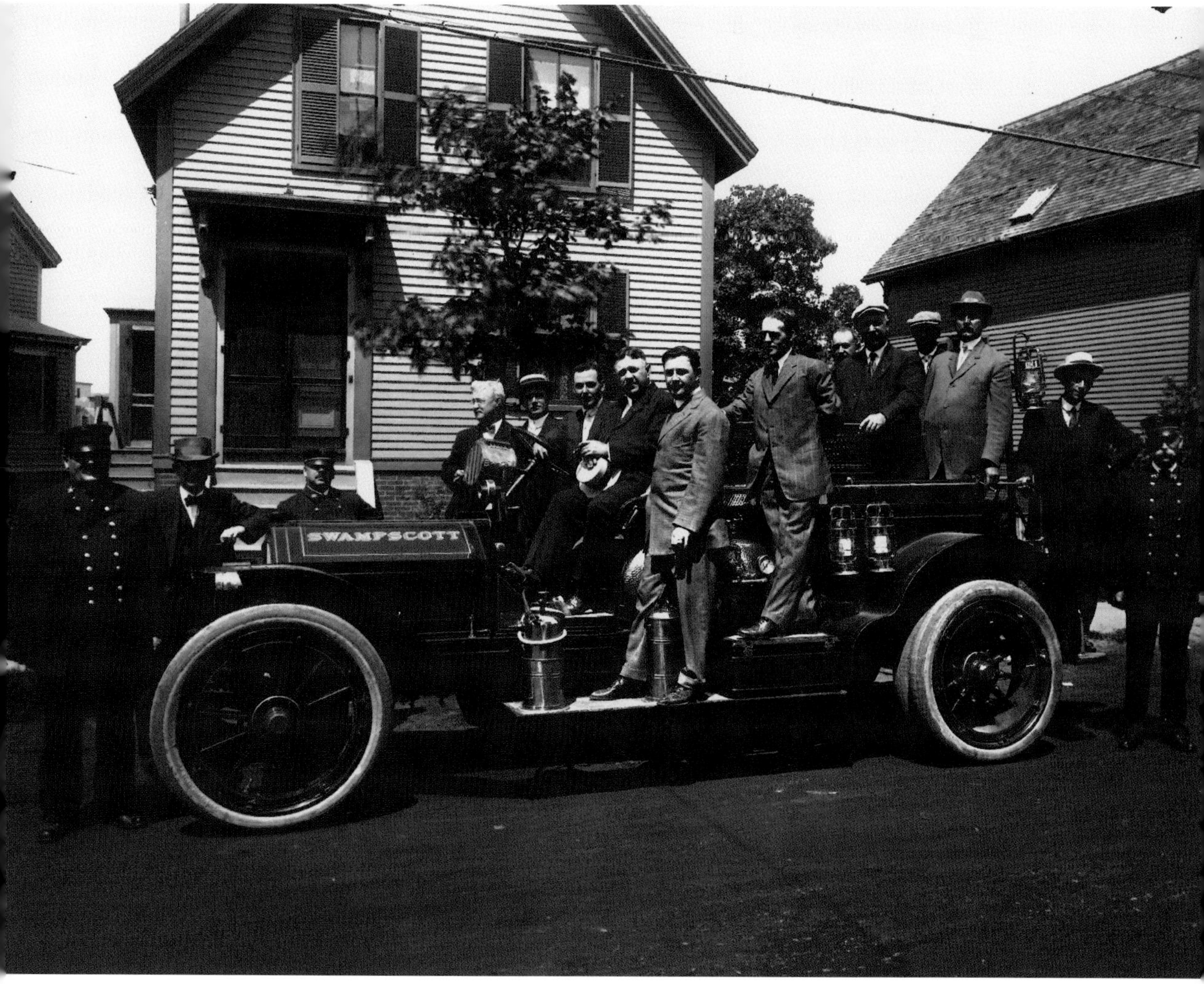

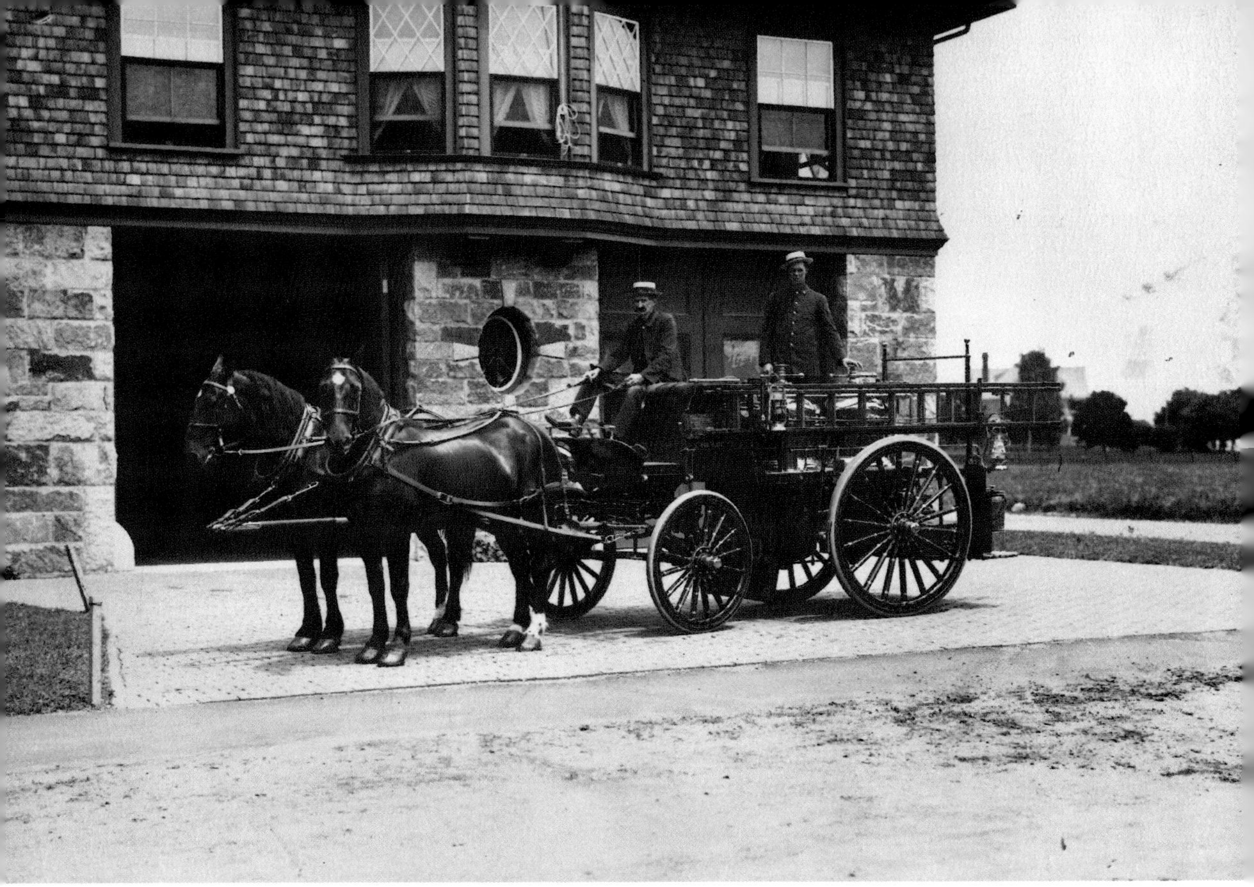

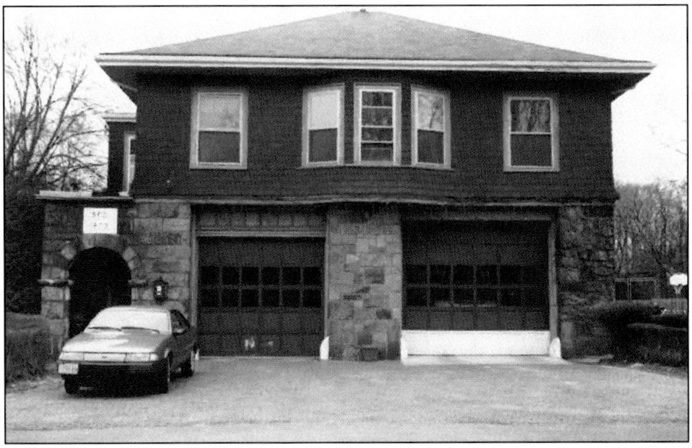

Known as the Phillips Beach Chemical Firehouse in 1905, the building on Phillips Avenue remains today. For years, it was a second fire station for the town until budget constraints closed it down in the 1990s. In the early-20th-century view (opposite page), the building serves as a backdrop for the call firemen. It is currently used by a private ambulance company that serves the town. (Courtesy Swampscott Historical Commission and Swampscott Public Library.)

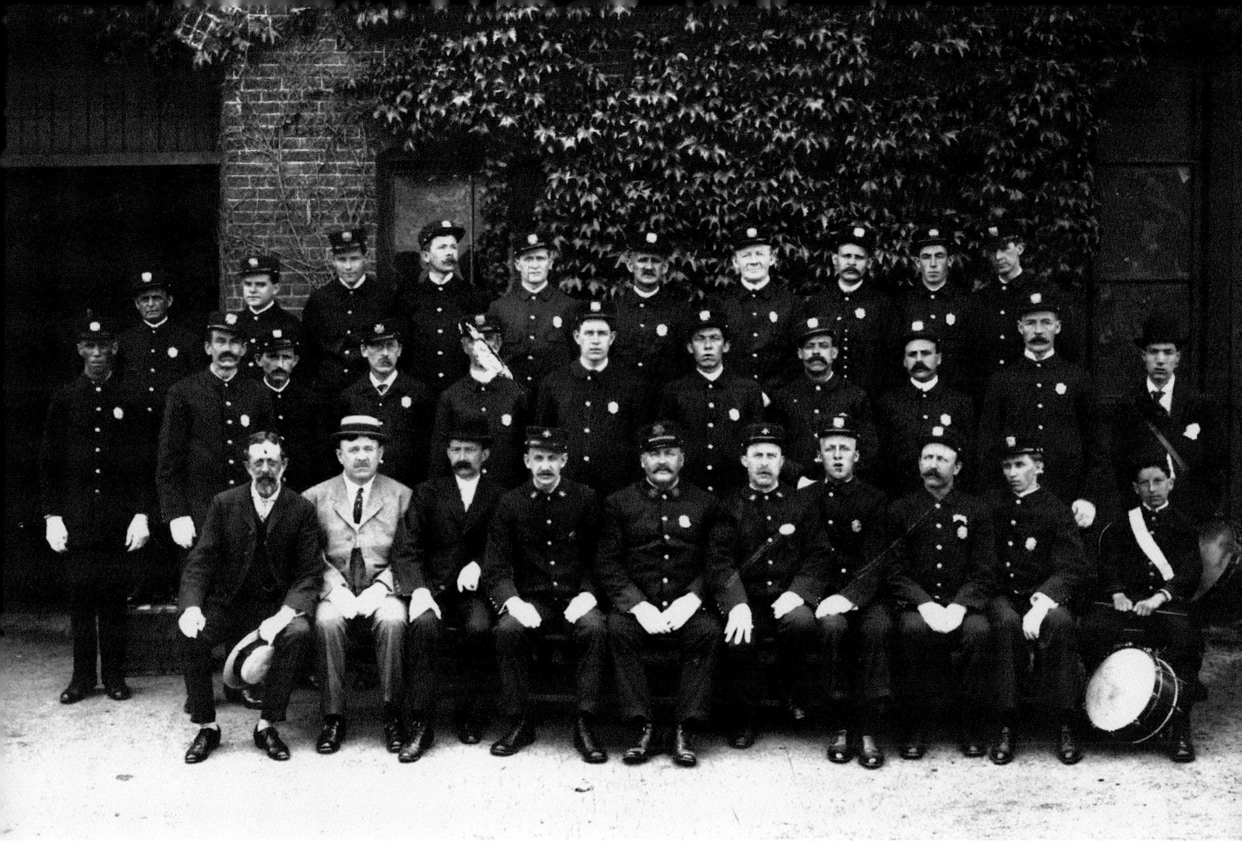

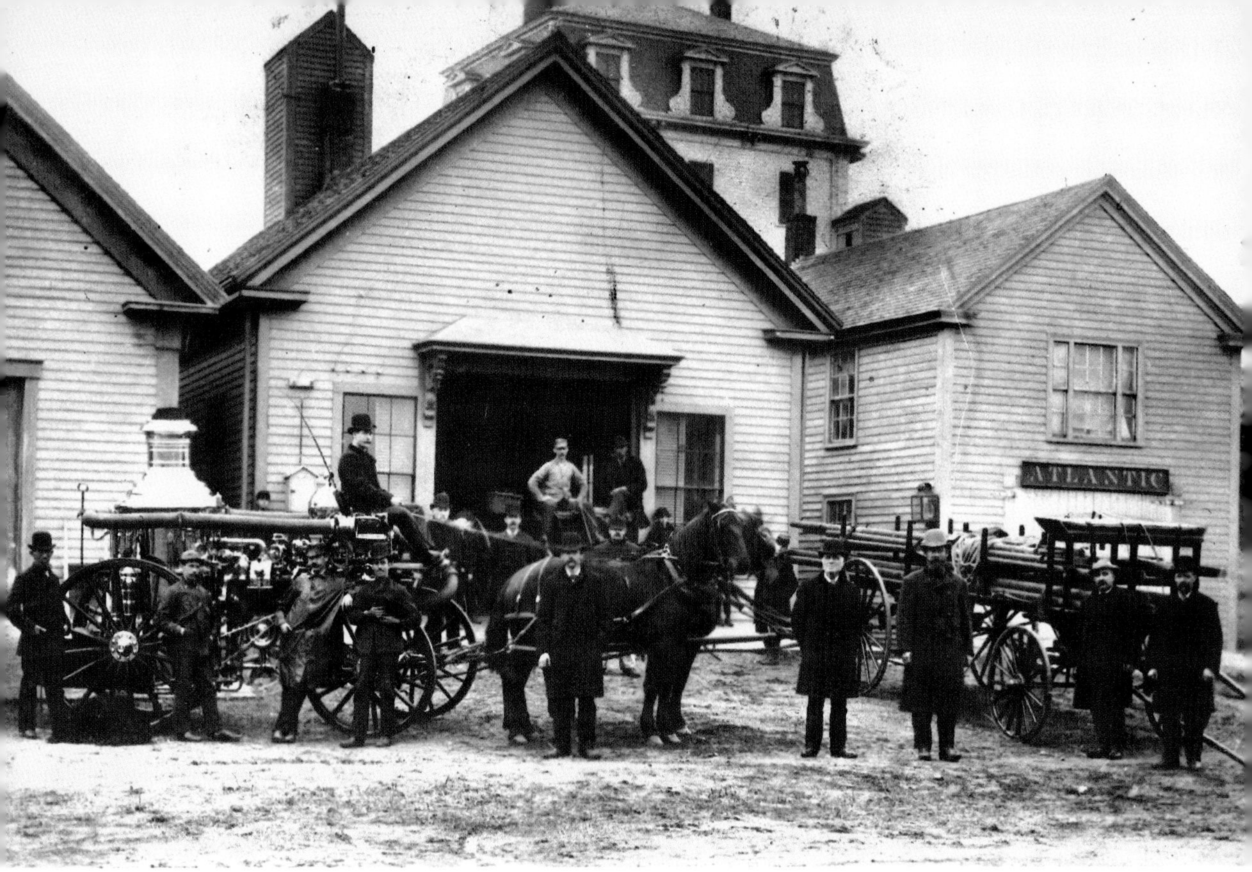

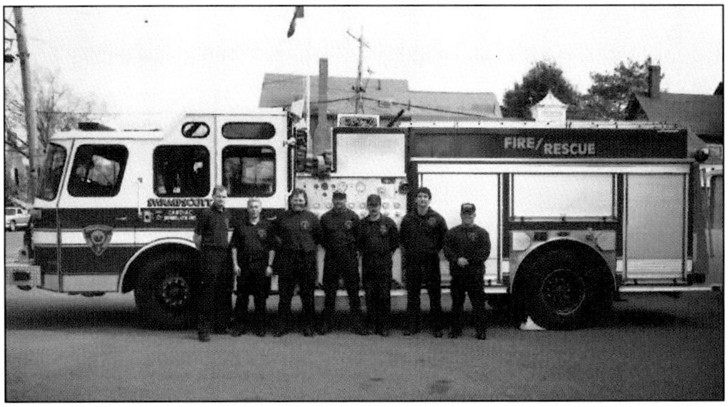

Photographed *c.* 1888, Swampscott firefighters show off their modern equipment in front of the firehouse on New Ocean Street. Today, firefighters make their home on Burrill Street and even carry equipment to treat heart attack victims. From left to right, with Engine 21, are Capt. Kevin Thompson; firefighters Remo Zimbaldi, Bill Hyde Jr., Bob Pickett Jr., and Tim Sweeney; Lt. John Quinn; and firefighter Bob Surette. (Courtesy Louis A. Gallo.)

Pulling these wagons along Blaney Beach could not have been easy, but young men from the Lincoln House stables knew nothing different in the 1870s. From left to right are an unidentified coachman, little Frederic H. Lewis, Edward Albree, and Weston K. Lewis. (Courtesy Swampscott Public Library.)

Chapter 4
SEASIDE SWAMPSCOTT

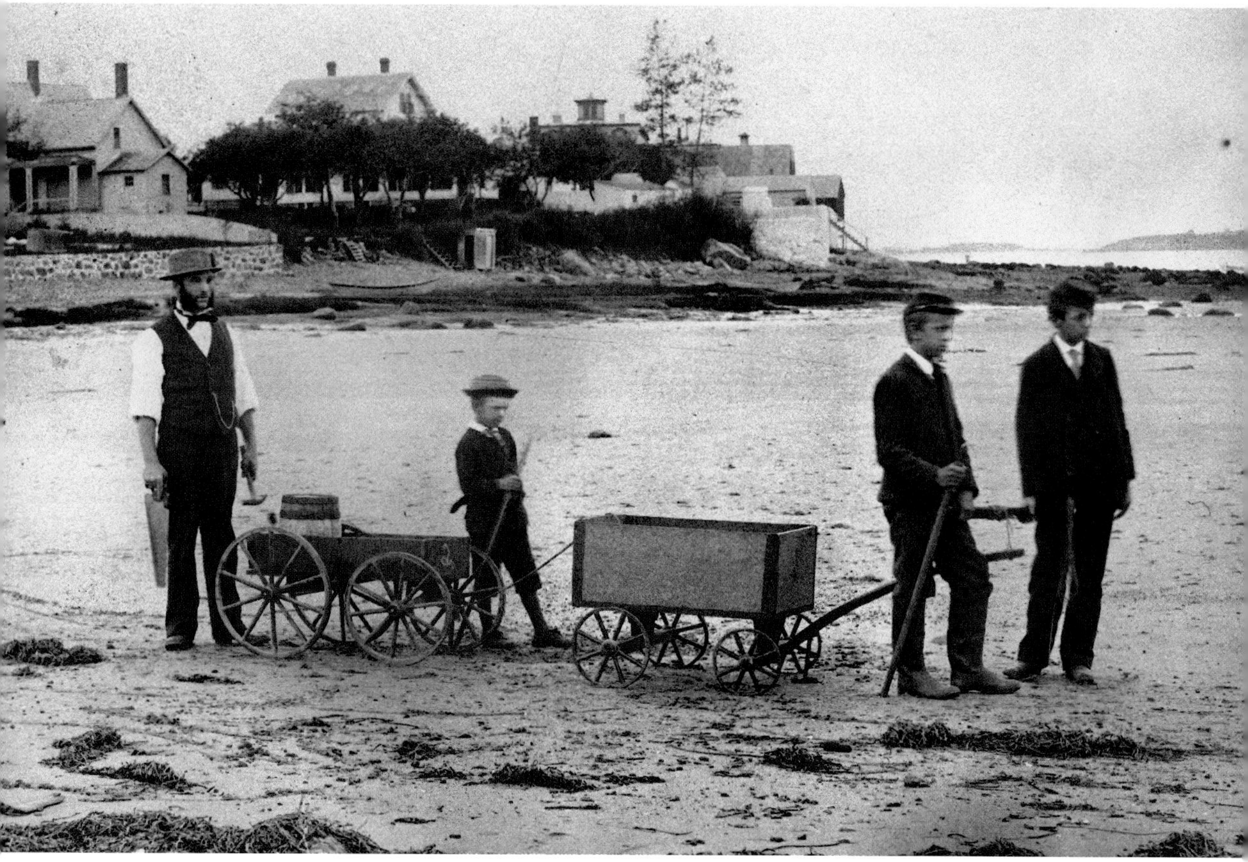

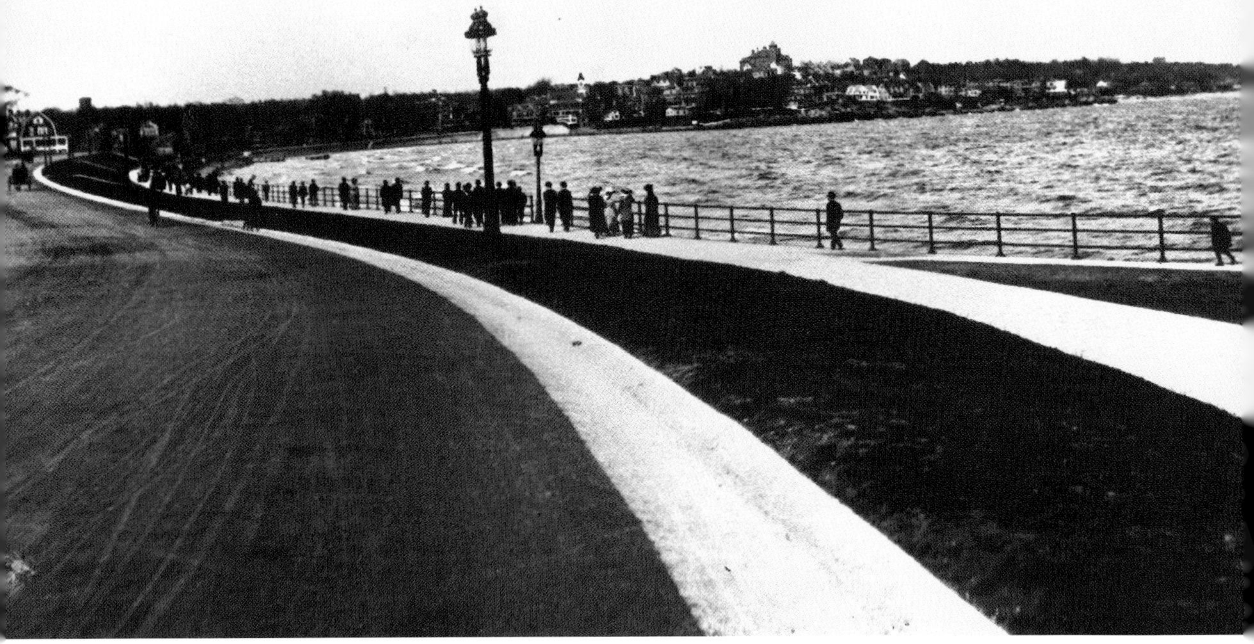

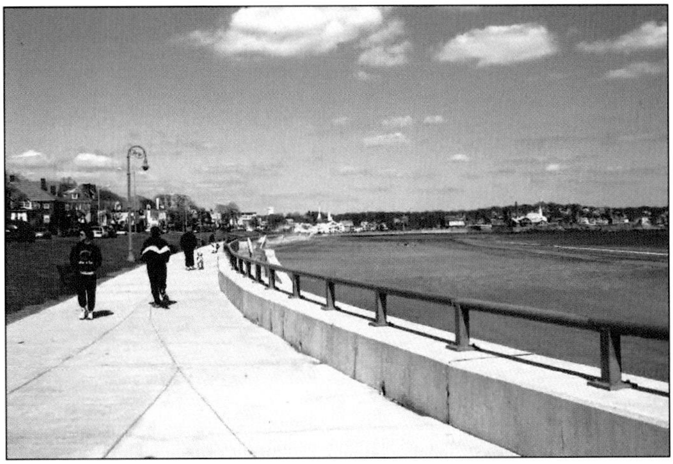

In a view looking from Red Rock in Lynn along Kings Beach, the Swampscott skyline is easily recognizable, with the highest building being the old Swampscott High School on Greenwood Avenue. One thing that has not changed is the love of walking along the stretch of sidewalk from Lynn to Swampscott. (Courtesy Swampscott Public Library.)

Kings Beach extends from Lynn to Swampscott and, over the years, the sea has deposited everything from boats to whales upon the beach. In 1991, this minke whale washed up on the beach, drawing great interest. The public works department assisted the New England Aquarium in burying the whale on the beach. (Courtesy Louis A. Gallo.)

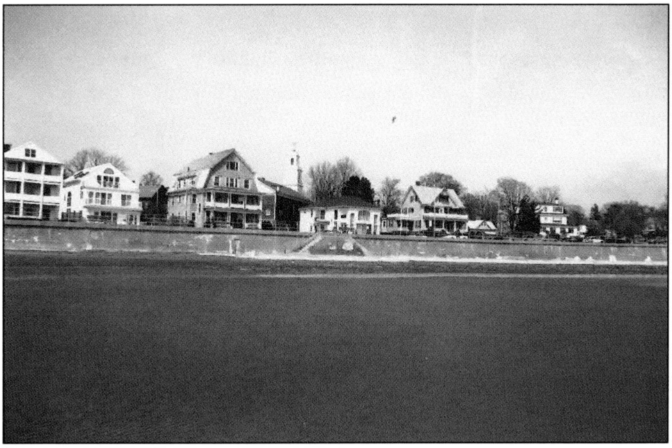

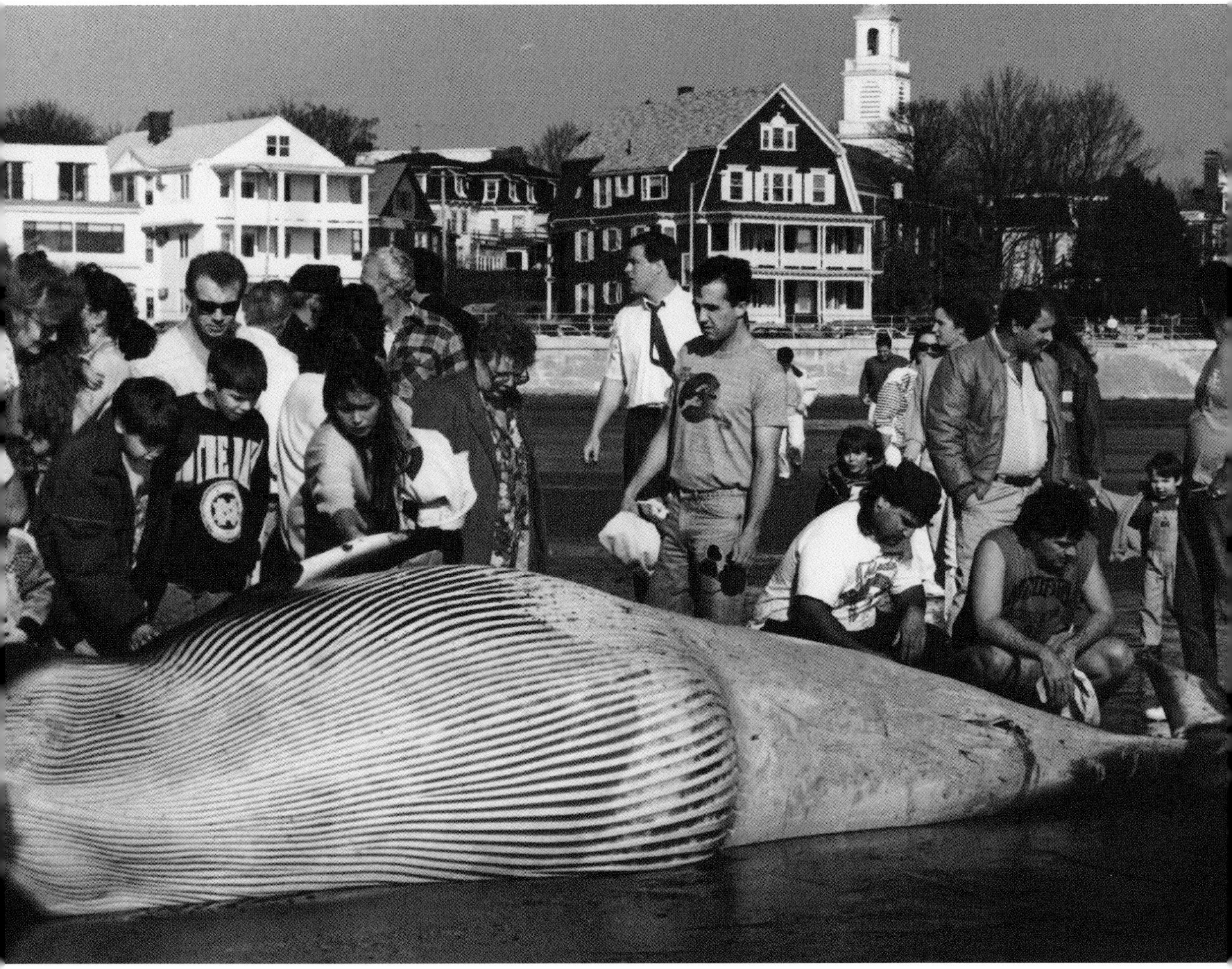

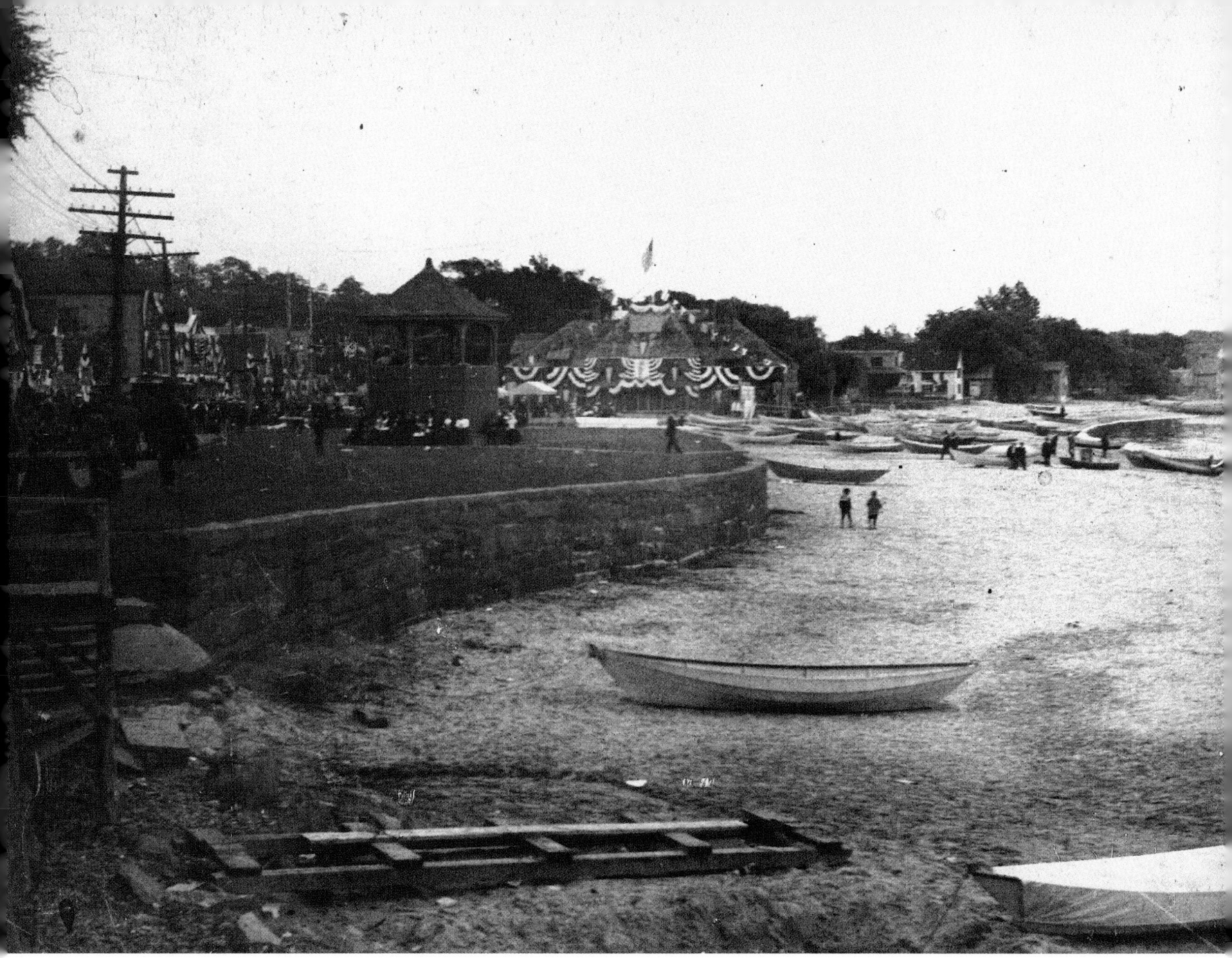

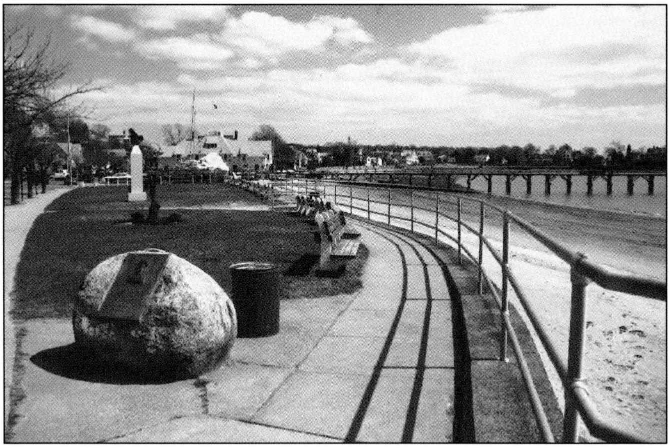

In 1902, Fisherman's Beach (complete with a gazebo over it), Humphrey Street, and the Fish House all were decked out in red, white, and blue for the celebration of the town's 50th birthday. Today, the beach has changed little, but the park above it has been dedicated to Lt. Gen. John R. Chaisson, former chief of staff of the U.S. Marine Corps. (Courtesy Louis A. Gallo.)

Lincoln House Point can be seen in the distance from Fisherman's Beach. From 1864 to 1915, the Lincoln House Hotel, named to honor Pres. Abraham Lincoln, rose above the sea. The beach was also a popular spot for painters, especially during the Beach Painters era in the 1890s. (Courtesy Louis A. Gallo.)

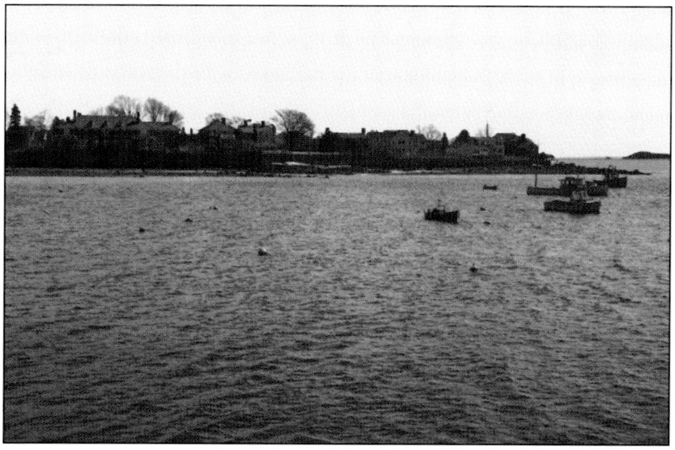

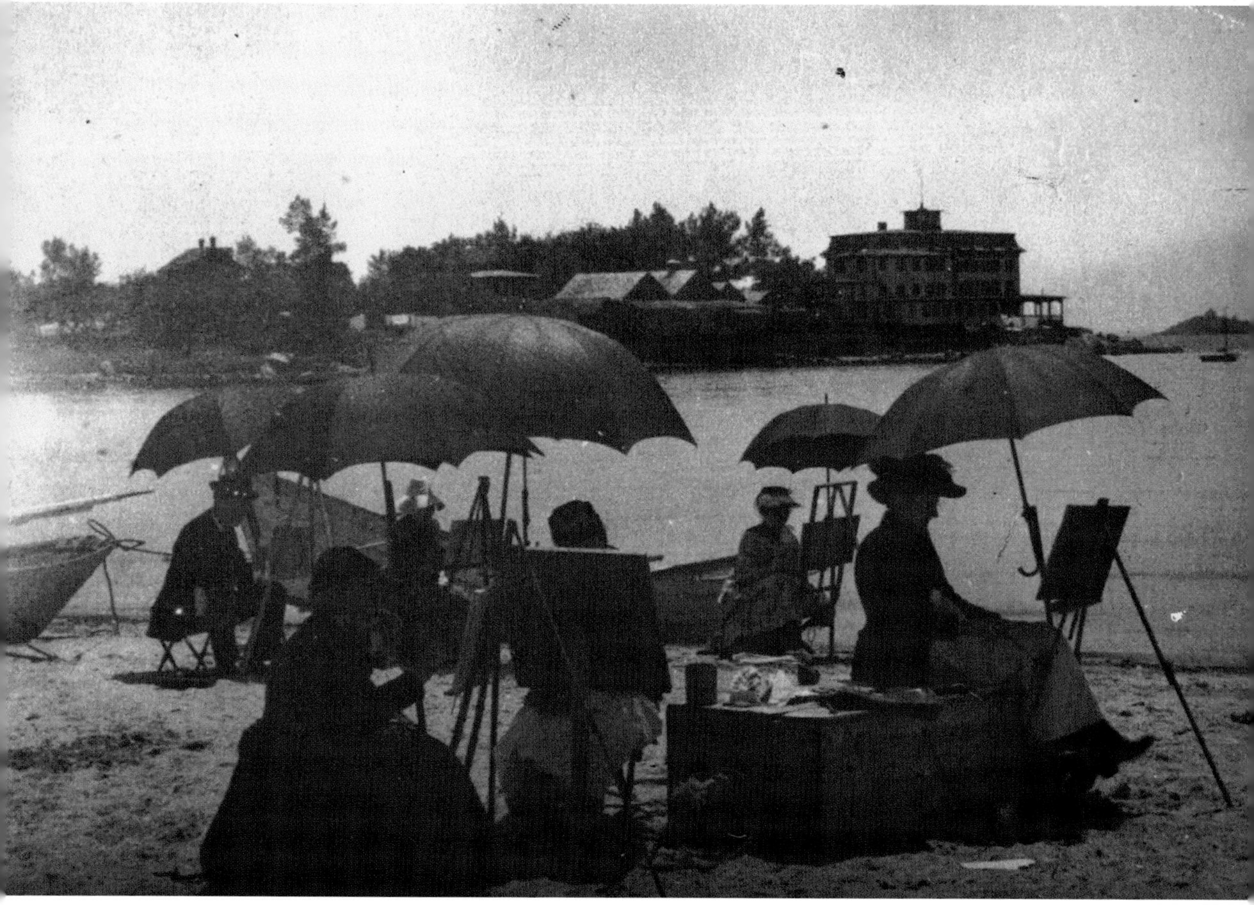

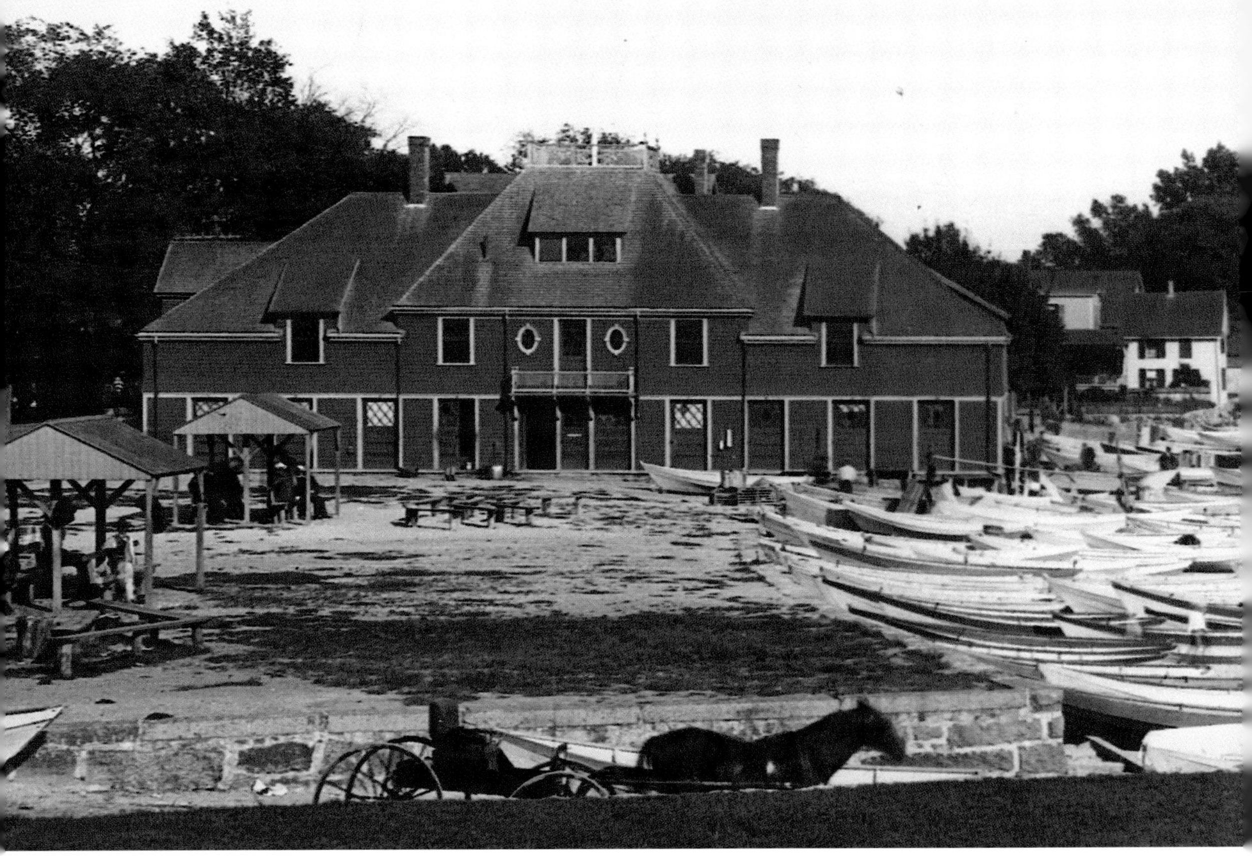

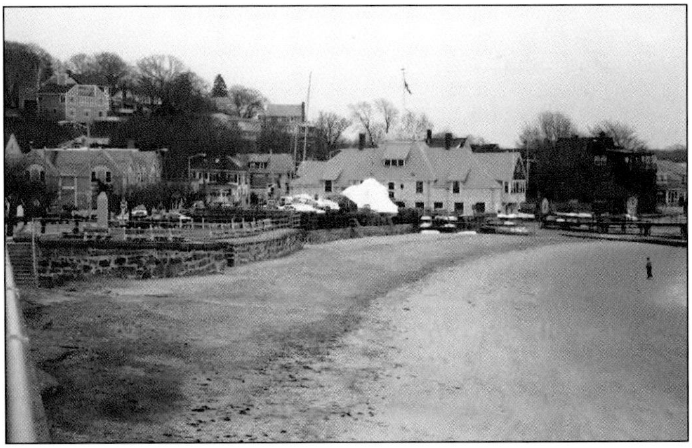

The Fish House on Humphrey Street was built in 1894 to replace the numerous fishing shanties on Fisherman's Beach. Today, fishermen use its lockers, the Swampscott Yacht Club uses its second floor, and the Fish House is listed on the National Register of Historic Landmarks. (Courtesy Louis A. Gallo.)

Fishermen still use the beach in front of the Fish House to offload the catch of the day. Each day, the fishermen row their catch of lobsters from their boat moored in the harbor to the beach; however, trucks rather than horses pull the boat ashore. (Courtesy Swampscott Historical Society.)

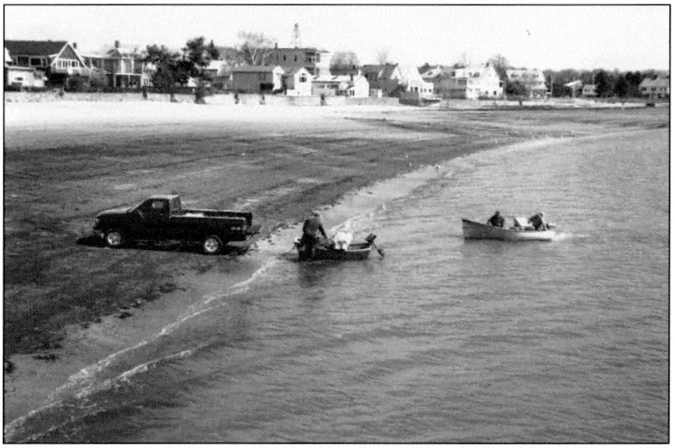

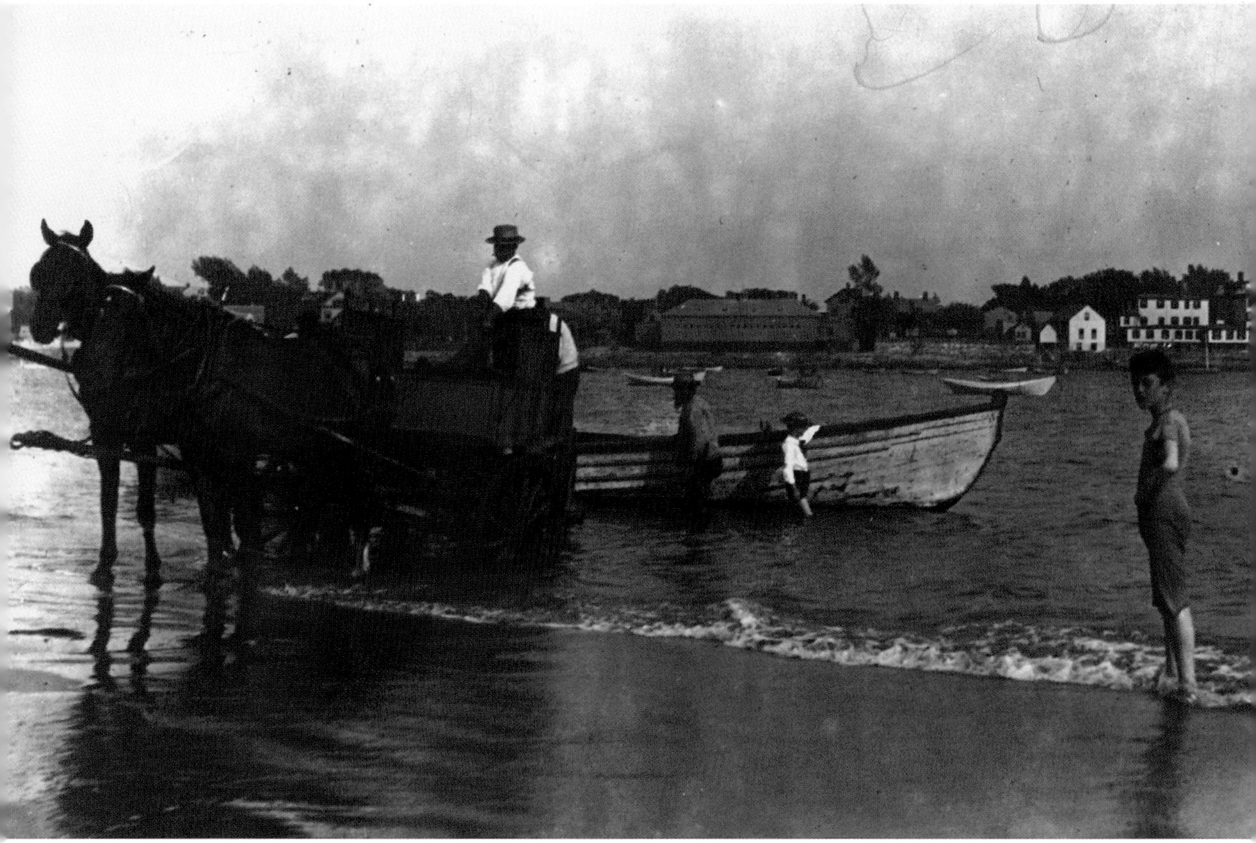

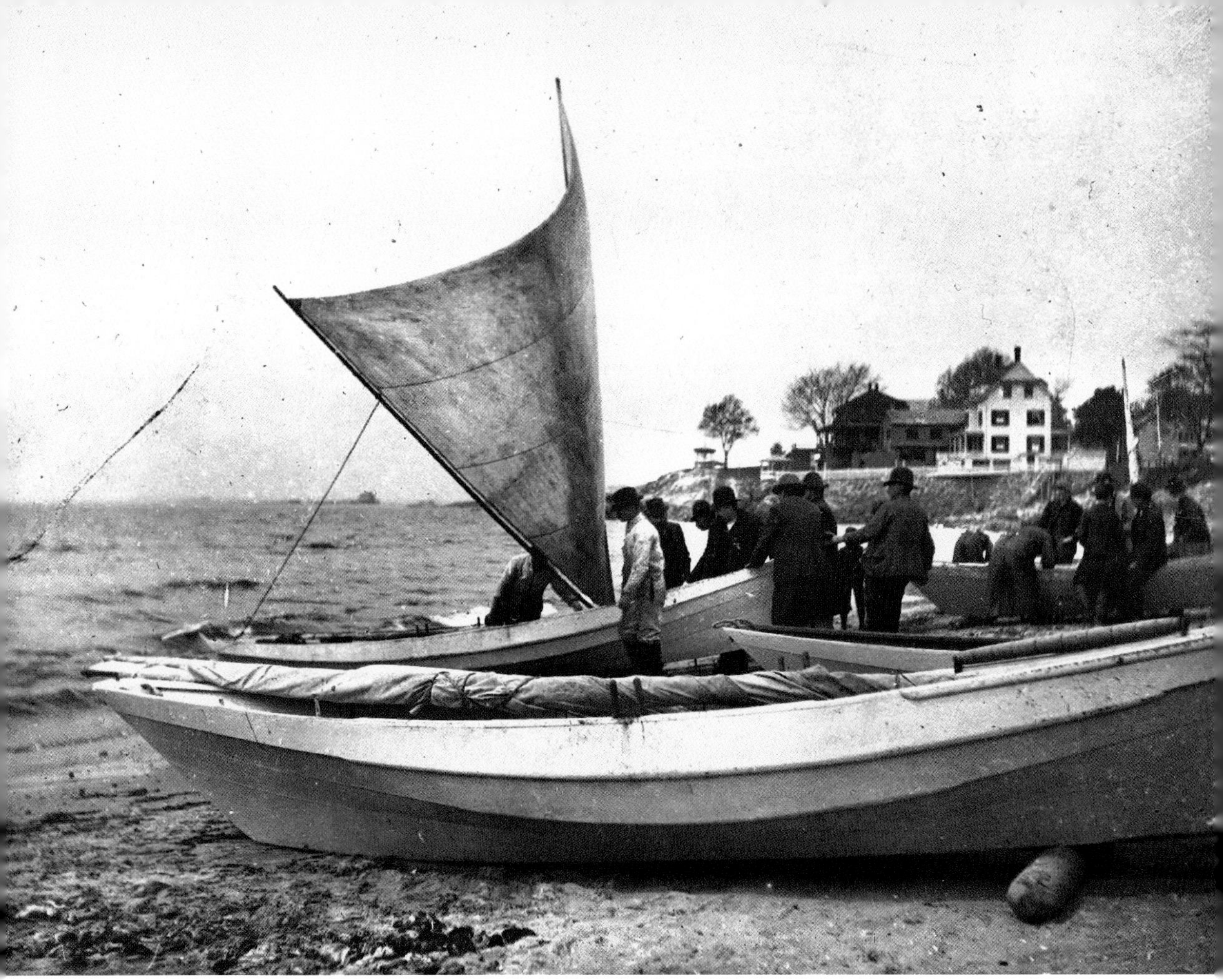

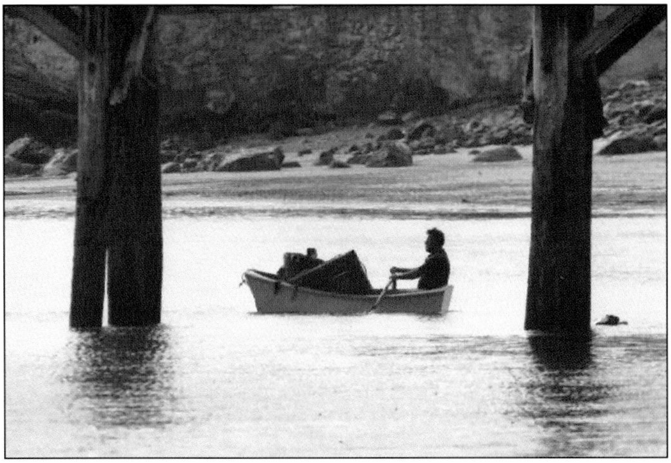

Fishermen in the 1890s unload their catch after beaching their sail-powered vessels on Fisherman's Beach. Today, a fisherman is more likely to row in his catch after mooring his fishing boat in the harbor. (Courtesy Swampscott Historical Commission.)

In the 1970s and 1980s, finding a catamaran sailboat on Fisherman's Beach seemed a far cry from the sailing dories of the 19th century. Swampscott Harbor and surrounding waters have always been a safe place for young sailors to learn the sport. (Courtesy Swampscott Historical Commission.)

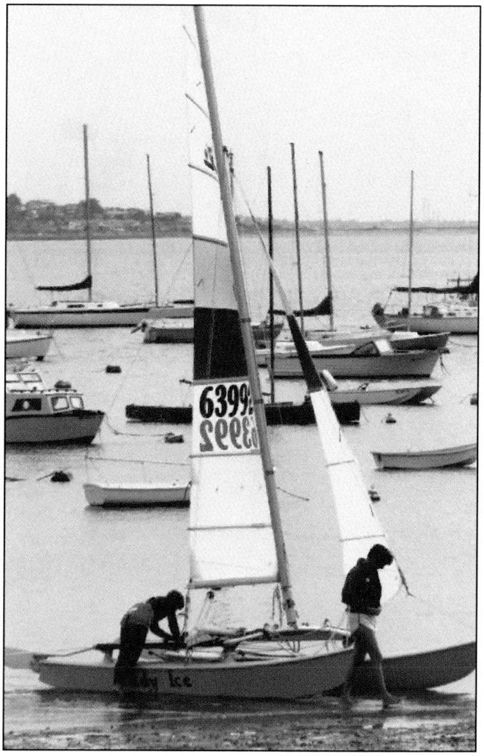

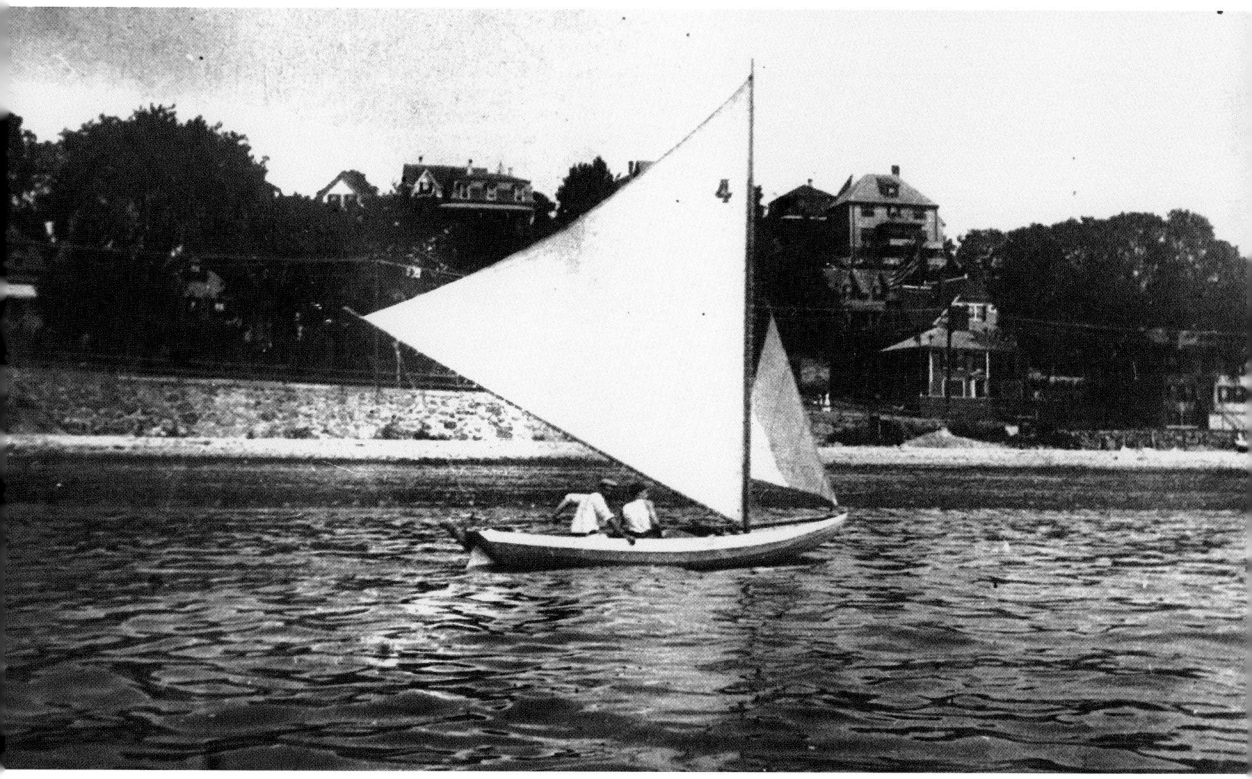

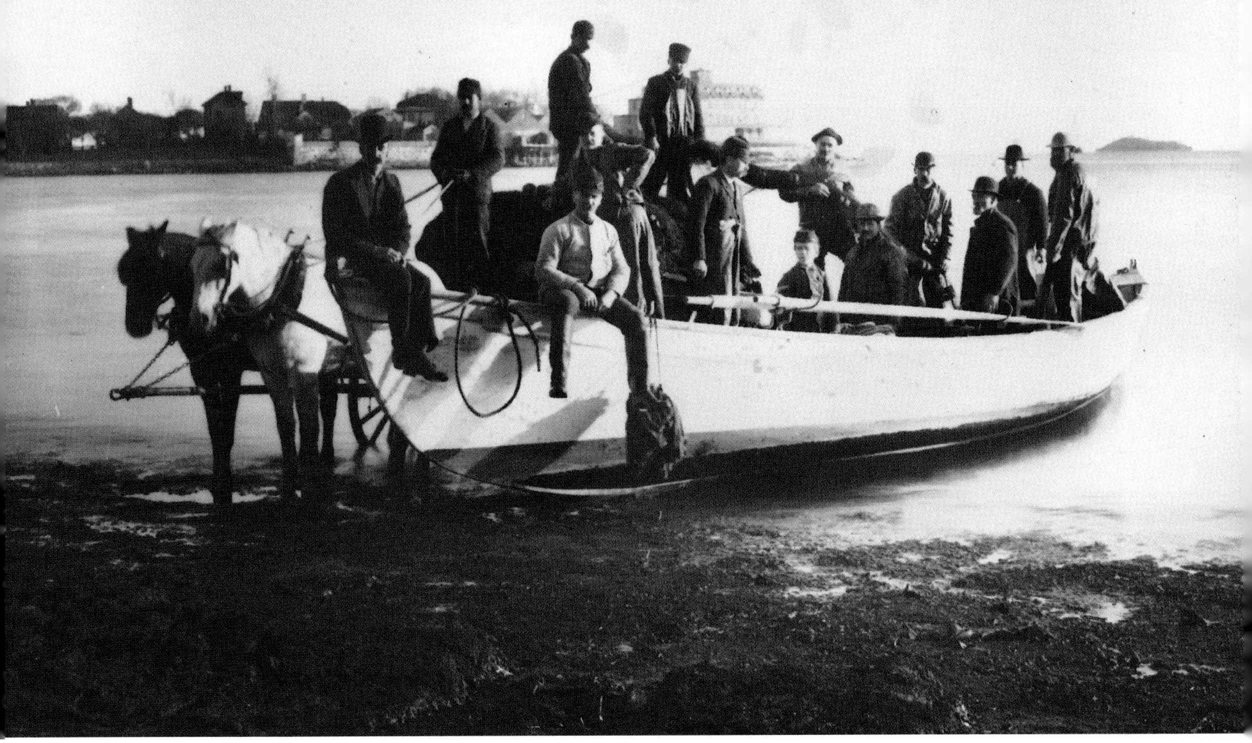

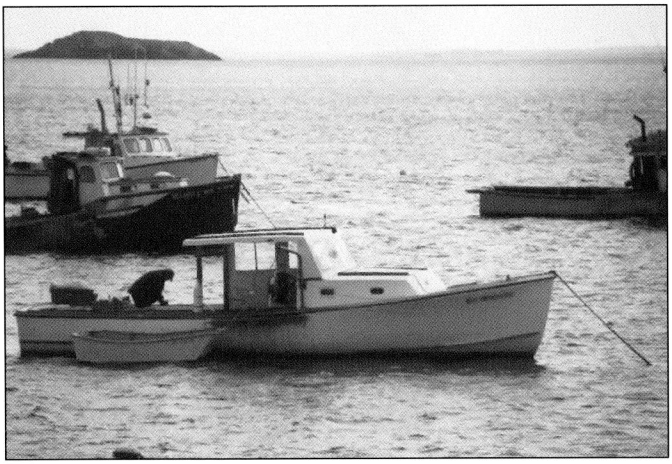

Fishermen in the late 1800s loaded a larger fishing vessel with nets, brought down to the boat by horse and wagon. Lobstermen of today have the luxury of motorized fishing boats, complete with winches to pull lobster traps from the ocean floor. (Courtesy Swampscott Historical Commission.)

Fisherman Chuck Domenicis unloads a bin of herring outside the Fish House. The fish will be used as bait in lobster traps. Back in the late 19th century, local fishermen donned their foul weather gear for a photograph of the "Fishermans Team." (Courtesy Louis A. Gallo.)

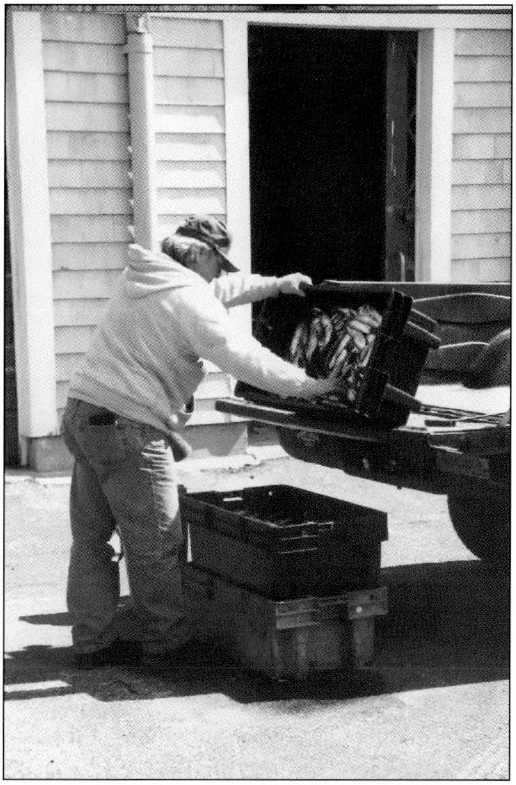

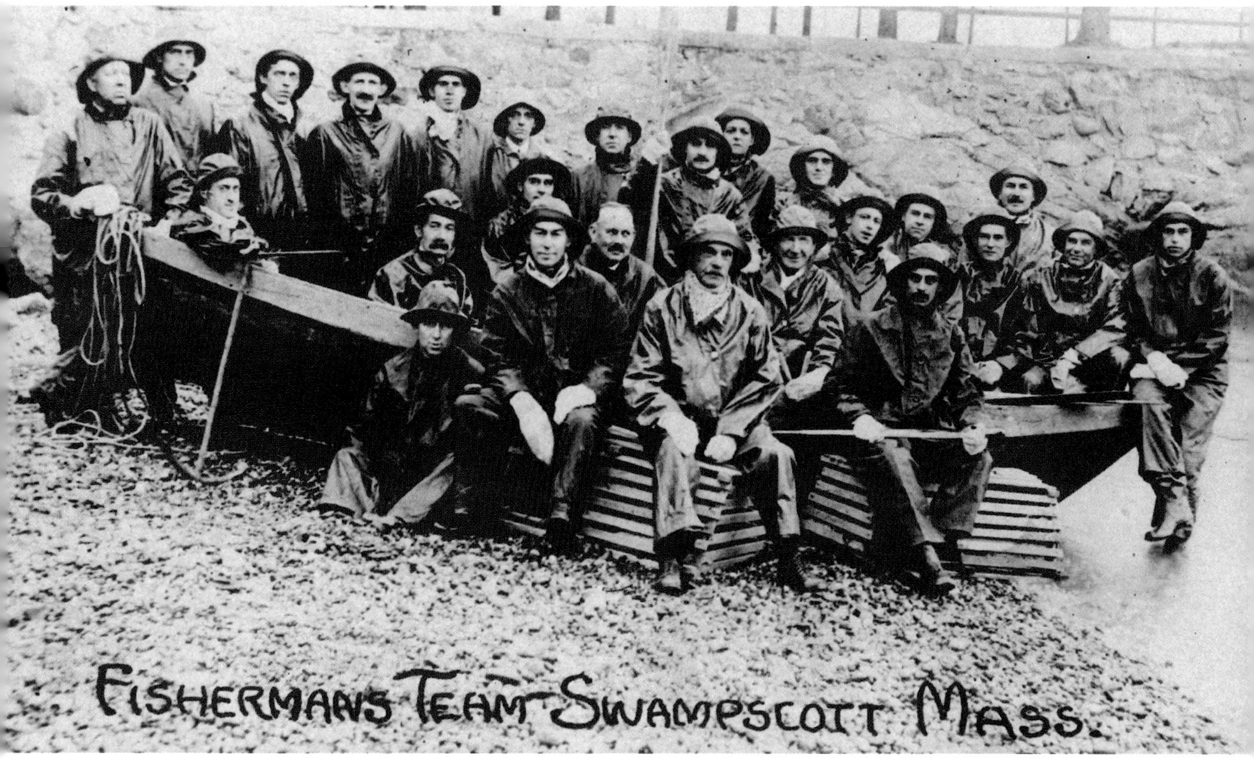

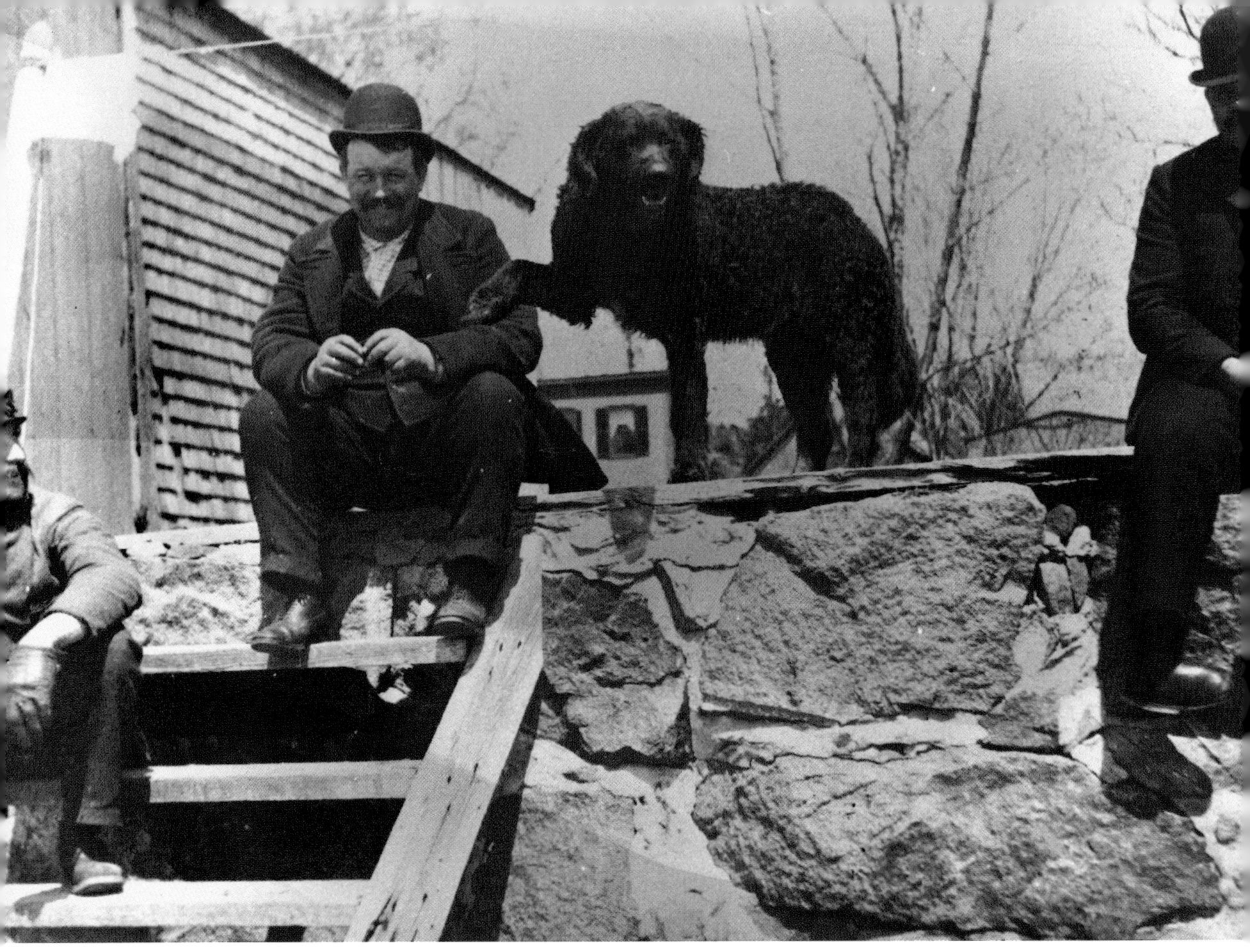

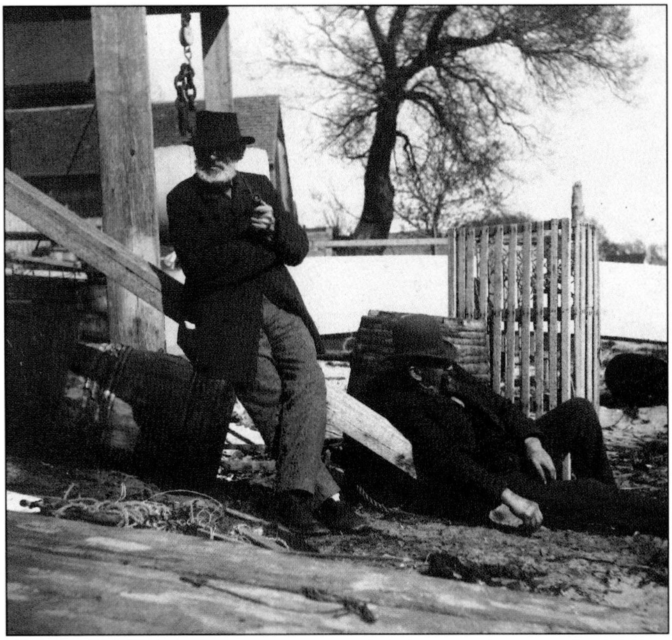

Wearing bowler hats, Henry and Jack Cullen and their curly-coated retriever spend some time with an unidentified man (left) near the Swampscott fishing shanties at Fisherman's Beach (above). Alonzo Carey (left) and Si Nickerson prefer to spend more time relaxing than fishing (left). Today, lobstermen haul their gear up to the historic Fish House (opposite page, above). In the late 1800s, fishermen also used Kings Beach as a base. (Courtesy Swampscott Historical Commission.)

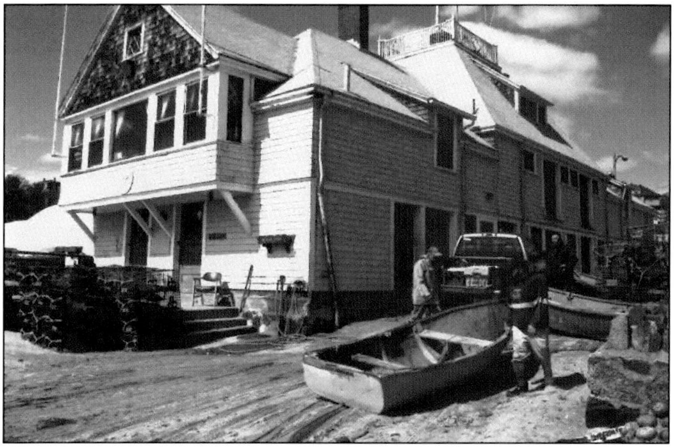

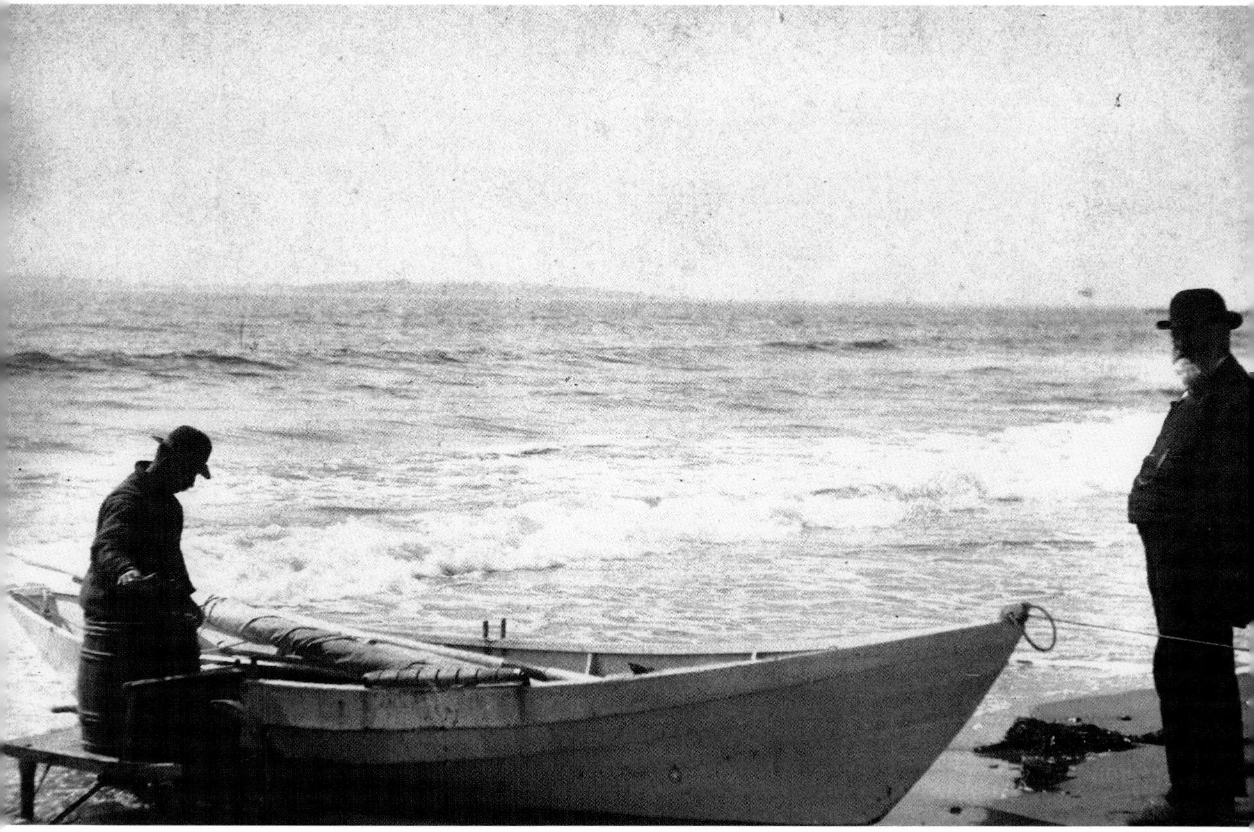

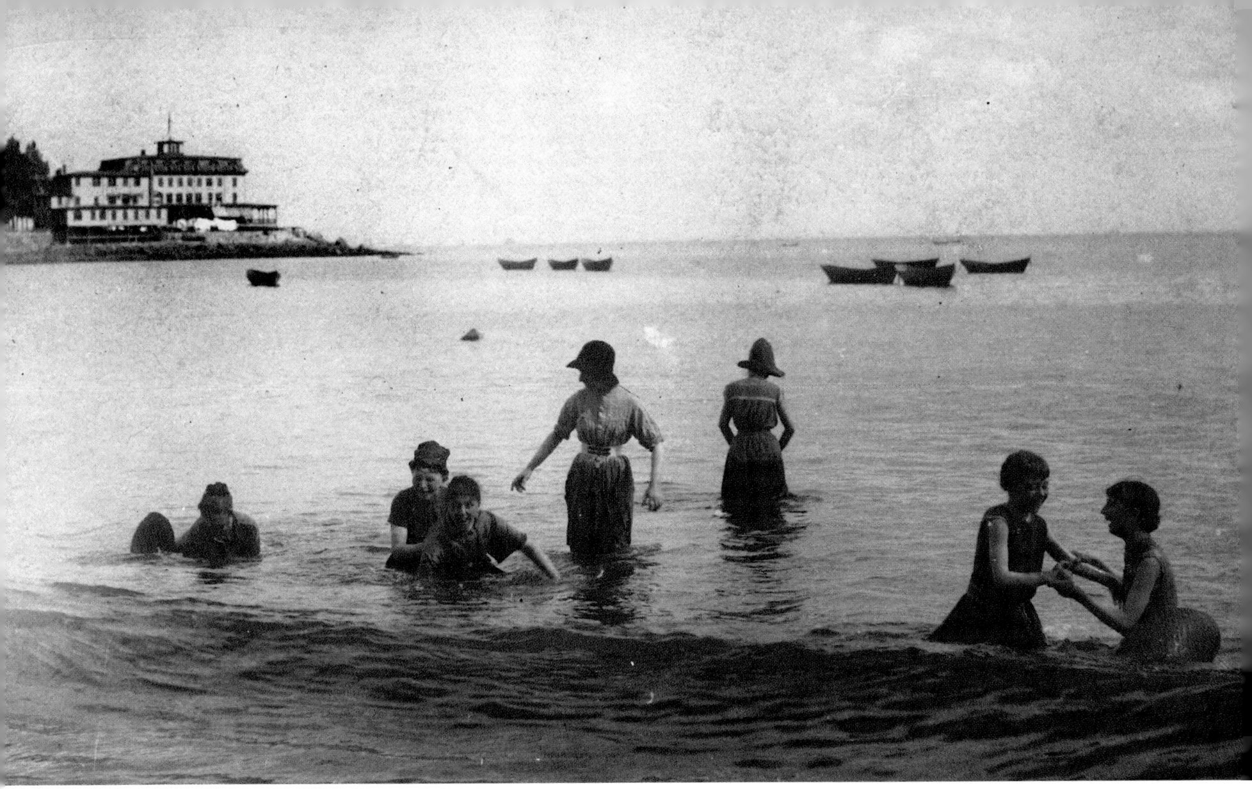

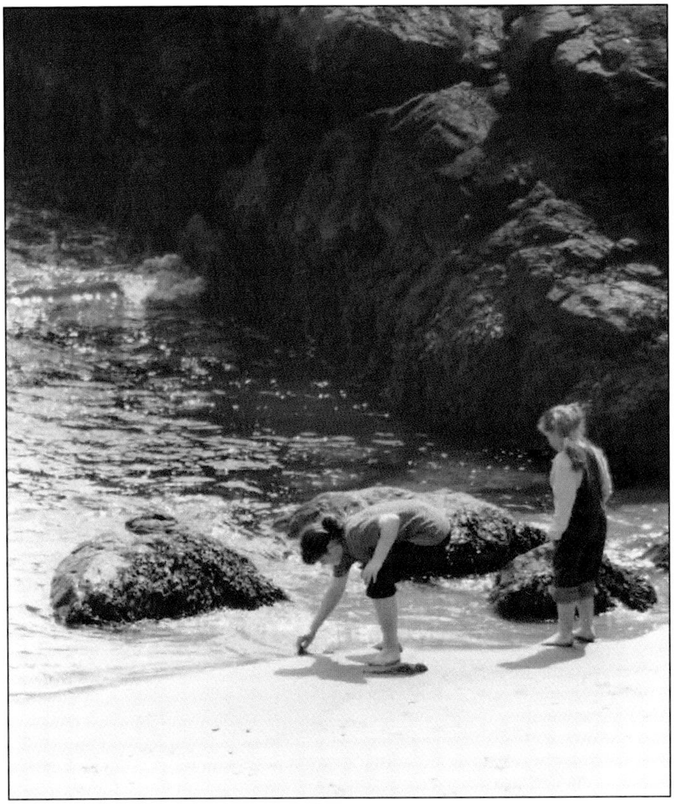

Young women go for a dip in the ocean off Fisherman's Beach, with the Lincoln House Hotel in the background. The swimmers were well-covered with their swimming suits, which more closely resembled dresses. Young girls at the beach today can be found not only swimming but also beachcombing. (Courtesy Louis A. Gallo.)

Finding a pickup truck on the beach today is not uncommon, but back in 1914, it was the horse and cart that hauled fish and even sand for the building of the seawall along Humphrey Street. (Courtesy Louis A. Gallo.)

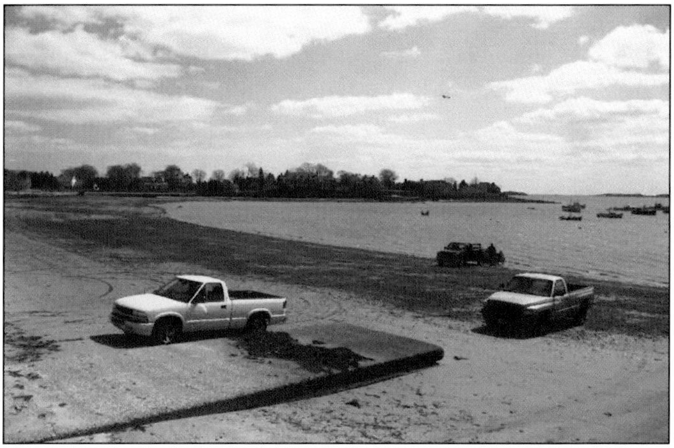

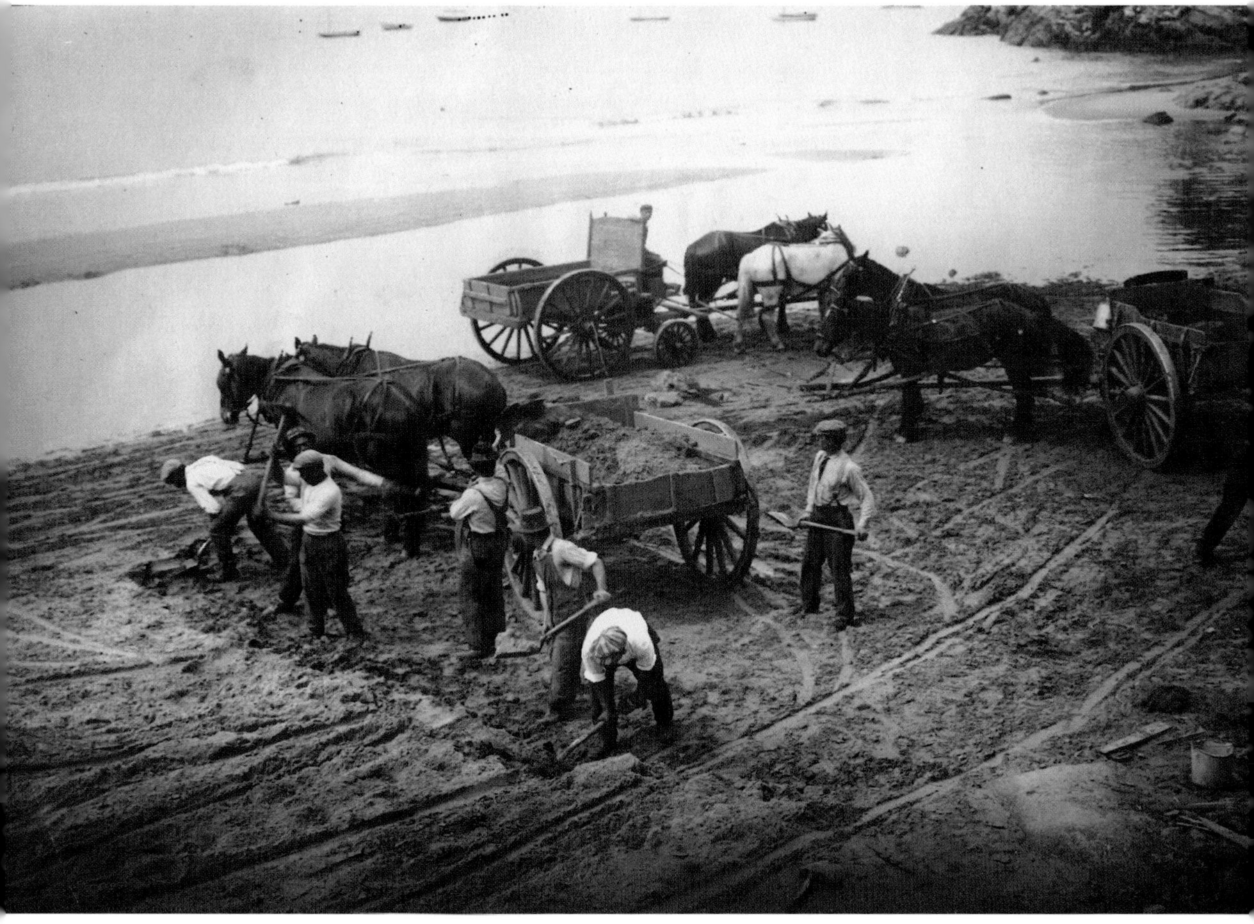

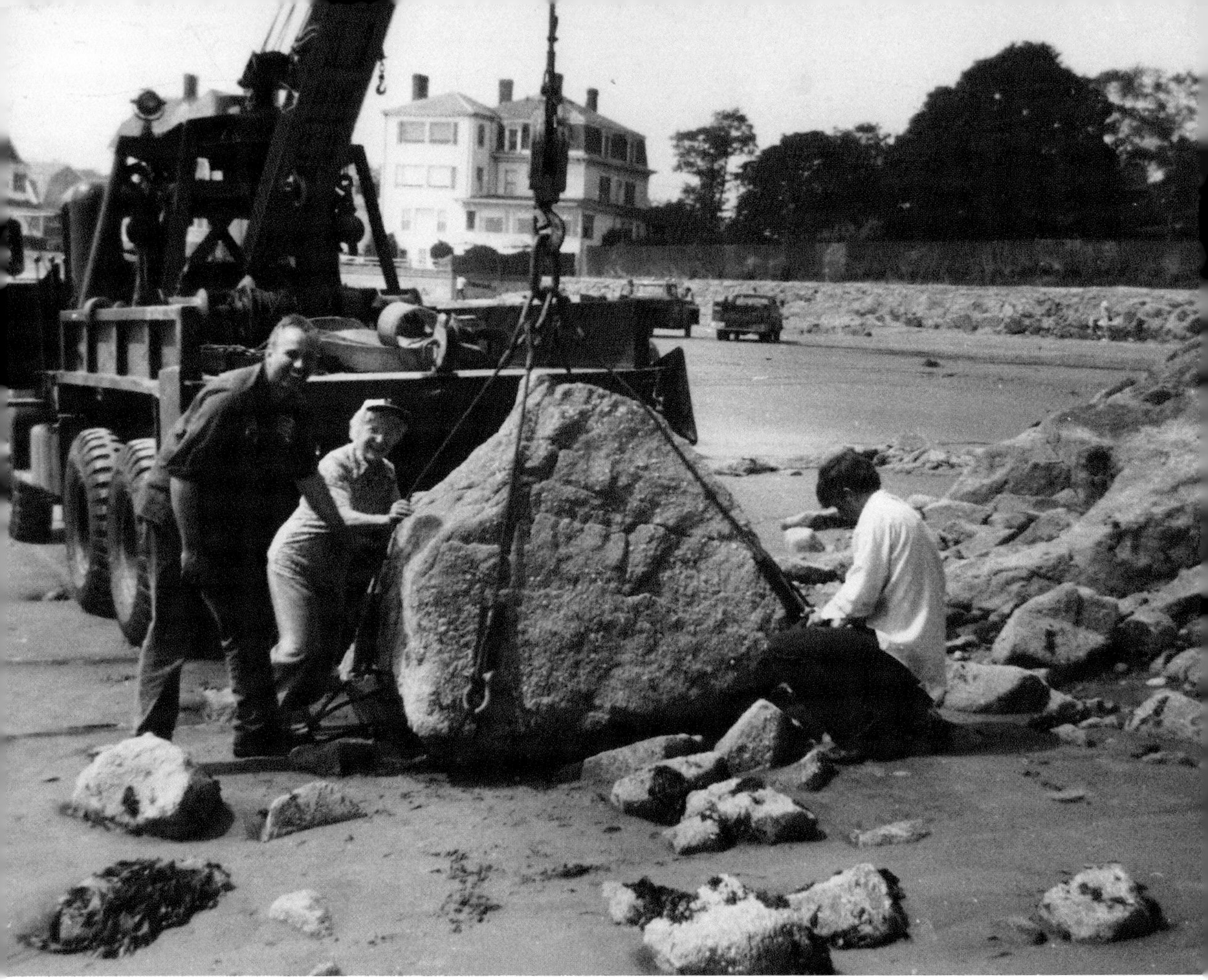

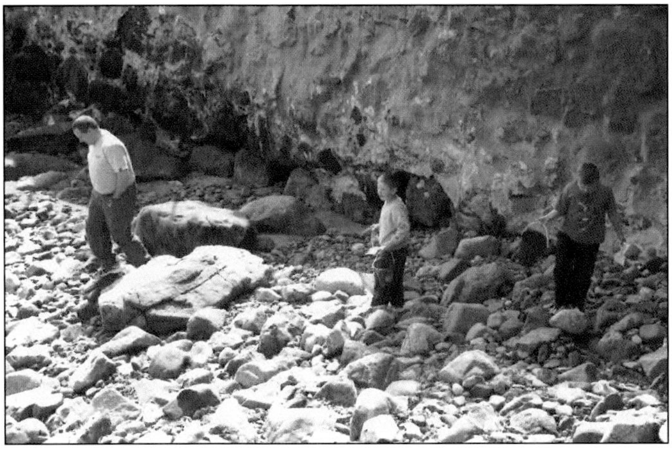

Crane owner Larry Durkee (left) helps Margaret Tatro, a member of the town Bicentennial Committee, and a public works employee move a boulder from Whales Beach to be used for the Revolutionary War monument-plaque on Monument Avenue. The boulders and rocks at nearby Fisherman's Beach have always invited explorers. (Courtesy Swampscott Historical Society.)

High atop Greenwood Avenue, the view of Lincoln House Point and the surrounding area is impressive, especially after walking up one of the steepest streets in town. In the early part of the 20th century, the view included the Fish House without a pier, the New Ocean House Hotel (back left), and the Lincoln House Hotel. (Courtesy Swampscott Historical Commission.)

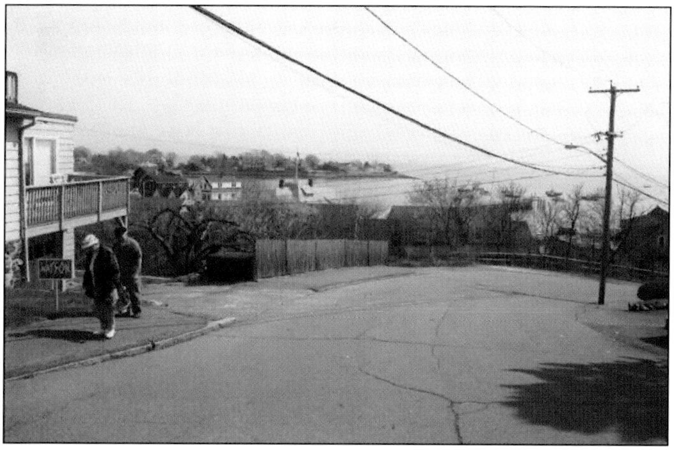

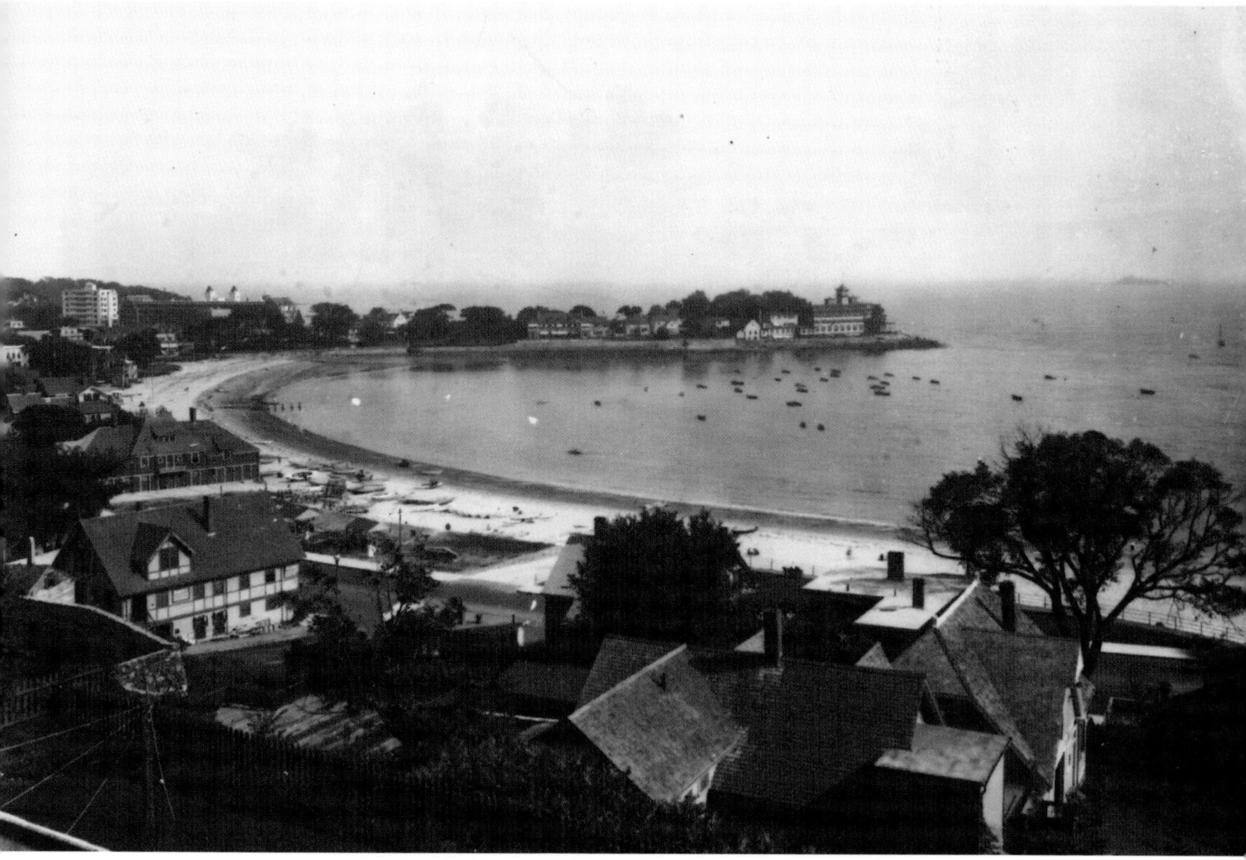

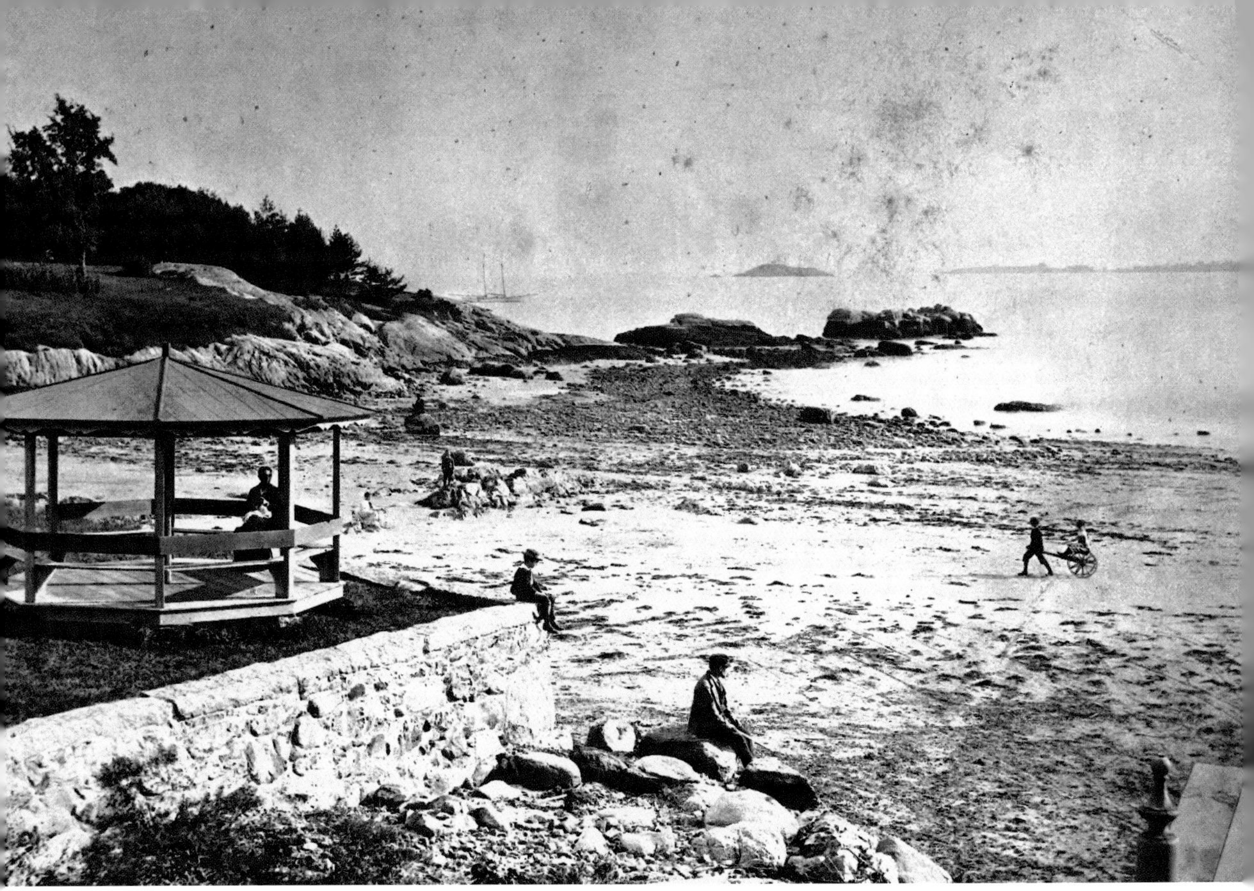

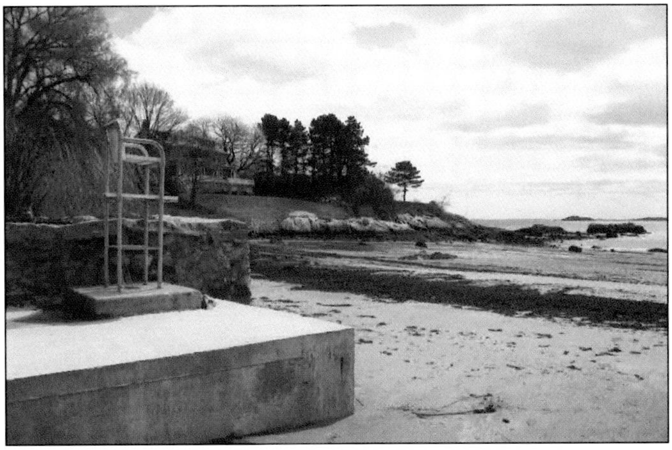

A view from the Little Anawan summerhouse includes Whales Beach with children at play and adults relaxing. Today, a lifeguard's chair sits at nearly the same location off Puritan Road. The beach is popular in the summer, with private homes abutting it. (Courtesy Swampscott Historical Commission.)

Upscale condominiums on Atlantic Avenue replaced the Hotel Preston, which was built high on a bluff on the Swampscott-Marblehead town line in 1872. After the hotel burned in 1957, the bluff was used as fill for Boston's Logan Airport runway extension. (Courtesy Swampscott Public Library.)

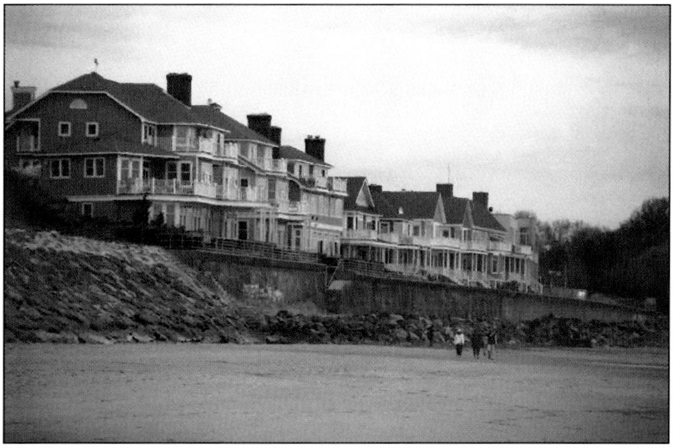

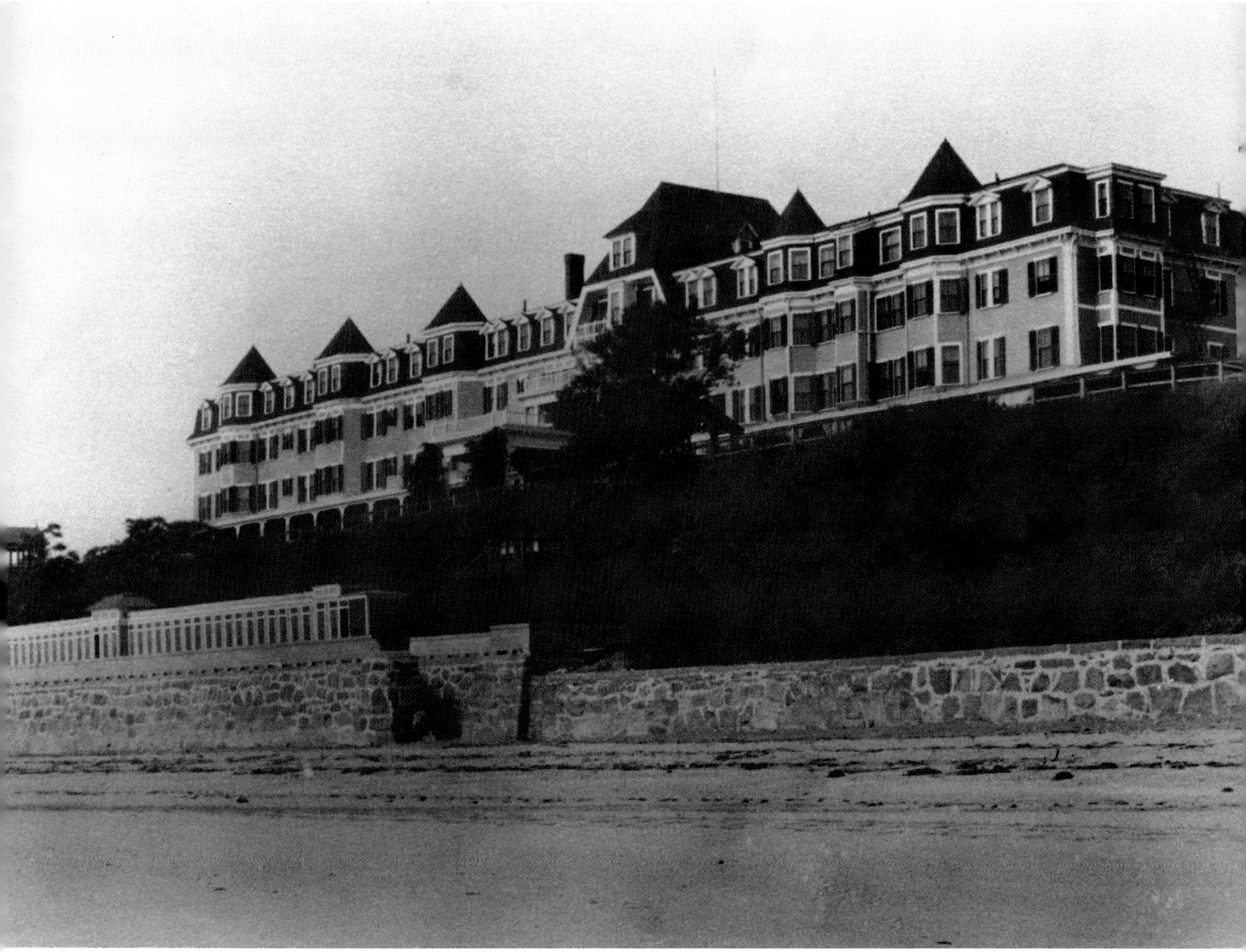

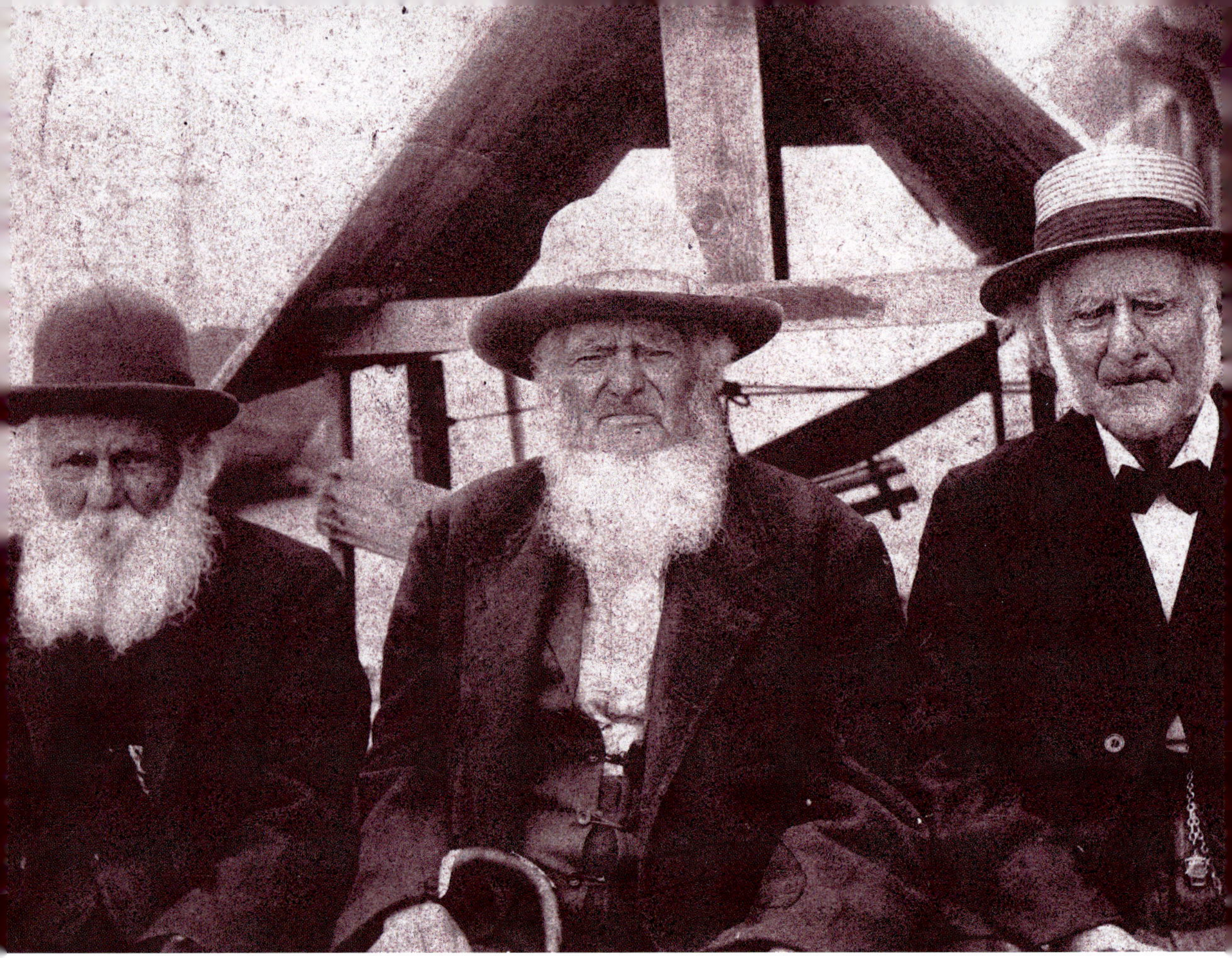

Small towns always have a character or two, and it looks like these three old salts could weave some good tales of life in Swampscott. From left to right are Frank Nesbit, an unidentified man, and Tom Stanley. (Courtesy Swampscott Historical Commission.)